CONTENTS

List of figures and tables ix
About the authors xii
Walkthrough of textbook features and online resources xiii
Acknowledgements xvi

Introduction: Events and the triple bottom line 1
Exploring events management in the 21st century 1
Exploring sustainability in the 21st century 1
Exploring events management and sustainability in the 21st century 2
Exploring events management and sustainability in the 21st century from a children's perspective: an example-based approach 3
Textbook structure 5
Structure of the book 5
References 9

01   Overview: The events industry and sustainability 12
Introduction 12
Typology of planned events 14
Events and sustainability 22
Events and the sustainability of a changing society 24
The role of disempowered groups in events 29
Summary 32
Further reading 33
References 34

02   The 'why' and 'how' of the sustainable event 39
Introduction 39
Sustainable practices and their applications in events management 40
Planning and designing sustainable events 45
Identifying and responding to the needs of stakeholders 47
Post-event evaluation of sustainability strategies 49
Future staging of sustainable events: recommendations 55
Summary 59
Further reading 59
References 60

03   The targets of sustainable events 63
Introduction 63
Definitions of sustainable events 64
Sustainability in events 64
Characteristics of sustainable events 66
Variability in sustainability 67
The targets of sustainable events 68
Key stakeholders in sustainable events targets 75
Summary 83
Further reading 84
References 84

04   Choosing a sustainable venue 88
Introduction 88
Types of event venues 89
Venue selection in events management 92
What is a sustainable venue? 95
Staff and community engagement 101
Venue grading and sustainability certification 101
Meeting the expectations of clients and event attendees 103
The role of the venue in event planning 104
The future of sustainable venues 106
Summary 107
Further reading 108
References 108

05   Stakeholders in sustainable events 110
Introduction 110
Types of stakeholders 111
Considerations and challenges when working with stakeholders 115
Summary 128
Further reading 128
References 129

06   Designing the sustainable event 132
Introduction 132
What is a sustainably designed event and why design one? 134
Brainstorming ideas for events 135
Setting sustainability goals 136
Event psychology 138
Event theming 141

PRAISE FOR *SUSTAINABILITY IN EVENTS MANAGEMENT*

"*Sustainability in Events Management* offers a timely and comprehensive contribution to one of the most pressing challenges facing the events sector today. By thoughtfully integrating the principles of the triple bottom line with practical guidance on planning, venues, stakeholders, safety, management and marketing, this textbook achieves the rare balance of conceptual depth and hands-on relevance. It provides a clear roadmap for both students and practitioners seeking to design and deliver events that are not only impactful but also responsible and future-ready. A valuable and much-needed resource for the field."
Dr Jason García-Portilla, Winchester Business School, University of Winchester

"*Sustainability in Events Management* is a timely and comprehensive exploration of how the event industry can – and must – align with the principles of the triple bottom line. This book offers an impressive synthesis of theory, practice and forward-thinking strategies that make it an essential addition to the event sustainability body of knowledge. From foundational concepts of sustainable event management to nuanced discussions of venue selection, stakeholder engagement and digital innovation, it provides readers with both depth and practical application. Particularly notable is its holistic approach: connecting environmental responsibility, social inclusion and economic resilience with clear frameworks such as the BCOPS model and evidence-based examples. The inclusion of emerging perspectives – such as biophilic design, intersectionality, and children's views of events – demonstrates a refreshing, inclusive vision for the future of the field. Accessible, insightful and rigorously structured with clear chapter learning outcomes, reader activities, checklists, references for further reading and online resources, this text serves as both a guide for practitioners seeking actionable sustainability tools and a vital academic resource for those shaping the next generation of event professionals."
Professor David Hind, Chief Executive, UK Event Industry Academy, President, Asia Pacific Institute for Events Management

"*Sustainability in Events Management* is a rigorous and highly accessible contribution to events literature that succeeds in translating the often abstract language of sustainability into a clear, operational agenda for practice. Grounded in the triple bottom line and the UN's SDGs, the book systematically follows the event cycle from planning and stakeholder engagement through venue selection, design, delivery, safety, procurement and legacy, while consistently foregrounding equity, diversity and inclusion and the rights and needs

of children and other less empowered groups. As a researcher in sustainable tourism and destination management, I particularly value the way the authors combine conceptual clarity with an impressive range of pedagogical tools, typologies, models such as BCOPS, real-world examples, checklists and reflective questions, that will support critical thinking and genuinely inform decision-making in both education and professional contexts. This volume will, in my view, become an important reference for students, scholars and practitioners seeking to position events as catalysts for environmental responsibility, social justice and long-term community wellbeing."
Dr Ante Mandić, Associate Professor of Sustainable Tourism, University of Split

"*Sustainability in Events Management* is a timely and essential contribution to the evolving discourse on responsible event planning. Drawing on the triple bottom line framework and the UN Sustainable Development Goals, the authors offer a comprehensive and practical guide that bridges theory, policy and practice. With its inclusive lens, highlighting the voices of children, marginalized communities and diverse stakeholders, this book redefines what it means to design and deliver events that are socially equitable, environmentally conscious and economically viable. Rich with real-world examples, innovative frameworks like the BCOPS model, and actionable checklists, this text is not only academically rigorous but also deeply relevant for practitioners, educators, and policymakers committed to shaping a more sustainable future for the events industry. This is a must read for any student and any course on which sustainability is now the core."
Professor Ian Yeoman, Hotel Management School Leeuwarden

"Events and sustainability, as two independent concepts, have been increasingly on the agenda of scholarly research, education and practice for the last few decades. This textbook, one of the first to bring these two concepts together, serves as a particularly important guidebook for the industry. While specifically emphasizing the rationale for sustainable events and how they should be implemented, this book also provides a comprehensive analysis of two key aspects: marketing (e.g., product selection, location choice and digitalization) and management (e.g., stakeholder engagement and planning). This book will be a valuable resource."
Professor Metin Kozak, Kadir Has University

Sustainability in Events Management

Planning, designing and delivering

Hugues Séraphin, Emma Delaney,
Chris Smith and Vanessa Gowreesunkar

Publisher's note

Every possible effort has been made to ensure that the information contained in this book is accurate at the time of going to press, and the publishers and authors cannot accept responsibility for any errors or omissions, however caused. No responsibility for loss or damage occasioned to any person acting, or refraining from action, as a result of the material in this publication can be accepted by the editor, the publisher or the author.

First published in Great Britain and the United States in 2026 by Kogan Page Limited

All rights reserved. No part of this publication may be reproduced, stored in a retrieval system or transmitted in any form or by any means – including electronic, mechanical, photocopying, recording or by any artificial intelligence (AI) or machine learning system – without the prior written permission of the publisher. Unauthorized use, including the use of text or images to train AI models, is strictly prohibited and may result in legal action.

Kogan Page
Kogan Page Ltd, 2nd Floor, 45 Gee Street, London EC1V 3RS, United Kingdom
Kogan Page Inc, 8 W 38th Street, Suite 902, New York, NY 10018, USA
www.koganpage.com

EU Representative (GPSR)
eucomply OÜ, Pärnu mnt 139b–14 11317, Tallinn, Estonia
www.eucompliancepartner.com

Kogan Page books are printed on paper from sustainable forests.

© Kogan Page, 2026

The moral rights of the authors have been asserted in accordance with the Copyright, Designs and Patents Act 1988.

ISBNs
Hardback   978 1 3986 2353 8
Paperback   978 1 3986 2351 4
Ebook   978 1 3986 2354 5

British Library Cataloguing-in-Publication Data
A CIP record for this book is available from the British Library.

Library of Congress Cataloging in Publication Data
A CIP record for this book is available from the Library of Congress.

Typeset by Integra Software Services, Pondicherry
Printed and bound by CPI Group (UK) Ltd, Croydon CR0 4YY

Biophilic event design 141
Ambience and sustainable décor 144
Digital solutions 146
Incorporating co-creation in event design 147
Intersectionality, equality, diversity and inclusion in event design 149
Designing events for engagement 151
Summary 153
Further reading and viewing 153
References 153

07 Delivering and evaluating the sustainable event 155
Introduction 155
Delivery 156
Framework 161
Pre-event staffing for sustainable events 162
Building the right team 165
The most unusual and unique festivals in the world: a question on sustainability 166
Central criteria for the sustainability of events 168
Training for sustainability 170
Monitoring and feedback 172
The BCOPS framework: a holistic approach to sustainable events 173
Summary 179
Further reading 181
References 182

08 Making the event safe as an important aspect of sustainability 184
Risk management: an overview 184
Core groups in safety planning 185
Operational management 191
Political challenges 200
Long-term planning and returning customers 203
Summary 206
Further reading 206
References 206

09 What is needed to run the sustainable event? 210
Introduction 210
Sustainable procurement 211
Registration and ticketing 217

Working with the venue and their preferred suppliers 218
Technology 219
Catering 221
Food waste 223
Additional furniture and props 223
Speakers, artists and performers 225
Supplier requirements 226
Staffing 227
Summary 229
Further reading and viewing 230
References 230

10 **Digital marketing: the way forward for sustainable events** 232
Introduction 233
Digital marketing and sustainable events 234
Audience expectations and digital media engagement 236
Audience expectations for sustainable events 237
Understanding the target market and demographics 239
Digital tools for demographic targeting and sustainability 241
PESO model in sustainable event marketing 243
The future of digital marketing for sustainable events 247
Summary 251
Further reading 252
References 252

11 **Conclusion: the future of sustainable events** 254
Introduction 254
Future propositions for the events industry 254
Events and their purpose: a futuristic approach 259
Summary 262
Further reading 263
References 263

Index 265

LIST OF FIGURES AND TABLES

Figures

Figure 0.1	Selection of venues for children	5
Figure 1.1	Sustainability of the events industry	14
Figure 1.2	Summary of typology of planned events	18
Figure 1.3	Size of planned events	19
Figure 1.4	Updated typology of planned events	21
Figure 1.5	Sequences of the triple bottom line	23
Figure 1.6	Alberts and Niendorf (2021) sequence of the triple bottom line	24
Figure 1.7	Sustainability and the challenges for the event industry	28
Figure 2.1	Sustainability as a value	46
Figure 2.2	Events objectives and sustainability (Quinn, 2013)	50
Figure 2.3	Events objectives and sustainability (Shone and Parry, 2004)	51
Figure 2.4	Areas for evaluation	52
Figure 2.5	Evaluating an event	52
Figure 2.6	The five dimensions of sustainability	54
Figure 2.7	The five dimensions of change, innovation and creativity	55
Figure 2.8	Societal changes to be addressed by events	56
Figure 2.9	Sequencing of the triple bottom line (Alberts and Niendorf, 2021)	58
Figure 3.1	Essence of sustainable events	65
Figure 3.2	Sustainability targets	69
Figure 3.3	Children in sustainability targets	82
Figure 4.1	Categories of types of venues	89
Figure 4.2	The Convention Centre Dublin © The CCD	93
Figure 4.3	Factors influencing the choice of venue	93
Figure 4.4	Indicators of venue sustainability	95
Figure 4.5	Excel London © Excel London	98
Figure 4.6	Supply chain management	99
Figure 5.1	Decision-making process and influence from stakeholders in event planning	115
Figure 5.2	Socially used terms in the context of a company/business	119
Figure 5.3	Example risk assessment questions when considering tree planting as part of offsetting emissions	120
Figure 5.4	Five steps	120
Figure 5.5	Elkington's triple bottom line	123
Figure 6.1	Elements of an event programme	133
Figure 6.2	Contextual questions for setting event sustainability goals list	137

Figure 6.3	Event sustainability goals list (adapted from Jain, 2024)	138
Figure 6.4	Behaviourism	139
Figure 6.5	Positive and negative stimuli	139
Figure 6.6	Event design	140
Figure 6.7	Event elements list	141
Figure 6.8	Embedding technology into event design list	146
Figure 6.9	Six Steps to co-creation (adapted from Morgan, 2016)	148
Figure 6.10	Participation ideas for event guests	152
Figure 8.1	Risk assessment procedure (adapted from Dowson and Bassett, 2018; Edger and Oddy, 2018; Jeynes, 2002)	186
Figure 9.1	Key stages in the procurement process	212
Figure 9.2	The Event Cycle Team © Event Cycle	217
Figure 11.1	The triple bottom line: people, planet, profit (adapted from Alberts and Niendorf, 2021)	259
Figure 11.2	Planet and people (adapted from Craig, 2013)	259
Figure 11.3	Innovation for sustainable events (I4SE)	260

Tables

Table 0.1	Spaces for children	4
Table 1.1	Keywords associated with planned events	15
Table 1.2	Typology of events	15
Table 1.3	Occurrence of ranking of the triple bottom line	23
Table 1.4	Motivations behind the organization of events in the UK	26
Table 1.5	Examples of actions of the UK event industry towards sustainability	26
Table 2.1	List of events happening in Winchester	44
Table 2.2	Self-reflection	54
Table 4.1	Checklist of indicators of venue sustainability	96
Table 5.1	Issues related to sustainability in festivals and events tourism (adapted by Pinar, 2019)	126
Table 6.1	A checklist for shortlisting event ideas (adapted from Powell, 2015)	136
Table 6.2	Tips for designing sustainable events	145
Table 7.1	UK venues	157
Table 7.2	Paris venues	158
Table 7.3	Assistance for event organizers in considering social aspects of an event	161
Table 8.1	Risk assessment form template (adapted from Shone and Parry, 2004: 171)	186
Table 8.2	Risk control plan form template (adapted from Shone and Parry, 2004: 172)	187

Table 9.1	Checklist of sustainability questions for event suppliers	213
Table 9.2	Checklist of questions and instructions for suppliers	226
Table 10.1	PESO integration strategy for sustainable events (adapted from Anastasiia, 2024)	246
Table 11.1	Top 20 new technology trends (adapted from AI Uncovered, YouTube, 2025)	256
Table 11.2	Top 20 new technology trends and their impacts on the event industry	257

ABOUT THE AUTHORS

Hugues Séraphin

Hugues Séraphin is Associate Professor and also the Principal Lecturer and People Lead for the Tourism, Hospitality and Events subject group at Oxford Brookes Business School, UK. His research focuses on children in tourism, hospitality and events.

Emma Delaney

Emma Delaney is Associate Professor in Events Management at the University of Surrey, UK, and prior to working in education she enjoyed a varied and successful career in the tourism and events industries. She is an award-winning teacher and researcher, interested in venue and destination management for business events.

Chris Smith

Chris Smith is Senior Lecturer in Events Management at the University of Winchester, UK. He has worked across a range of live events for 20 years and continues to work in operational roles at festivals and cultural events.

Vanessa Gowreesunkar

Vanessa Gowreesunkar is Associate Professor at the Indian Institute of Management, Sirmaur, India. She is the Vice President of the International Tourism Studies Association. Her research focuses on tourism management, tourism marketing, island tourism and sustainable tourism among others.

WALKTHROUGH OF TEXTBOOK FEATURES AND ONLINE RESOURCES

Learning outcomes

A bulleted list at the beginning of each chapter summarizes what you can expect to learn, to help you track your progress.

LEARNING OUTCOMES

By the end of Chapter 4, you should be able to:

- recognize the different types of event venues assess the significant role of the venue in event design and delivery
- compare venues based on indicators of their sustainability
- identify the contribution of the venue to sustainable supply chain management
- evaluate venue sustainability accreditation and certification schemes, including ISO 20121.

Real-world examples

Global examples from the events industry illustrate how key ideas and theories are operating in practice.

REAL-WORLD EXAMPLE The Convention Centre Dublin

The Convention Centre Dublin (CCD, 2025) is the first carbon-neutral constructed convention centre and it aims to become the Republic of Ireland's most sustainable venue and a leading expert in sustainable events management. The venue has a comprehensive waste management policy in place to help manage the generation and segregation of waste and the its recycling figures are consistently above 95 per cent. The venue will assess how to best manage the creation, segregation and recycling of waste, not only within the building, but also for every event, and to achieve this, it has custom-built recycle-friendly bins to help event guests in this mission to reduce, reuse and recycle.

Activity

Interactive questions and activities throughout to encourage you to reflect on what you have learned and apply your knowledge and skills in practice.

ACTIVITY 4.1

Using the indicators of venue sustainability in Table 4.1, choose an events venue from each of the categories shown in Figure 4.1 and compare and contrast them to identify which you believe to be the most sustainable venue.

Checklists

Key details to remember when planning your own sustainable event.

CHECKLIST

Sustainable events succeed when sustainability is embedded throughout behaviour, communication, operations, policy and strategy and is planned in advance, delivered with care, reviewed with honesty and improved for the future.

Here is a checklist that may help in sustainable event planning and evaluation.

Pre-event planning

- Define clear sustainability goals aligned with ISO 20121 and the UN SDGs.
- Integrate sustainability targets into feasibility studies and operational planning (Bowdin 2024).
- Select venues and suppliers that align with sustainability criteria such as the TBL (Elkington, 1994).
- Develop SMART indicators for carbon reduction, community involvement and social impacts.
- Build sustainability into staff recruitment, onboarding and training plans.

Further reading

Additional resources to further your learning, from books to videos.

References

Detailed references provide quick and easy access to the research and underpinning sources behind the chapter.

Online resources:

This book includes online resources for lecturers and students.
These resources can be accessed through the Kogan Page website: www.koganpage.com/SIEM

ACKNOWLEDGEMENTS

Life is not a race or a marathon… It is a triathlon!

Agnès Séraphin (the Alpha), Sala and Adisa Mahama (the Omega), you are the calories I need to keep running.
Hugues

I am truly blessed to be surrounded by good people whose presence, encouragement and support make every academic journey meaningful. My first words of gratitude go to my long-term publication partner, Hugues Séraphin, who has consistently thought of me whenever embarking on new projects. Since we began our careers together in 2012, we have been sailing side by side, navigating both challenges and opportunities, and building not just a professional partnership but also a cherished friendship.

I also extend my heartfelt appreciation to my family members and well-wishers, who remain my unwavering support system. Their encouragement provides me with the strength and inspiration to pursue new ventures with passion and commitment.

I wish to acknowledge the wonderful collaboration with Chris, Emma and Susan (along with Hugues, of course). Together, we have been more than co-editors; we have been a team bound by trust, enthusiasm and shared vision. The journey of shaping this book has been immensely rewarding, and it is the spirit of collaboration and friendship that has truly made it special.

Finally, this book is the outcome of a collective endeavour, and it is a privilege to have been part of such a committed and dynamic team. To all who have contributed, directly or indirectly, I extend my heartfelt gratitude.
Vanessa

Many thanks to my co-authors Chris and Vanessa, for their collegiality and commitment to this project, and particularly to my long-term colleague and dear friend, Hugues Sèraphin. My personal thanks go to Mark for your unwavering support and encouragement, through this, and many other endeavours.
Emma

Huge thanks go to my wonderful supportive co-authors Emma, Vanessa and a special mention to Hugues. Thank you to industry colleagues who provided insight and comments to this book. You make the industry what it is, delivering wonderful experiences for others. Personal thanks go to my beautiful daughter Edie for helping me count words and reminding me that sustainable planning is so that the next generation can enjoy it.
Chris

Introduction

Events and the triple bottom line

Exploring events management in the 21st century

Since the breakout of Covid-19 in 2020, the society we live in has changed tremendously (Gössling et al, 2020). Our lifestyles and ways of consuming (Everingham and Chassagne, 2020), and more specifically the way we socialise (Higgins-Desbiolles, 2020); the importance we give to our wellbeing (Séraphin and Dosquet, 2020); how technology is now integrated and used in our daily life (Zeng et al, 2020); and the emergence of sustainability as a buzz word influencing behaviour and attitude (Ioannides and Gyimothy, 2020) in relation to issues such as climate change (Prideaux et al, 2020). As a response to the pandemic and changes in society, the events industry has also had to change the way it operates (Rowen, 2020), and equally important, consider its long-term legacy through the education of the younger generation (Edelheim, 2020). Despite the post-pandemic changes that have occurred in society, events have remained very important for individuals, societies and communities (Dowson et al, 2022; Evans, 2024; Getz and Page, 2019).

Exploring sustainability in the 21st century

For sustainability to be effective, every industry needs to conduct a holistic analysis of their environment, and not just consider their physical environment (Dodds, 2024). Indeed, the political context, the image of the destination, the stakeholders involved in the management of a destination and the level of economic development are factors that impact on the life cycle of an activity (Butler, 2024). Subsequently, this textbook explores sustainability from three dimensions:

- Planet – actions related to tackling issues such as pollution, waste management and, environmental stewardship (Slater et al, 2020; Spenceley et al, 2021).
- People – which is essentially about addressing health, safety and other human needs (Rhama, 2023).
- Profit – the economic dimension of the triple bottom line (TBL) (Késenne, 2005).

Exploring events management and sustainability in the 21st century

Environmental sustainability (planet) is a major global issue that concerns every industry, including the events industry. Higham et al (2021) state there is a code red on, which is impacting on the event industry in multiple ways, such as the need for event organizers to work with partners (suppliers, contractors, etc) who are also committed to sustainability, as well as the need to develop greening strategies. Sustainability can also be viewed from a social perspective and so is directly concerned with the 'people' dimension of the TBL. With the emerging importance of equality/equity, diversity and inclusion (EDI), event organizers have to ensure that events 'welcome everyone and enable them to participate fully, on their own terms' (Finkel and Dashper, 2020, pp. 475–91). Because of the many compliances events must now adhere to, this has impacted on the cost of running events, including venue costs (which vary according to location, capacity, parking, facilities, layout, accessibility); staffing costs; catering costs; entertainment costs (again, which vary according to the type, theme, size, location and length of the events); equipment costs; travel and accommodation costs (e.g. for a band, key speakers, etc.), marketing and promotion costs (Eventbrite, 2023).

Despite the challenges faced by event organizers and the pressure faced by the public sector (Getz, 2012), the feeling is that the 'show must go on' as 'planned, live events, both personal and societal in scale and meaning, will always be a prominent feature of civilization, in all societies and cultures' (Getz, 2012, p. 382; Séraphin, 2021). As predicted by Getz (2012) and fuelled by both the Covid pandemic and development of technologies, virtual events are gaining in importance. Beyond the environmental and social dimension of events, it should be noted that the events industry was worth £800 billion worldwide in 2021 and is expected to reach £2 trillion by 2028 (Quadrant2 Design, 2022). In the UK it is predicted that in 2025 the income generated by events will break down into food and beverage (47%) sponsorship (37%), contests and raffles (29%), merchandising (27%) and VIP packaging (26%) (Eventbrite, 2023).

Sustainable management of events from a TBL perspective means taking care equally of the 'people', 'planet' and 'profit', which subsequently implies meeting the economic, sociocultural and environmental needs of every single stakeholder, without exception.

The purpose of this textbook is to highlight and understand the 'new world' of events management and to provide guidelines for both those working in the industry and those learning about the industry. Although the approach of the book is holistic, the focus remains on sustainability from the perspective of the TBL. The operational and management approach of events adopted in this textbook will allow readers (whether learners and/or practitioners) to understand the evolution of events as a result of the evolution of the needs of society. Specific examples of events, good practice and case studies are provided to support and illustrate arguments. The textbook also takes a novel approach by discussing events management from the perspective of children and young people, as outlined below.

Exploring events management and sustainability in the 21st century from a children's perspective: an example-based approach

Choosing a venue for children's events

The selection of child-centric events should follow a three-step approach. First, identifying the main needs of children and carers. Second, identifying spaces that can meet those needs. Finally, selecting a suitable venue. These three stages are the primary stages. Secondary stages include location, access, nearby amenities, capacity and flow, facilities, catering and décor (Delaney, 2023). This introduction focuses exclusively on the primary stages because they have not yet been covered in the literature. Delaney (2023) investigated child-centric events and found that the secondary stages are no different to other events. Indeed, Powell (2023: 121) argues: 'All well-planned events share the same core principals whatever their size or type. Children's events are no different. Events designed with children in mind require no less time or effort.'

Stage 1 Main needs of children and carers when attending events

1. Events for children need to have an empowering dimension, which can be achieved by including in the designing and planning of the event activities that enable children to showcase what they are capable of, giving them as much importance as their adult counterparts (Borstlap and Saayman, 2019; Krasil'nikov, 2020).

2. To guarantee the health and safety of children, it is important to consider the age of the children. Clear signage and emergency procedures, information sent to carers prior to the event to ensure that they provide equipment such as ear defenders and other safety equipment, if appropriate, and provision of suitable food/snacks; as well as breaks and relaxation time (Brackenridge et al, 2015; Department for Education, 2023).

3. Clear rules for behaviour need to be communicated with children, which plays a role in the sense of freedom they can experience (Clark, 2008; Müller, 2020).

4. The event needs to be fun, while also contributing to learning (education and entertainment) and strengthen family connections and wellbeing of participants. These are particularly important for children from underserved communities (Jepson et al, 2019; Krasil'nikov, 2020; Sadeghi et al, 2023; Tayler et al, 2006; Zhou et al, 2018).

5. Because 'children' are not a homogeneous group, it is important that equipment at the event meets the needs of all age groups targeted (Frey, 2019; Hixson, 2014).

Stage 2 Identifying spaces for children

Research by Francis and Lorenzo (2002) and Rasmussen (2004) indicates that children's spaces are multiple, and include:

- institutional places (e.g. theme parks, sports parks, schools, day care)
- public spaces (e.g. beaches, parks, malls, waterfronts)
- private spaces (e.g. home, cars)
- found places (e.g. natural areas, waterfronts)
- found/off limit places (e.g. adventure places)
- wilderness (e.g. urban wilderness, natural areas)
- new and innovative places (e.g. town trails, community gardens, city farms).

These spaces may be divided into two main categories – indoor and outdoor – and are all suitable spaces for events (see Table 0.1).

Stage 3: Selecting a suitable space

The final stage is to identify the most suitable venue (Figure 0.1). Event managers need to identify the space which most closely matches the needs of the targeted group and the theme/objective of the event. This could involve the use of multi-criteria decision analysis (MCDA), which is 'a general term for methods providing a quantitative approach to support decision making in problems involving several criteria and choices' (Botti and Peypoch, 2013: 109).

Table 0.1 Spaces for children

Space	Example	Further information
Institutional places	Theme park e.g. Gulliver Land resort)	www.gulliverslandresort.co.uk
Public spaces	Park, e.g. Hat Fair	www.hatfair.co.uk/
Private spaces	Home, e.g. birthday party	
Found places	Natural areas, e.g. family learning event at Camley Street Natural Park	www.wildlondon.org.uk/family-learning-events/camley-street-natural-park
Wilderness	Nene Park Adventure Nature Tots – groups for toddlers and their guardians	www.nenepark.org.uk/nature-tots
New and innovative	Town trail, e.g. Winchester treasure trail	www.dayoutwiththekids.co.uk/attractions/the-winchester-treasure-trail-4cce705c

Introduction

Figure 0.1 Selection of venues for children

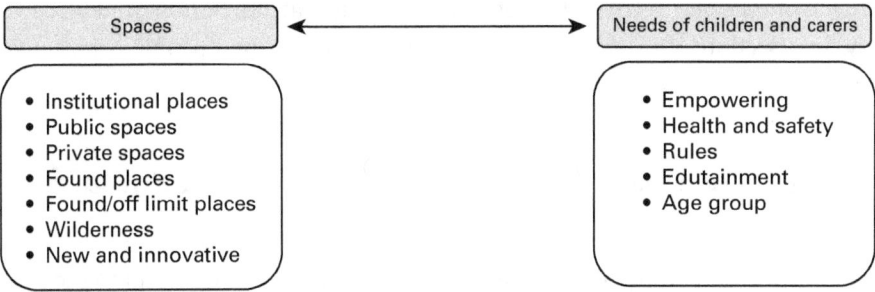

Further explanation regarding the design, planning and delivery of events for children is disseminated throughout the book, but can be found specifically in Chapters 1 and 5.

Textbook structure

This book is written from the viewpoint that an event is an experience in which sustainability (taken holistically) must play a significant role. For the experience to be successful, the book aligns with Edger and Oddy (2018) who argue that six functions are important in the design, planning and delivery of successful events, namely:

1 Exploration – of the needs of the market and customers.
2 Engineering – the conceptualisation and planning of the experience of attendees
3 Engagement – of all stakeholders involved
4 Execution – planning and operations before the delivery of the event
5 Evaluation – of the impacts of the event
6 Evolution – what can be done to enhance the existing version of the event.

For the six stages to happen, the event manager (who is responsible for the conception, planning and staging of the event), the venue manager (who is in charge of the operational aspect of the event) and the customer experience manager (who is responsible for customer experience) need to work together.

Structure of the book

Introduction: events and the triple bottom line

This book is written from the perspective that sustainable events need to be planned, designed and delivered with the triple bottom line (TBL) in mind, as well as aiming to address the 17 UN Sustainable Development Goals (SDGs). The book is therefore written from the perspective of events under existing categorizations, but also events at the intersection of other industries. A children and young people perspective of events is also considered.

Chapter 1: Overview: the events industry and sustainability

The chapter starts by providing an updated version of the existing categorization of events which differs from the one developed by Getz (2012) and Getz and Page (2019). Indeed, existing categorizations of events do not take into consideration those that are at the intersection of the events industry with other industries (for example, speed dating events which are at the intersection of the dating industry and hospitality industry). Chapter 1 goes on to review the existing literature on events and sustainability (the triple bottom line), while identifying gaps and explaining how events viewed from an intersection perspective can help to address these gaps (for instance, romantic loneliness, which is a major societal issue, can be tackled by the events industry if events are thought, planned and designed from an intersection perspective). Other contributions of events to society are also explored through concepts such as hospitality and tourism in a post-Covid-19 context. Similarly, some gaps in sustainability from an event perspective can be tackled if viewed from a children's perspective.

Chapter 2: The 'why' and 'how' of the sustainable event

This chapter is written from the perspective that for sustainability to be achieved, every single objective in the planning, design and delivery process must be considered from a TBL and SDG perspective. Thus, the first step in planning is to analyse the brief from the client. Second, explore what can be done to meet the requirements of the client, in other words the objectives of the event. This chapter also discusses the need to include ethical aspects and the decision-making around balancing costs and benefits of sustainability practice in events.

Chapter 3: The targets of sustainable events

The design and delivery of the event will vary according to who the event is aimed at. Indeed, the perception, understanding and importance of sustainability varies according to demographics. These variations therefore need to be taken into consideration when designing, communicating and delivering the event, as the expectations of attendees and other stakeholders involved will be different. The information provided should connect with the social aspects of sustainability and include a range of perspectives of attendees, for example, those who are mobility impaired, of a different ethnicity, or from different socioeconomic groups. This chapter is also written from both adults' and children's perspectives.

Chapter 4: Choosing a sustainable venue

The choice of venue for any event is a major decision that will influence the design and delivery of the event programme and the experience of attendees. The venue itself will be one of the main assets of the event and the venue management team will be key event stakeholders. As such, it may be prudent to choose a venue that has the principles of sustainability at its core and is both strategically and operationally focused on responsibly hosting events. Choosing a venue with such values and processes will help to ensure a synthesis between the venue and the event. This chapter will explore sustainability from an event venue perspective. It will illustrate how sustainable venues can be used to complement and advance the goal of planning and delivering a sustainable event.

Chapter 5: Stakeholders in sustainable events

This chapter considers the traditional stakeholders of events, namely attendees, host organizations, host community, sponsors, media and staff. The chapter focuses on the importance of the strategy used to select stakeholders involved in the event with regard to sustainability. The chapter reviews past events to show that a poor choice of sponsor (e.g. BP for the London 2012 Olympics) can impact negatively on the sustainability of an event. Chapter 5 also considers how events targeting particular stakeholders might attract other stakeholders who are sometimes unnoticed (e.g. children attending events that are primarily for a different age group) and the importance of catering for them. Finally, the chapter considers sustainability initiatives and stakeholders including issues such as greenwashing.

Chapter 6: Designing the sustainable event

Designing a sustainable event is central to the whole concept of events management. This section covers the choice of venue, decor, theme, event programme, catering and potential take away goods for participants. The concepts of atmosphere and co-creation are also considered. Taking the example of speed dating events (intersectionality), this chapter illustrates the difficulties and importance of creating the right atmosphere for the right audience. For children, the right atmosphere is also important as part of their safety and contributing to their wellbeing. Chapter 6 also looks at how event design influences behaviours, for example, promoting sustainable practices as well as onsite compliance with issues relating to EDI as an important aspect of the planning, designing and delivery of events and how addressing EDI is part of the 'people' aspect of the TBL.

Chapter 7: Delivering and evaluating the sustainable event

Chapter 7 explores the run up to an event (logistics, staffing) as well as the aftermath of the event (debrief, reporting). It considers what people need to understand, check for, plan and prepare for in terms of delivery as well as what should be measured during the event and evaluated afterwards. The chapter also delves into the importance and outcome of collaboration with local communities, suppliers, and stakeholders and seeking feedback after an event. The emphasis of the chapter is on the criteria to be used to evaluate the level of sustainability of an event and its long-term impacts, along with the significance of this for future event planning. ISO20121 or BCorps are also discussed.

Chapter 8: Making the event safe as an important aspect of sustainability

Conducting a thorough risk assessment of an event is an important part of ensuring its sustainability. Equally important, is consideration of safety at events targeting children and the balance between 'what is required' in order for the event to be safe alongside what can be considered sustainable practice. The chapter also discusses the role and importance of operations management, specifically aspects such as contingency planning and crowd management. Indeed, crowds are an important aspect of the marketing strategy for events (images of events often include crowds as a way of evidencing the event's popularity). Although a crowd may be a good selling point, this aspect of events is often discussed negatively.

Chapter 9: What is needed to run the sustainable event?

Chapter 9 mainly focuses on the inventory, and the importance of the choice of material, equipment, etc., needed to run an event. There is increasing pressure on event organizers to use resources that are eco-friendly, as well as to ensure events are cost effective (particularly when they are financed with public money). Procurement and funding are explored, building on the event design and operational aspects. This chapter also discusses emerging technologies such as AI and automation in events management in a post-pandemic world. These areas are increasingly relevant for sustainability.

Chapter 10: Digital marketing: The way forward for the sustainable events

This chapter focuses on sustainability in terms of marketing practices and audience expectations in events management, and the articulation of this in marketing strategies. The challenge with marketing a sustainable event is to attract the targeted number of attendees at a reduced cost, while being inclusive, knowing that individuals get information from different channels according to their particular demographic. Chapter 10 provides pointers for a successful marketing strategy and ticketing of events. To achieve its objectives, the chapter explores a variety of the PESO (paid, earned, shared, owner) model, from both the manager and the consumer perspectives. This requires an understanding of the target market, too. Finally, the environment aspect of sustainability is also considered.

Chapter 11: Conclusion: the future of sustainable events

Much has been said, written and done towards the sustainability of the event industry. This section adopts a forward-looking approach to planning, designing, and delivering events, with an exploration of future thoughts of the industry from Getz (2012), Yeoman (2013) and Séraphin (2021). Questions include: What will come after the SDGs run out in 2030? What about the impact of virtual and hybrid events? Is the metaverse more sustainable than live? How can the event industry be integrated within a circular economy process? Could the events industry lead the way in making sustainable practice the norm? Where might new innovations come from?

References

Borstlap, H and Saayman, M (2019) From crayons to canvas: The enlightenment of children at an arts festival, *African Journal of Hospitality, Tourism & Leisure*, 8 (2), 1–12

Botti, L and Peypoch, N (2013) Multi-criteria ELECTRE method and destination competitiveness, *Tourism Management Perspectives*, 6, 108–13.

Brackenridge, C H, Rhind, D and Palmer-Felgate, S (2015) Locating and mitigating risks to children associated with major sporting events, *Journal of Policy Research in Tourism, Leisure and Events*, 7 (3), 237–50

Butler, R (2024) 23 Final thoughts: revisions and modifications to the TALC model, *The Tourism Area Life Cycle: Review, Relevance and Revision*, 100

Clark, C D (2008) Tricks of festival: Children, enculturation, and American Halloween, *ETHOS*, 33 (2), 180–205

Delaney, E (2023) Venue considerations when planning child centric events. In: H Séraphin (ed) *Events Management for the Infant and Youth Market*, 139–52, Emerald Publishing Limited, Leeds

Department for Education (2023) *Using after-school clubs, tuition and community activities*. Department for Education, UK

Dodds, R. (2024). KESTAVA–food waste and sustainability in a Finnish restaurant. In *International Case Studies in Innovation and Entrepreneurship in Tourism* (pp. 161–165). Routledge.

Dowson, R, Albert, B and Lomax, D (2022) *Event planning and management: Principles, planning and practice*. Kogan Page Publishers.

Edelheim, J (2020) How should tourism education values be transformed after 2020? Global Tourism Geographies, 22 (3) 1–8

Edger, C and Oddy, R E (2018) *Events management: 87 key models for event, venue and experience (EVE) managers*, Libri Publishing, Farringdon

Evans, N G (2024) *Strategic Management for Tourism, Hospitality and Events*, Routledge, Abingdon

Eventbrite (2023) The event budget template you need to keep on track. www.eventbrite.co.uk/l/gc-event-budget-template-2/?submissionGuid=bb8099af-4dd6-4c48-9c47-6554a1f19ab9

Everingham, P and Chassagne, N (2020) Post-Covid-19 ecological and social reset: moving away from capitalist growth models towards tourism as Buen Vivir. In: *Global Tourism and Covid-19*, 101–12, Routledge, Abingdon

Finkel, R and Dashper, K (2020) Accessibility, diversity and inclusion in events. In: *The Routledge Handbook of Events*, 475–90, Routledge, Abingdon

Francis, M and Lorenzo, R (2002) Seven realms of children's participation, *Journal of Environmental Psychology*, 22 (1–2), 157–69

Frey, H F (2019) A small festival for small people. The WeeFestival as Advocacy. *Theatre Research in Canada*, 40 (1–2), 64–82

Getz, D (2012) Event studies: Discourses and future directions, *Event Management*, 16 (2), 171–87

Getz, D and Page, S J (2019) *Event Studies: Theory, research and policy for planned events*, Routledge, Abingdon

Gössling, S, Scott, D and Hall, C M (2020) Pandemics, tourism and global change: a rapid assessment of Covid-19, *Journal of Sustainable Tourism*, 29 (1), 1–20

Higgins-Desbiolles, F (2021) Socialising tourism for social and ecological justice after Covid-19. In: *Global tourism and Covid-19*, 156–69, Routledge, Abingdon

Higham, J, Font, X and Wu, J (2021) Code red for sustainable tourism, *Journal of Sustainable Tourism*, 30 (1), 1–13

Hixson, E (2014) The impact of young people's participation in events: Developing a model of social event impact, *International Journal of Event and Festival Management*, 5 (3), 198–218

Ioannides, D and Gyimóthy, S (2020) The Covid-19 crisis as an opportunity for escaping the unsustainable global tourism path, *Tourism Geographies*, 22(3), 624–32

Jepson, A, Stadler, R and Spencer, N (2019) Making positive family memories together and improving quality-of-life through thick sociality and bonding at local community festivals and events, *Tourism Management*, 75, 34–50

Késenne, S (2005) Do we need an economic impact study or a cost-benefit analysis of a sports event? *European Sport Management Quarterly*, 5(2), 133–42

Krasil'nikov, I (2020) Child and adolescent socialization in the 'Music-Making for All' festival and competition project, *Propósitos y Representaciones*, 8

Müller, J (2020) The children of the revolution, the nation's future: understanding the multigenerational audience of the Rock in Rio music festival, *International Journal of Communication*, 14, 18

Powell, C (2023) 7 Steps to the perfect children's event. In: *Events Management for the Infant and Youth Market*, 121–37, Emerald Publishing Limited, Leeds

Prideaux, B, Thompson, M and Pabel, A (2020) Lessons from Covid-19 can prepare global tourism for the economic transformation needed to combat climate change, *Tourism Geographies*, 22 (3), 667–78

Quadrant2design (2022) The events industry key statistics, www.quadrant2design.com/the-events-industry-key-statistics/

Rasmussen, K (2004) Places for children – children's places, *Childhood*, 11(2), 155–73

Rhama, B (2023) Sustainable rural tourism from the perspective of triple bottom line scientific framework, *Journal of Policy Research in Tourism, Leisure and Events*, 17 (1), 1–14

Rowen, I (2020) The transformational festival as a subversive toolbox for a transformed tourism: lessons from Burning Man for a Covid-19 world, *Tourism Geographies*, 22(3), 695–702

Sadeghi Shahdani, H, Torabi Farsani, N, Moslehi, M and Zahedi, M (2023) Designing an event calendar for children and teenagers: A tool for educational tourism, *Journal of Hospitality & Tourism Education*, 36 (2), 192–200.

Séraphin, H (2021) Covid-19: An opportunity to review existing grounded theories in event studies, *Journal of Convention & Event Tourism*, 22 (1), 3–35

Séraphin, H and Dosquet, F (2020) Mountain tourism and second home tourism as post Covid-19 lockdown placebo? *Worldwide Hospitality and Tourism Themes*, 12 (4), 485–500

Slater, S J, Christiana, R W and Gustat, J (2020) Recommendations for keeping parks and green space accessible for mental and physical health during Covid-19 and other pandemics, *Preventing Chronic Disease*, 17, E59

Spenceley, A, McCool, S, Newsome, D, Báez, A, Barborak, J R, Blye, C J, Bricker, K, Cahyadi, H S, Corrigan, K, Halpenny, E and Hvenegaard, G (2021) Tourism in protected and conserved areas amid the COVID-19 pandemic, *Parks*, 27, 103–18

Tayler, C, Mcardle, F, Richer, S, Brennan, C and Weier, K (2006) Learning partnerships with parents of young children: Studying the impact of a major festival of early childhood in Australia, *European Early Childhood Education Research Journal*, 14 (2), 7–19

Yeoman, I (2013) A futurist's thoughts on consumer trends shaping festivals and events, *International Journal of Event and Festival Management* 4 (3), 249–60

Zeng, Z, Chen, P J and Lew, A A (2020) From high-touch to high-tech: Covid-19 drives robotics adoption, *Tourism Geographies*, 22 (3), 724–34

Zhou, J, Zhou, J, Xie, T, Tang J and Zhu, Z (2018) *Materialistic vs. meaningful festival celebration for children on Sina microblog*, 5th International Conference on Behavioral, Economic, and Socio-Cultural Computing (BESC), Kaohsiung, Taiwan, 270–75

01 | Overview: The events industry and sustainability

LEARNING OUTCOMES

By the end of Chapter 1, you will be able to:
- reflect on the typology and meaning of planned events
- explain how the evolution (in terms of its role and importance) of the events industry reflects the evolution of society and the demand for sustainability
- identify key concepts related to the sustainability of planned events such as the partnership ecosystem, the Helix model and related concepts, events professionals as agents of change, sustainable development goals and events, and disempowered groups of people.

Introduction

Events and the evolution of pre-modern, modern and post-modern society are entwined, and as such, events could be used to discuss the evolution of the former. Indeed, throughout history, it has been noted that the role, purpose, number, types, importance, impacts, morphing, size, delivery, location, attendance and attendees of events have changed to reflect the evolution of society (Andrews and Leopold, 2013).

As a result of the morphing of events, it is also important that literature in the field reflects that evolution. Subsequently, this chapter provides a classification of planned events that mirrors the types and needs of contemporary consumers, while also pointing out how existing events contribute to the economic, social and environmental sustainability of the post-modern society we live in. This opening chapter positions itself alongside O'Regan et al (2022) who argue that a discursive formation around a particular topic is not static and should constantly be challenged to advance knowledge. Subsequently, the chapter adopts a radical innovation approach (as opposed to an incremental approach), aimed at advancing knowledge in service industries such as events and related fields such as hospitality and tourism (Brooker and Joppe, 2014). Practically, this translates into a discussion of types of events and consumers, who are often overlooked by the literature and sometimes also overlooked by the industry. Such an approach enables the first chapter to provide an alternative typology of events, while also discussing how to address the new and emerging needs of consumers (Getz, 2012; Getz and Page, 2019).

Taking the impacts that Covid-19 had on the event industry, Séraphin (2021) indicated that major changes in society, and subsequently in events, offer opportunities to review grounded theories in the field. These reviews are important, particularly for theories that are now outdated. However, this chapter also adopts a Janusian-thinking approach, acknowledging that advancing knowledge in a field is not about a tabula rasa; instead, it is about acknowledging and embracing long-existing grounded theories as still being valid, while also suggesting that an accurate depiction implies updating some of the existing grounded theories, such as Getz's (2012) Future Propositions (FPs) and the typology of events, etc.

Influenced by the research by Ziakas and Getz (2020), Ziakas and Costa (2011) and Ziakas (2019), this chapter adopts an intersectional approach, which translates into looking at events which are intersectional in terms of the industry they belong to. Finally, we consider adopting the position that no members of society should be considered as passive and/or powerlessness, as it is currently the case. The current situation results in some segments of society being under-represented or not represented in research and/or industry (Dashper, 2020; Grande and Séraphin, 2025).

By giving visibility to the disempowered, by adopting a multidisciplinary approach, and finally by adopting a Janusian-thinking approach, this chapter disrupts the current approach of discursive formation of event studies. This disruption contributes to the sustainability of the industry through the 'people' dimension of the triple bottom line (TBL), while also addressing the United Nations Sustainable Development Goal 10 (Reduced inequalities), which in turn contributes to the 'planet' and 'profit' dimensions of the TBL. Indeed, when individuals are empowered, they adjust their behaviour and attitudes and turn into sustainability thinkers, actioners and transformers, resulting in the achievement of SDGs such as SDG 11 (Sustainable cities and communities), SDG 12 (Responsible consumption and production) and SDG 13 (Climate action) (Bocken et al, 2014; Schill et al, 2020).

An equality, diversity and inclusion (EDI) approach to the research, planning, design and delivery of events is believed to be the corner stone of the long-term sustainability of the events industry. Indeed, this approach alongside empowerment has led to a version of George Orwell's 'Newspeak', understood as the destruction of former beliefs, attitudes, ways of thinking and perceptions and the adoption of new ones (Borman, 1998; Napolitano et al, 2020). Despite the fact the event industry has already adopted Newspeak in the form of a greenwashing strategy, with the existence of phrases such as 'greening events' and the emergence of the green version of events that are not known

Figure 1.1 Sustainability of the events industry

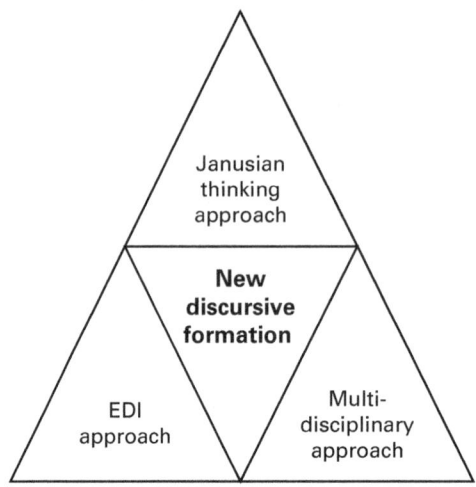

to be the opposite of eco-friendly, such as Formula E's 'green challenge', it is believed that Newspeak is not fully achieved yet, as it happens when no other alternative is possible (Dodds, 2018; Mair and Popely, 2019; Sturm, 2019; Borman, 1998). However, current issues such as Covid, the development of technology and virtual events etc., have had a major impact on the delivery of events. Their implications will be discussed later in the chapter. Figure 1.1 outlines the perspective of this chapter to provide an overview of the sustainability of the events industry.

Typology of planned events

Definitions of planned events

Events are often defined by their duration and frequency (Table 1.1). They are temporary as they have a start and finish time and occur at specific times during the year. Events include a gathering of people (such as a community, customers, competitors, colleagues, family and friends) for a specific purpose, which may be cultural, commercial, a celebration or a funeral, for example. Other elements that help to define an event include place (regional, national, international, pan-continental), geography (city, county, country, field, etc.), size (small or large), value (income generated) and the experience conveyed to participants. Ownership (private and for profit or public and non-profit) and the proximity of the event to local communities may also be used to define events.

To facilitate the understanding of events, frameworks or typology of events have been developed. Although the overall categorization of events is broadly similar, some differences do exist, which provides evidence that the typology of events has not been agreed upon among academics, as indicated in Table 1.2.

Table 1.1 Keywords associated with planned events

Keywords associated with events	References
Temporary	Bladen et al, 2022; Dowson et al, 2022; Dawson and Bassett, 2018
Calendar	Dowson et al, 2022; Getz and Page, 2019
Gathering of individuals	Bladen et al, 2022; Dowson et al, 2022; Dawson and Bassett, 2018; Raj et al, 2017
Specific purpose	Bladen et al, 2022; Dowson et al, 2022; Dawson and Bassett, 2018; Raj et al, 2017
Location, size, value, experience, ownership	Getz and Page, 2019; Reic, 2016

Table 1.2 Typology of events

Typology of events	Sources
• Sporting events • Corporate events • Musical events • Cultural events • Commercial/business events • Political/government events • Personal/private events • Religious events	Raj et al (2016)
Type • Cultural celebrations • Business and trade • Arts and entertainment • Political and state • Private events • Sport and recreation Size • Local events • Major events • Hallmark events • Mega-events • Virtual events	Dawson et al (2023)

(continued)

Table 1.2 (Continued)

Typology of events	Sources
• Cultural celebrations • Business and trade • Arts and entertainment • Sport and recreation • Political and state • Private functions	Getz & Page (2019)
• Cultural celebrations • Business and trade • Arts and entertainment • Political and state • Private events • Educational and scientific • Recreational	Getz (2007, 2012)
Type • Cultural events • Business events • Sports events • Local or community events Size • Major events • Hallmark events • Mega-events	Bowdin et al (2011)
Type • Cultural celebrations • Business and trade • Arts and entertainment • Sport competition • Political and state • Private events • Recreational Size • Local events • Major events • Hallmark events • Mega-events	Dawson & Bassett (2018)

(continued)

Table 1.2 (Continued)

Typology of events	Sources
Type • Musical • Sporting • Business • Cultural • Arts • Religious • Political • Family • Generational • Fundraising Size • Micro • Minor • Major • Hallmark • Mega	Reic (2017)
• Business and corporate events • Cause-related and fund-raising events • Exhibitions, expositions and fairs • Entertainment and leisure events • Festivals • Government and civic events • Hallmark events • Marketing events • Meeting and convention events • Social/life-cycle events • Sport events	Berridge (2007)

Convergence of typology of events

Despite the different existing typologies of events, overlaps can be seen, as shown in Table 1.2. Figure 1.2 provides a summary of existing typologies.

Sporting events and competitions

Sporting events involve both an audience and performers. They are often designed as championship. According to Bowdin et al (2023), there are four types of sporting

Figure 1.2 Summary of typology of planned events

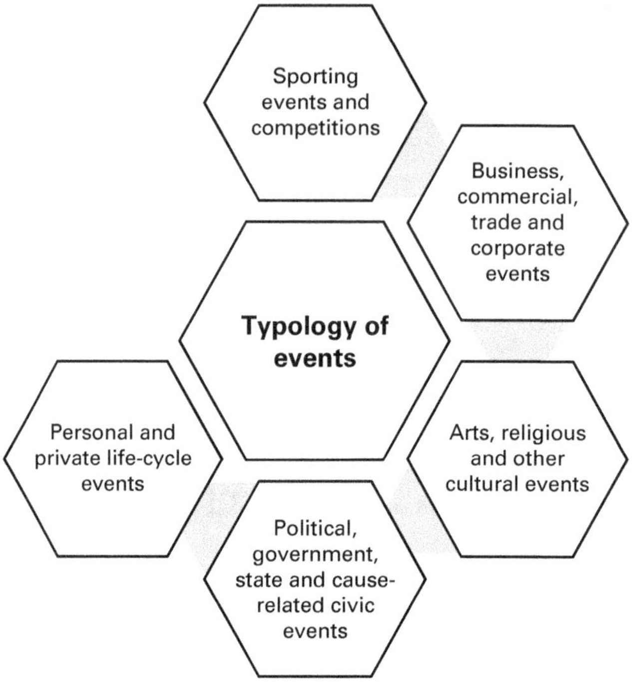

```
         Sporting
       events and
       competitions
                            Business,
                           commercial,
                            trade and
                            corporate
                              events
           Typology of
             events

Personal and                 Arts, religious
private life-cycle            and other
    events                   cultural events

            Political,
           government,
         state and cause-
          related civic
             events
```

events: mega-events, calendar events, one-off events and finally showcase events. Because of the image and impact of sporting events (particularly mega-events), they are often part of political and government marketing strategies.

Business, commercial, trade and corporate events

Business, commercial, trade and corporate events are used to support the objectives and ambitions of organizations (Berridge, 2007). They are usually associated with experiential or live marketing. The main purpose of these commerce-oriented events is to bring together buyers and sellers and develop the image of a brand, while also building and sustaining a relationship with internal and external customers (Berridge, 2007; Getz and Page, 2019). The purpose of these events can also be to exchange information, debate on a topic, educate, etc. Exhibitions or fairs such as the World Travel Market and the Hampshire Business Show are examples of business, commercial, trade and corporate events (Berridge, 2007).

Arts, religious and other cultural events

Cultural events can be commercial or non-commercial. Religious events which are also cultural events, are the largest events in the world when it comes to the number of attendees. The pilgrimage of Muslims in Saudi Arabia for the Hajj in Makkah is an example by excellence (Raj et al, 2017).

Political, government, state and cause-related civic events

Events to promote a cause usually have a social function (Getz and Page, 2019). The most striking examples are fund-raising events which help with research and raising awareness of conditions such as cancer, diabetes, etc. (Getz and Page, 2019). Events may also be organized for political reasons and will be organized by political parties, communities or other government entities (Berridge, 2007). Their main objectives are to promote political, economic or social change (Raj et al, 2017).

Personal and private life-cycle events

Personal and private life-cycle events are usually attended by people who have been invited, such as family and friends (Berridge, 2007; Raj et al, 2017). According to the convergence of the typologies discussed in Table 1.2, the size of such events can be split into five categories (Figure 1.3).

Local events

Local events are usually organized by and for the local community. They have enormous potential in terms of development of social capital among members of the local community. These events tend not to attract interest and audiences outside the local area. From a financial perspective, their cost is relatively low (Dawson and Bassett, 2018).

Figure 1.3 Size of planned events

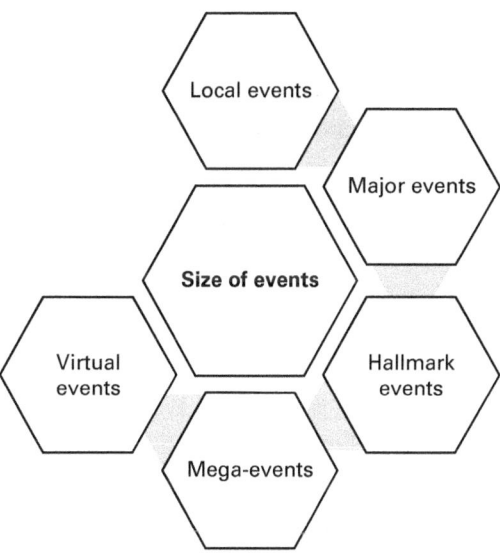

Major events

As opposed to local events, major events attract both locals and an international audience. Because of their significance in terms of audience and economic impact, they attract interest from the media and commercially oriented organizations (Dawson and Bassett, 2018).

Hallmark events

These events are characterized by their authenticity and play a significant role in the branding of a destination because of their regional and local positive impacts. Indeed, they have often became synonymous of destinations (Dawson and Bassett, 2018; Getz and Page, 2019). Examples of hallmark events include the Rio Carnival, Venice Carnival and La Tomatina in Spain.

Mega-events

Mega-events are the largest type of events. They usually attract attendees from all over the world. The Olympics and similar sporting events are examples of mega-events. Countries bid to host these events, often many years in advance. The cost of hosting these events is enormous, but so are the impacts (Bowdin et al, 2023; Dawson and Bassett, 2018). However, local and community events could also be argued to have 'mega' economic and social impacts on a destination (Getz and Page, 2019).

Virtual events

Virtual events are events that are held online, rather than in a physical space. The breakout of Covid played a significant role in the development of these events (Dowson et al, 2022). Séraphin (2021) argued that the pandemic played a significant role in reviewing some grounding theories such as the one formulated by Getz (2012: 382):

> FP1: Planned, live events, both personal and societal in scale and meaning, will always be a prominent feature of civilization, in all societies and culture.

> FP2: Virtual events will gain in frequency and importance in response to advances in global technology, and because of globalisation forces and the costs or risks of travel, but they will be in addition to, and not a substitute for, live event experiences.

Séraphin (2021) in turn argued that:

> New Future Proposition (NFP1): Planned, live events, both personal and societal in scale and meaning, will always be a prominent feature of civilization, in all societies and cultures. However, in time of pandemics or other crisis, live events will be perturbed, before a staggered returned to normal under certain conditions, and strict controls.

New Future Proposition (NFP2): Virtual events will gain in frequency and importance in response to advances in global technology, and because of globalization forces and the costs or risks of travel, but they will be in addition to, and not a substitute for, live event experiences.

Updating the typology of events

Existing research offering a typology of events is based exclusively on a specific industry or sector (Table 1.2). Some events also happen to be at the intersection of different sectors and/or industries. Speed-dating events, for example, are at the intersection of the dating industry, the event industry and the hospitality industry. Equally important, events such as speed-dating events and those aimed at adults fall into the category of intersectional events dedicated exclusively to adults, hence the reason, Séraphin (2024) refers to them as 'adultainment' events (Séraphin, 2024; Séraphin & Chaney, 2024; Yallop et al, 2025; Turley et al, 2017). See Figure 1.4. The main difference between these events and other personal and private life-cycle events such as weddings and birthdays is that the former can also be attended by those aged under 18. Other examples of events not aimed purely at adults include events delivered by children (for example in mini-clubs in hospitality settings, particularly in family

Figure 1.4 Updated typology of planned events

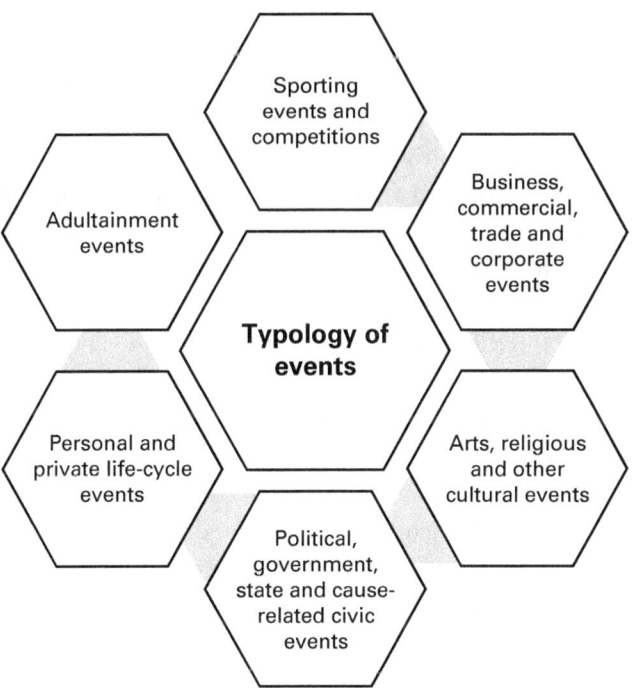

resorts) to their parents and other customers of the resort. These events are advertainment (advertizement and entertainment) events as their purpose is to encourage families to come back to the resorts, and to encourage parents who have not registered their children to the mini clubs to do so. The benefits of these types of events are referred as psychic income, namely events with positive psychological and emotional benefits (Delaney, 2025). These events contribute to the economic sustainability of resorts ('Profit' aspect of the Triple Bottom Line).

Events and sustainability

The triple bottom line (TBL)

The triple bottom line (TBL) includes three different dimensions namely planet, profit, and people. The 'planet' dimension focuses on sustainability strategy for an eco-friendly planet with actions related to tackling issues such as pollution, waste management and environmental stewardship (Slater et al, 2020; Spenceley et al, 2021). The 'people' dimension is essentially about addressing health, safety and other human needs (Rhama, 2023). Finally, 'profit' is the economic dimension of the TBL. It is about finding and maintaining a balance between economic growth and societal wellbeing (Rhama, 2023). Note that there are a variety of sequences for the TBL (Alberts and Niendorf, 2021; Craig, 2013; Munoz and Cohen, 2018; Woodroof, 2009). These reflect a non-unified or agreed discursive formation around sustainability, which could be perceived as both a challenge – as diverse perceptions can lead to confusion – but also an opportunity for continual updating and reviewing of knowledge (O'Regan et al, 2022; El-Sawad et al, 2004).

For Craig (2013) sustainability only includes two parameters: planet and people. Woodroof (2009) also considers two parameters as being very important for sustainability, namely profit and planet. Both Craig and Woodroof acknowledge the importance of the planet dimension, but there is no consensus on the order of people and profit as parameters of sustainability. After Munoz and Cohen (2019), sustainability started to include all three dimensions of the TBL as they are known today. However, Munoz and Cohen (2019) sequence the TBL as people, profit and planet, while Alberts and Niendorf (2021) rank the TBL as people, planet and profit. Figure 1.5 provides a visual representation of these differences in ranking.

Table 1.3 is obtained by crossing the research from Alberts and Niendorf (2021), Craig (2013), Munoz and Cohen (2019) and Woodroof (2009). This suggests that 'profit' is the dimension that no one agrees on the level of importance, as opposed to 'people' and 'planet' which are both considered as important, but with some degrees of difference.

A consensual sequencing from Alberts and Niendorf (2021), Craig (2013), Munoz and Cohen (2019) and Woodroof (2009) could be:

1 People
2 Planet
3 Profit

The sequence suggested by Alberts and Niendorf (2021) appears to be the most consensual one (Figure 1.6). It is also the positioning of this book with regard to sustainability in the event industry.

Figure 1.5 Sequences of the triple bottom line

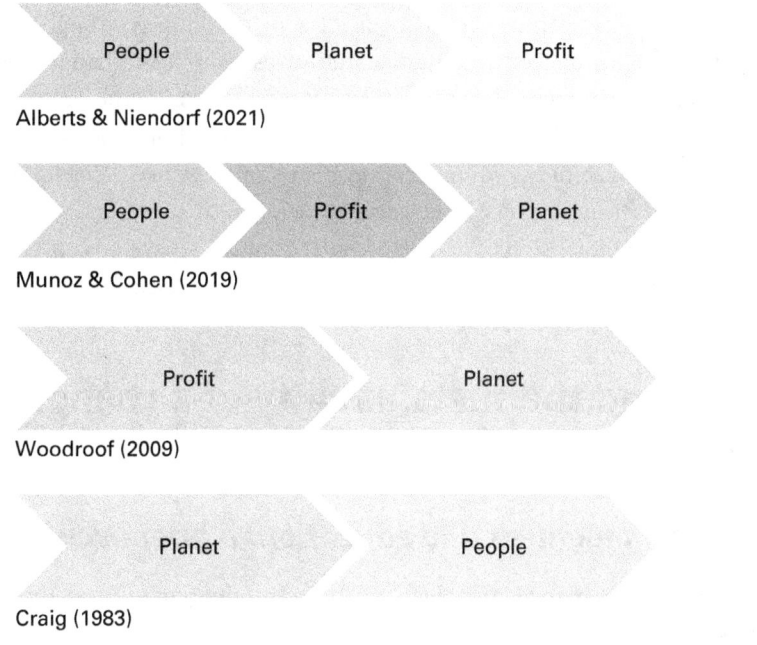

Table 1.3 Occurrence of ranking of the triple bottom line

Dimensions	OCCURRENCE OF RANKING		
	1st	2nd	3rd
People	√√	√	
Planet	√	√√	√
Profit	√	√	√

Figure 1.6 Alberts and Niendorf (2021) sequence of the triple bottom line

The TBL and planned events

Events are a central part in the life of individuals ('people') and cover all aspects of their life course, including contextual and person changes across the lifespan (Zacher and Froidevaux, 2021). 'Planet' is an underlying dimension in all these events as sustainability is central for the event industry, but also for the long-term sustainability of life on the planet (Séraphin and Nolan, 2019). Indeed, there is now a code red for sustainability in everything we do regardless of the industry (Higham et al, 2022; Schill et al, 2020), hence the different initiatives to unlock changes (Visser, 2016). While business, commercial, trade and corporate events are the only types of events directly related to profit, as with any other event, they should be organized in such a way as to minimize negative impacts on people and planet (Wickham et al, 2021). Despite the lesser importance that seems to be given to 'profit' in terms of the TBL, it is an underlying dimension of all events, since running an event is costly and so needs to be profitable, even if that is not its primary objective (Getz, 2012; Késenne, 2005).

Events and the sustainability of a changing society

Events management and education: a brief overview

Historically, events management was covered as modules in tourism and/or hospitality courses. However, over the years, higher education providers progressively developed dedicated and specialized courses in events management. As part of this, also emerged events management modules dedicated to sustainability. For universities which are part of the Principles for Responsible Management Education (PRME) network, the inclusion of sustainability in the curriculum is compulsory as it is part of the foundation of the network (Séraphin et al, 2021).

Events professionals as agents of change

When empowered to be sustainable agents of change, individuals and particularly young people can turn into sustainability thinkers, actioners and transformers (Séraphin et al, 2022). Being an agent of change is not a panacea however, as pointed out by Smith et al (2023). As Getz (2012, p.382) pointed out: 'The event professional of the future will be competent in events management theory and applications, knowledgeable about the importance of events in society, an effective advocate for event-related policy, and a constant learner within the field of event studies.'

Indeed, students studying events management are fully aware of the positive and negative impacts of events on society. They are also perfectly aware of strategies to put in place to minimize the negative and maximize the negative.

Application of sustainability

The seventeen UN Sustainable Development Goals (SDGs) are criteria that can be used by the event industry to evaluate its level of sustainability (Whitfield et al, 2024). Through the SDGs, events organizers can consider:

- social and cultural responsibility, including elements such as the reporting of impacts, legacies, well-being, inclusion, safeguarding, gender and sexual orientations
- economic sustainability, which is the umbrella for strategies such as alleviating poverty
- environmental sustainability, including recycling strategies, environmental leveraging and the use of technology
- events management and education, with a focus on how education can impact consumer attitude and behaviour regarding sustainability, greenwashing (Whitfield et al, 2024).

REAL-WORLD EXAMPLE A more sustainable model for live music?

Lollapalooza India 2025 presented a strong response to climate concerns. With more than 140,000 attendees, the Mumbai edition of the festival partnered with the Earth Day Organization (EDO) to imbed sustainability throughout the entire event. For instance, the festival hosted an Earth Action Day Area, offering games and exhibits made from recycled materials.

For its Music of the Spheres tour, Coldplay halved its direct emissions compared to its previous global tour and committed to planting one tree for every ticket sold (Darley, 2025).

The UK events management industry is quite active when it comes to sustainability. For instance, many higher education (HE) institutions delivering events management courses are part of the PRME network (education and training) and so must integrate sustainability in their curriculum. In the UK, there are also many organizations/networks such as The Power of Events, The Network of Women in Events and the Event Industry Forum contributing to the sustainability of the industry. Table 1.4 shows the response of event organizers to the question, 'What is the main reason you or your organization organize events?' The activities of some of the different bodies involved in the UK sector and their coverage of the span of SDGs is shown in Table 1.5.

Towards a partner ecosystem strategy for sustainability

Collaboration and partnership among stakeholders (Figure 1.7) involved in an industry are often perceived as a source of value co-creation and economic performance (Mendes et al, 2023). They are also associated with an enhancement of competitiveness, as a result of shared expertise, knowledge, ideas, innovation, etc. (Camilleri et al, 2023).

Table 1.4 Motivations behind the organization of events in the UK

2017	2018	TBL	SDGs
Education and training (29%)	Education and training (38%)	People	4
Generate profit (24%)	Generate profit (25%)	Profit	8
Networking/build relationships (16%)	Networking/build relationships (26%)	People	17
Bring people together/community building (8%)	Bring people together/community building (32%)	People	11
Raise money for charity (4%)	Raise money for charity (17%)	People	10
Lead generation (4%)	Lead generation (13%)	People	11

SOURCE Eventbrite (2018)

Table 1.5 Examples of actions of the UK event industry towards sustainability

SDGs	Sources	About
SDG 4: Quality education	The Power of Events www.thepowerofevents.org/about/	School engagement programme to inspire the future generation about the events industry
SDG 5: Gender equality SDG 10: Reduced inequalities	The Network of Women in Events (NOWIE) https://female-founders.org/events/?gad_source=1	Advocating for better opportunities for women in the event industry
SDG 9: Industry innovation and infrastructure	Attitude attitudeiseverything.org.uk/	Improving access to events people with disabilities
SDG 3: Good health and wellbeing SDG 12: Responsible consumption and production	DEFRA www.gov.uk/government/organizations/department-for-environment-food-rural-affairs	Protection/guidance related to food production and standards
SDG 11: Sustainable cities and communities SDG 17: Partnerships for the goals	Events Industry Forum www.eventsindustryforum.co.uk/	Provide guidance to event practitioners

To ensure that all stakeholders of the industry work within a flourishing ecosystem, Yallop et al (2025) and Pansiri (2008) suggest that it is important for the partners to be: (1) compatible in terms of values and also goals for the future; (2) capable of working and complementing each other using their tangible and intangible resources to increase their performance and therefore competitiveness; (3) committed to make the partnership a success for all those involved; (4) able to maintain a certain level of control over each other to avoid partners taking decisions not agreed by all; (5) able to trust each other, which implies a transparent discussion of all aspects of the organization.

Commitment and trust are presented by Yallop et al (2025) as central. Indeed, taking the case of speed dating events, they show that despite a high level of compatibility and capabilities, the hospitality industry and the dating industry have failed to work together effectively due to a low commitment and trust. This reconciliation is the *sine qua non* condition for the development of new concepts such as 'dinner date' (Séraphin and Abou Hamdan, 2023). Working in partnership within an ecosystem contributes to sustainable development goals such as SDG 9 (Industry, innovation and infrastructure) and SDG 17 (Partnerships for the goals).

There are instances of events management education providers and event industry companies or organizations working together. The University of East London and organizers of the London After Dark festivals are working together to develop an education programme aimed at increasing community engagement, while also providing students with the opportunity to work on the design and planning of an event (Curtis and Jones, 2024). Collaboration between industry and academia is also a way for both parties to further understanding of event attendees, which would advance academic research, while enabling practitioners to deliver better events (Stadler, 2015). Collaboration between academia and industry has led to the emergence of a practice referred to as research-led and research-informed teaching. This practice has 'become an important element of higher education teaching and learning in the UK' (Stadler, 2024: 204). As seen earlier in this chapter, collaborations can also be among industry partners and/or other supporting/network/advisory bodies. The event industry and its stakeholders seem to have fully embraced the importance of SDG 17 (Partnerships for the goals).

The partner ecosystem approach discussed in this section echoes the concept of the Helix model. The Triple Helix model refers to the interaction among three entities, namely academia, industry and government, with the objective to offer quality education to learners and foster knowledge exchange between industry and academia (Etzkowitz, 2015; Page, 2014). There is also the Quad Helix model (Kimatu, 2016), which involves four entities such as academia, supporting organizations, government and industry. As for the Quintuple or Penta Helix model, it offers a structure for five partners to be involved (Kholiavko et al, 2021).

Partner ecosystem and Helix model are also related to the concept of 'clustering'. The term 'clustering' referred to as 'innovative milieu', 'industrial complex' or 'agglomeration' by Peck and McGuinness (2003) is often associated with competitive advantage and performance improvement (Lai et al, 2014). If we take the case of businesses, clusters help to lower their investment costs, facilitate the recruitment of highly skilled staff, improve leverage with suppliers, enhance their ability to innovate in terms of development of new products and services, increase social networks and contacts and help them gain legitimacy (Lai et al, 2014). All this is possible if there is a good knowledge management system in place among partners (Lai et al, 2014). Finally, the concept of 'Belt' can be used alongside cluster, partnership ecosystem and Helix model. This is a very old concept based on the principle of cooperation, extensive consultation and contribution, and shared benefits (Li et al, 2020).

The development of an ecosystem in the events industry can lead to the development of events management 'knowledge cities'. Their development presents a variety of benefits for stakeholders, including (1) students, who can more easily find a job after graduation due to prior placements within the sector; (2) academia, who have an opportunity to be more innovative in their pedagogic and research approach, and to access private funding; (3) businesses, who have an opportunity to be more innovative and therefore improve their performance in the market, as well as contribute to the local community's well-being. The same benefits described in points 1–3 above could also be said about eventful destinations (Richards and Palmer, 2010; Rullani, 2012).

Visser (2015) points out that stakeholders' engagement plays a role in unlocking changes towards sustainability. This section of the chapter on partner ecosystems has discussed this aspect of sustainability in depth and is summarized in Figure 1.7. The next section provides examples of challenges for the industry in terms of customer engagement.

Figure 1.7 Sustainability and the challenges for the event industry

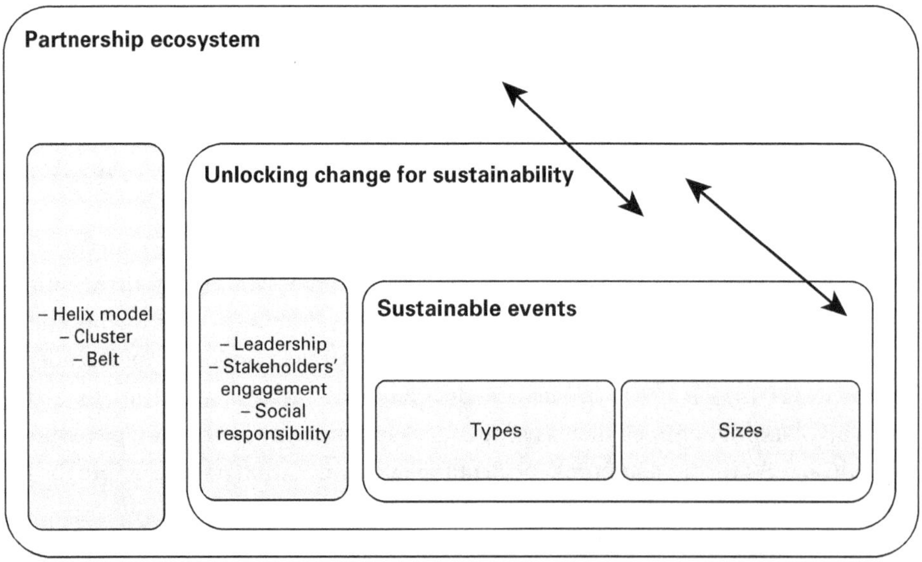

The role of disempowered groups in events

The event industry: children's place or place for children?

Society and organizations are offering children a place because the current social environment is not naturally a children's place (Rasmussen, 2004). This is even the more the case for the event industry, which is considered to have a rigid format and one that is not always suitable for children, while those that have a disability often face barriers that prevent them being involved in the event industry (Carlyle, 2023).

REAL-WORLD EXAMPLE   Global children's festivals

The Győr Kids Festival

The Győr Kids Festival is a free outdoor festival for disadvantaged children aged 3 to 14 years which aims to provide access to cultural activities. It is now the largest free outdoor festival for children and young people in Hungary. In 2015, the event was attended by 50,000 visitors, including 26,000 children and young people. As a calendar event, the Győr Kids Festival is scheduled every year in July in the city centre of Győr (Győrkőc-Festival, 2024).

The International Children's Festival of the Arts

The International Children's Festival of the Arts (May–June) in the City of St Albert in Canada aims to bring together children and arts for cultural experiences to remove barriers, foster joy and creativity, develop social capital and, equally important, inspire the next generation of artists. The festival aims to create safe, inclusive and creative spaces where children can explore and further their understanding of themselves, others and the surrounding environment.

Dowse et al (2017:197) argued that children are undermined as members of the community. The same could be said of the events industry which offers children a 'place' but is not a children's 'Place'. Taking the example of weddings, Haverly (2023) explains that while they can be attended by children, they are not the most suitable event for them because of the length of the event, which can be perceived as boring by them. Children are considered to bring stress to the event, while also being perceived as contributing to the fun of the event. Green (2023) suggests that outside the school environment, more specific products and services must be planned, designed and delivered to children. Using the example of Kids TEDx, 'an event which children and young people create, host and attend' (Carlyle, 2023: 209), it is clear that the events industry, if backed up with transformational leadership, industry reform, stakeholder engagement, social responsibility, integrated values and future-fitness, can unlock change (Visser, 2015). This approach is important as events, and more specifically family events, have a lasting impact on children, which have repercussions on them even when adults (Maingi and Gowreesunkar, 2023). Venues and events promoting environmental sustainability are particularly strong in terms of learning and impacts on children (Lestar and Pelligrini-Masini, 2023).

Empowering the disempowered

Other disempowered members of society that the events industry needs to cater for include (but is not limited to) individuals with cognitive impairments such as autism and dementia, individuals with physical impairments such as epilepsy and cancer, and socially marginalized and vulnerable individuals such as migrants, refugees and older people. Batec Mobility is a company which provides mobility solutions and they compiled a list of the world's most inclusive and accessible music festivals, including the following (Batec Mobility, n.d.):

- B-Side Festival (UK)
- Coachella (USA)
- Coca-Cola Music Experience (Spain)
- Festival Inclusivo por la Diversidad Asturias (Spain)
- Glastonbury (UK)
- Hellfest (France)
- Lollapalooza (USA)
- Mallorca Live Festival (Spain)
- Primavera Sound (Spain)
- Reading Festival (UK)
- Sziget Festival (Budapest)

Measures to promote inclusivity at events

Batec Mobility (n.d.) also suggest the following to promote inclusivity at events. Steps to enhance accessibility for people with reduced mobility (PRM) include:

- designated parking spaces
- specific camping areas close to the entrance
- adapted showers and bathrooms
- platforms near the main stage for optimal concert viewing

- improved lighting to mitigate potential obstacles
- creation of refuge zones
- trained staff available to provide assistance when needed
- barrier-free spaces without uneven surfaces or obstructions and ramps or lifts where there are changes in elevation
- information points and accessible interaction with other services (e.g. ticket validation, wristband placement, festival currency purchase or recharge).

Steps to improve cognitive accessibility:

- Clear and understandable information, for example websites designed with a user-friendly interface and programmes presented in a readable format.
- Effective event signage including use of icons for bathrooms, reserved areas and exit signs.

Steps to improve accessibility for individuals with visual impairments:

- Provision of audio descriptions, Braille systems, audio guides, tactile maps and acoustic messages within the venue.
- Measures to enhance reading and viewing of venue information and visual signals for those with low vision, including adjustments to character size, contrast and brightness.
- Increased lighting around signs and information points.
- Access allowed for guide dogs for those requiring assistance.

Steps to improve accessibility for individuals with hearing impairments:

- Individual induction loop systems ensuring clear audio for users of hearing aids and cochlear implants.
- Availability of subtitling resources.
- Sign language interpretation, for example trained personnel providing interpretation services at concerts.
- Vibrating backpacks provided for individuals with severe hearing impairments.

ACTIVITY 1.1

Create an outline proposal for a fun and creative event for children and young people (3–18 years old). The purpose of the event is to raise awareness about sustainability.

1 Provide a list of fun activities you could offer to educate children about sustainability.

2. Justify your choice (for instance, identify which Sustainable Development Goals would be achieved by these activities).

3. As part of your proposal, make a list of the likely needs that children and their carers would have when attending such an event.

When planning this event, you also need to take into consideration the needs of children and carers when attending events. Their needs are listed here (see Figure 2): www.eventsindustryforum.co.uk/images/documents/EIF_Report-Oxford_Brookes.pdf

CHECKLIST

The questions below support this chapter's discussion around the typology of events and the evolution of the events industry with regard to sustainability.

Typology and meaning of planned events

1. What type of event are you organizing?
2. What is the purpose of the event?
3. Does your event meet societal needs?

Events and society

4. Who are you working with to ensure the sustainability of your event?
5. How can you evaluate the performance of your event from a sustainability perspective?
6. Is your event inclusive?
7. What changes could you make to your event to make it suitable for disempowered groups?

Summary

Environmental sustainability ('planet' in the triple bottom line (TBL)) is a major global issue that industries, including the events industry, are concerned about. There is a code red on sustainability (Higham et al, 2022), which is impacting on the events industry in multiple ways, including the need for event organizers to work with partners (suppliers, contractors, etc.) who are also committed to sustainability as well as the need to develop strategies that encourage the greening of events. From a social perspective, sustainability is directly concerned with the 'people' dimension of the TBL. With the emergence of equality/equity, diversity and inclusion (EDI), event organizers must ensure for instance that events 'welcome everyone and enable them to participate fully, on their own terms' (Finkel and Dashper, 2020:475–91). Because modern events management must be thought and planned with an open and innovative mind, adopting a combined EDI, multi-disciplinary and Janusian-thinking approach can help in this endeavour.

Additionally, it is important that the typology of events is reviewed and updated regularly to reflect the evolution of society, and the emergence of new events related to this evolution. The industry also needs to think increasingly in terms of sustainability (people, planet, profit) to ensure the long-term success of events. Collaboration and partnership among stakeholders of the industry is also a pre-requisite for sustainability. However, some challenges remain, such as ensuring that industry does not disempower those individuals with physical, cognitive or social impairments.

Because events must adhere to a variety of laws, regulations and standards, this has impacted the cost of running them, including venue costs (which vary according to location, capacity, parking, facilities, layout and accessibility); staffing costs; catering costs; entertainment costs (which vary according to the type, theme, size, location and duration of the event); equipment costs; travel and accommodation costs for performers etc.; and marketing and promotion costs (Eventbrite, 2023). Despite the challenges faced by events organizers and the pressure faced by the public sector (Getz, 2012), the 'show must go on' as 'Planned, live events, both personal and societal in scale and meaning, will always be a prominent feature of civilization, in all societies and cultures' (Getz, 2012: 382).

As predicted by Getz (2012) and fuelled by both the Covid pandemic and the development of technologies, virtual events are also gaining in importance.

The main takeaways from this chapter are that the event industry is dynamic when it comes to putting in place measures towards sustainability. Technology and changing perceptions will be the key drivers for an even more sustainable events industry.

Further reading

Lestar, T, Pilato, M M and Séraphin, H (2024) *Eating Together in the Twenty-First Century*, Routledge, Abingdon

Séraphin, H (ed) (2022) *Children in Sustainable and Responsible Tourism*, Emerald Publishing, Leeds

Séraphin, H (ed) (2023) *Events Management for the Infant and Youth Market*, Emerald Publishing, Leeds

Séraphin, H and Korstanje, M (2025) *Solo Travel, Tourism and Loneliness*, Routledge, Abingdon

References

Alberts, H C and Niendorf, B D (2021) Interdisciplinary learning about people, planet, and profit in Germany, *The Geography Teacher*, 18 (3–4), 158–63

Andrews, H and Leopold, T (2013) *Events and the Social Sciences*, Routledge, Abingdon

Batec Mobility (n.d.) Discover the best inclusive and accessible music festivals, batec-mobility.com/en/accessible-music-festivals/

Berridge, G (2007) *Events Design and Experience*, Routledge, Abingdon

Bladen, C, Kennell, J, Abson, E and Wilde, N (2022) *Events Management: An introduction*, Routledge, Abingdon

Bocken, N M, Short, S W, Rana, P and Evans, S (2014) A literature and practice review to develop sustainable business model archetypes, *Journal of Cleaner Production*, 65, 42–56

Borman, G (1998) *Cliffs Notes on Orwell's 1984*, CliffsNotes, Lincoln, Nebraska

Bowdin, G A, Allen, J, Harris, R, Jago, L, O'Toole, W and McDonnell, I (2023) *Events Management*, Routledge, Abingdon

Brooker, E and Joppe, M (2014) Developing a tourism innovation typology: Leveraging liminal insights, *Journal of Travel Research*, 53 (4), 500–8

Camilleri, M A, Troise, C, Strazzullo, S and Bresciani, S (2023) Creating shared value through open innovation approaches: opportunities and challenges for corporate sustainability, *Business Strategy and the Environment*, 32 (7), 4485–502

Carlyle, J (2023) A Kids TEDx? Handing over the microphone to children to bring us all inspiration, learning and wonder, In *Events Management for the Infant and Youth Market*, 209–17, Emerald Publishing Limited, Leeds

Craig, D H (2013) Healthy planet, healthy people, *Health Education*, 14 (5), 9–13

Curtis, M and Jones, A (2024) Measuring attitudinal change in community light festivals. In *Reimagining Community Festivals and Events*, 159–82, Routledge, Abingdon

Darley, J (2025) Coachella, Coldplay & Glastonbury: Can Festivals Go Green?, *Sustainability Magazine*, 10 April, sustainabilitymag.com/articles/coachella-coldplay-glastonbury-can-festivals-go-green

Dashper, K (2020) Mentoring for gender equality: Supporting female leaders in the hospitality industry, *International Journal of Hospitality Management*, 88, 102397

Dawson, R and Bassett, D (2018) *Event Planning and Management: Principles, planning and practice*, 2nd edition, Kogan Page, London

Delaney, E (2025) Applying the psychic income paradigm to business events, *Event Management*, 29 (4), 627–31

Dodds, R (2018) Strategies and best practices for greening festivals. In *Green Events and Green Tourism*, 11–17, Routledge, Abingdon

Dowse, S, Powell, S and Weed, M (2020) Mega-sporting events and children's rights and interests – towards a better future. In *Human Rights and Events, Leisure and Sport*, 97–108, Routledge, Abingdon

Dowson, R, Albert, B and Lomax, D (2022) *Event Planning and Management: Principles, planning and practice*, Kogan Page, London

El-Sawad, A, Arnold, J and Cohen, L (2004) 'Doublethink': The prevalence and function of contradiction in accounts of organizational life, *Human Relations*, 57 (9), 1179–203

Etzkowitz, H (2015) Rendezvous of the 'Third Kind': Triple Helix origins and future possibilities, *Industry & Higher Education*, 29 (4), 243–47

Eventbrite (2018) The Pulse Report: 2018 Event Industry Trends f.hubspotusercontent00.net/hubfs/8020908/DS01_The%20Pulse%20Report%20-%202018%20Event%20Industry%20Trends%203971.pdf

Eventbrite (2023) The Event Budget Template You Need to Keep on Track. www.eventbrite.co.uk/l/gc-event-budget-template-2/?submissionGuid=bb8099af-4dd6-4c48-9c47-6554a1f19ab9

Finkel, R and Dashper, K (2020) Accessibility, diversity and inclusion in events. In *The Routledge Handbook of Events*, 475–90), Routledge, Abingdon

Getz, D (2012) Event studies: Discourses and future directions, *Event Management*, 16 (2), 171–87

Getz, D and Page, S J (2019) *Event Studies: Theory, research and policy for planned events*, Routledge, Abingdon

Grande, K and Séraphin, H (2025) Children as a 'Left Behind' group by outdoor hospitality businesses (Campsites): A human resources perspective, *International Journal of Hospitality Management*, 125, 104001

Green, S (2023) Creating unique workshops and events for children: The case of Birdhouse Studio. In *Events Management for the Infant and Youth Market*, 181–95), Emerald Publishing, Leeds

Győrkőc-Festival 2024 wunderbaresungarn.de/veranstaltungen/festival-konzert/gyorkoc-festival-2024-gyor/

Haverly, M (2023) Children at weddings: How to manage parents and children before, during and after the wedding. In *Events Management for the Infant and Youth Market*, 171–79), Emerald Publishing, Leeds

Higham, J, Font, X and Wu, J (2021) Code red for sustainable tourism, *Journal of Sustainable Tourism*, 30 (1), 1–13

Késenne, S (2005) Do we need an economic impact study or a cost-benefit analysis of a sports event? *European Sport Management Quarterly*, 5 (2), 133–42 doi.org/10.1080/16184740500188789

Kholiavko, N, Grosu, V, Safonov, Y, Zhavoronok, A and Cosmulese, C G (2021) Quintuple Helix model: investment aspects of higher education impact on sustainability, *Management Theory and Studies for Rural Business and Infrastructure Development*, 43 (1), 111–28

Kimatu, J N (2016) Evolution of strategic interactions from the triple to quad helix innovation models for sustainable development in the era of globalization, *Journal of Innovation and Entrepreneurship*, 5 (1), 16

Lai, Y L, Hsu, M S, Lin, F J, Chen, Y M and Lin, Y H (2014) The effects of industry cluster knowledge management on innovation performance, *Journal of Business Research*, 67 (5), 734–39.

Lestar, T and Pellegrini-Masini, G P (2023) The agency of children and young people in sustainability traditions: Eco-spirituality events on Hare Krishna eco-farms in Europe. In Séraphin, H (ed) *Events Management for the Infant and Youth Market*, 67–84, Emerald Publishing, Leeds

Li, T, Shi, H, Yang, Z and Ren, Y (2020) Does the belt and road initiative boost tourism economy? *Asia Pacific Journal of Tourism Research*, 25 (3), 311–22

Maingi, S W and Gowreesunkar, V G (2023) Childhood family events, memories, nostalgia and sustainability discourse: Conceptual and theoretical perspectives. In Séraphin, H (ed) *Events Management for the Infant and Youth Market*, 25–38, Emerald Publishing, Leeds

Mair, J and Popely, D (2018) Greening in the MICE industry. In *Green Events and Green Tourism*, 50–60, Routledge, Abingdon

Mendes, T, Braga, V, Silva, C and Ratten, V (2023) Taking a closer look at the regionally clustered firms: How can ambidexterity explain the link between management, entrepreneurship, and innovation in a post-industrialized world? *The Journal of Technology Transfer*, 48 (6), 2007–53

Muñoz, P and Cohen, B (2018) Entrepreneurial narratives in sustainable venturing: Beyond people, profit, and planet, *Journal of Small Business Management*, 56, 154–76

Napolitano, C M, Hoff, K A, Ming, C W J, Tu, N and Rounds, J (2020) Great expectations: Adolescents' intentional self-regulation predicts career aspiration and expectation consistency, *Journal of Vocational Behavior*, 120, 103423

O'Regan, M, Salazar, N B, Choe, J and Buhalis, D (2022) Unpacking overtourism as a discursive formation through interdiscursivity, *Tourism Review*, 77 (1), 54–71

Page, S J (2014). *Tourism Management*, Routledge, Abingdon

Pansiri, J (2008) The effects of characteristics of partners on strategic alliance performance in the SME dominated travel sector, *Tourism Management*, 29, 101–15

Peck, F and McGuinness, D (2003) Regional development agencies and cluster strategies: Engaging the knowledge-base in the North of England, *Local Economy*, 18 (1), 49–62

Raj, R, Rashid, T and Walters, P (2017) *Events Management: Principles and practice*, SAGE, London

Rasmussen, K (2004) Places for children–children's places, *Childhood*, 11 (2), 155–73

Reic, I (2016) *Events Marketing Management: A consumer perspective*, Routledge, Abingdon

Rhama, B (2023) Sustainable rural tourism from the perspective of triple bottom line scientific framework, *Journal of Policy Research in Tourism, Leisure and Events*, 17 (1), 1–14

Richards, G and Palmer, R (2010) *Eventful Cities. Cultural management and revitalisation*, Routledge, Abingdon

Rullani, E (2012) Villes et régions comme écologie de la connaissance: Un terrain à explorer. In P Ingallina (ed) *Université et Enjeux Territoriaux*, 19–21, Presses Universitaires du Septentrion, Lille

Schill, M, Godefroit-Winkel, D and Hogg, M K (2020) Young children's consumer agency: The case of French children and recycling, *Journal of Business Research*, 110, 292–305

Séraphin, H (2021) COVID-19: An opportunity to review existing grounded theories in event studies, *Journal of Convention & Event Tourism*, 22 (1), 3–35

Séraphin, H (2024) Speed dating events: Introducing 'Special interest and meso-adultainment events' as a new type of event to existing literature, *Journal of Convention & Event Tourism*, 25 (1), 1–9

Séraphin, H and Abou Hamdan, O (2023) The 'Dinner Date' concept: Reconciling the dating and hospitality industries, *Journal of Tourism, Heritage & Services Marketing*, 9 (2), 73–77

Séraphin, H and Chaney, D (2024) Identifying and understanding the intersectional cues that matter for customers in speed dating events, *Event Management*, 28 (6), 933–48

Séraphin, H and Nolan, E (eds) (2019) *Green Events and Green Tourism: An international guide to good practice*, Routledge, Abingdon

Séraphin, H, Yallop, A C, Seyfi, S and Hall, C M (2022) Responsible tourism: The 'why' and 'how' of empowering children, *Tourism Recreation Research*, 47 (1), 62–77

Séraphin, H, Yallop, A C, Smith, S M and Modica, G (2021) The implementation of the Principles for Responsible Management Education within tourism higher education institutions: A comparative analysis of European Union countries, *The International Journal of Management Education*, 19 (3), 100518

Slater, S J, Christiana, R W and Gustat, J (2020) Recommendations for keeping parks and green space accessible for mental and physical health during COVID-19 and other pandemics, *Preventing Chronic Disease*, 17, E59

Smith, S M, Cripps, K, Stokes, P and Séraphin, H (2023) The principles for (ir)responsible management education: An exploration of the dynamics of paradox, the hidden curriculum, competencies and symbolization, *Management Learning*, 54 (3), 384–95

Spenceley, A, McCool, S, Newsome, D, Báez, A, Barborak, J R, Blye, C J, Bricker, K, Cahyadi, H S, Corrigan, K, Halpenny, E and Hvenegaard, G (2021) Tourism in protected and conserved areas amid the COVID-19 pandemic, *Parks*, (27), 103–18

Stadler, M (2015) *Innovation, industrial dynamics and economic growth*, University of Tübingen Working Papers in Economics and Finance, No. 84

Stadler, R (2024) Teaching community events, power and empowerment to final year Event Management students: Pedagogical considerations and reflections. In *Reimagining Community Festivals and Events*, 204–21, Routledge, Abingdon

Sturm, D (2018) Formula E's 'green' challenge to motorsport events, spaces and technologies: the London e-prix as a case study. In *Green Events and Green Tourism*, 145–53, Routledge, Abingdon

Turley, E L, Monro, S and King, N (2017) Adventures of pleasure: Conceptualising consensual bondage, discipline, dominance and submission, and sadism and masochism as a form of adult play, *International Journal of Play*, 6 (3), 324–34

Visser, W (ed) (2016) *The World Guide to Sustainable Enterprise – Volume 3: Europe*, Routledge, Abingdon

Visser, W (2015) *Sustainable Frontiers: Unlocking change through business, leadership and innovation*, Routledge, Abingdon

Whitfield, J, Gouthro, M B and Moital, M (eds) (2024) *The Routledge Handbook of Events and Sustainability*, Routledge, Abingdon

Wickham, M, Donnelly, T and French, L (2021) Strategic sustainability management in the event sector, *Event Management*, 25 (3), 279–96

Woodroof, E A (2009) 10 Profitable green strategies: Help your profits and the planet, *Strategic Planning for Energy and the Environment*, 28 (3), 26–36

Yallop, A C, Séraphin, H and Hamdan, O A (2025) Rethinking the relationship between dating services and the hospitality industry through speed dating events: A partner ecosystem strategy, *Event Management*, 29 (4), 565–83

Zacher, H and Froidevaux, A (2021) Life stage, lifespan, and life course perspectives on vocational behavior and development: A theoretical framework, review, and research agenda, *Journal of Vocational Behavior*, 126, 103476

Ziakas, V (2019) Issues, patterns and strategies in the development of event portfolios: configuring models, design and policy, *Journal of Policy Research in Tourism, Leisure and Events*, 11 (1), 121–58

Ziakas, V and Costa, C A (2011) The use of an event portfolio in regional community and tourism development: Creating synergy between sport and cultural events, *Journal of Sport & Tourism*, 16 (2), 149–75

Ziakas, V and Getz, D (2020) Shaping the event portfolio management field: premises and integration, *International Journal of Contemporary Hospitality Management*, 32 (11), 3523–44.

02 | The 'why' and 'how' of the sustainable event

LEARNING OUTCOMES

By the end of Chapter 2, you will be able to:

- demonstrate a sound understanding of discussions around sustainable practices and their application in events management
- plan and design a proposal for a staged event which conforms to current sustainability industry standards
- identify and respond to the needs of stakeholders while conforming to current sustainability industry standards
- evaluate post-event the outcomes of sustainability strategies using relevant techniques.

Introduction

This chapter is written from the perspective that for sustainability to be achieved, every single objective involved in the planning, design and delivery of the event must be considered from a triple bottom line (TBL) and sustainable development goals (SDGs) perspective. Thus, the first step in planning is to analyse the brief from the client and to explore what can be done to meet their requirements, in other words the objectives of the event.

This chapter also discusses the need to consider ethical aspects and the decision-making needed to balance costs with the benefits of sustainability practice in events. Once the event has been delivered, the team debrief should identify what went well and what went less well. Recommendations can then be formulated to maximize the positive aspects and improve the weaker aspects of the planning, design and delivery of events.

As mentioned in Chapter 1, sustainable practices cover the three dimensions of the TBL in a specific order: people, planet, profit. This chapter discussed all three aspects generally before applying them to the events management context.

Sustainable practices and their applications in events management

People

Sustainability and 'people' are generally expressed in relation to equality, diversity and inclusion (EDI). In a nutshell, this concept is about enforcing in the wider society (including working and leisure environments) the principles of equal opportunities in relation to gender, ethnicity, class, disability, age, sexual orientation, religion and other emerging forms of inequalities. The overall objective of EDI is the achievement of a fairer society. The application of EDI by organizations and broadly speaking in society contributes to the achievement of a number of SDGs, particularly SDG 1 (No poverty), SDG2 (No hunger), SDG 5 (Gender equality), SDG 8 (Decent work and economic growth), SDG 10 (Reduced inequalities) and SDG 16 (Peace, justice and strong institutions) (UN DESA, n.d.).

EDI is also at the forefront of a number of pieces of legislation. In the UK for instance, it is directly related to the Human Rights Act 1998 (right to education, freedom of expression, right to life, etc) and the Equality Act 2010, which is about the creation of a fair workplace, and as such covers gender, race, disability and sexual orientation. The Equality Act 2010 is the forerunner of nine earlier pieces of legislation:

- Equal Pay Act 1970
- Sex Discrimination Act 1975
- Race Relations Act 1976
- Disability Discrimination Act 1995
- Employment Equality (Religion or Belief) Regulations 2003
- Employment Equality (Sexual Orientation) Regulations 2003
- Employment Equality (Age) Regulations 2006
- Equality Act 2006, Part 2
- Equality Act (Sexual Orientation) Regulations 2007

The equivalent of the Equality Act 2010 in the USA would be the Equity and Inclusion Enforcement Act of 2021, which prohibits discrimination based on race, colour or national origin (Congress.gov, 2021).

02 | The 'why' and 'how' of the sustainable event

As far as events management research is concerned, EDI remains a marginal issue and is therefore poorly researched. This is especially true when compared with research on the operational and managerial aspects of events management, and yet, EDI impacts on both these aspects of events management (Calver et al, 2025). The events industry is very conscious of the integration of EDI in its sustainable planning practices. For instance, the Birmingham Commonwealth Games in 2020 held in the UK created 22,380 full time jobs and delivered around £1.2 billion economic outputs between 2018 and 2022. The vision behind the Games was that it had to be the 'Game for Everyone' (UK Event Report, 2024). Accessibility, safeguarding of vulnerable groups such as children and young people and staff working conditions are just some of the topics covered in the Purple Guide, which 'provides guidance for event organizers, suppliers, local authorities and others involved in the outdoor events industry' (Purple Guide).

EDI is not just about planning, designing and delivering events that are inclusive to all, but planning, designing and delivering events that meet the needs of those who are 'left behind' or marginalized by society. Loneliness, for example, is a major societal issue worldwide (Séraphin and Korstanje, 2025). Speed dating events, which are classed as 'adultainment' (adult entertainment), for individuals who are looking for romantic partners can be said to address SDGs such as SDG 3 (Good health and well-being), SDG 10 (Reduced inequalities) and SDG 11 (Sustainable cities and communities). Events such as bingo clubs also address SDGs such as SDG 10 (Reduced inequalities), SDG 11 (Sustainable cities and communities) and SDG 17 (Partnerships for the goals) (Séraphin, 2024).

REAL-WORLD EXAMPLE   Bingo: 'Generational' game gets reinvented for new crowd

Bingo can be been traced back to the late 16th century in Italy. After the First World War, bingo was popular in ex-servicemen's clubs and working men's clubs. On 2 January 1961, new legislation allowed bingo to be played in clubs in the UK. By the mid-1960s, there were six million members of bingo clubs. However, smoking bans impacted negatively on the popularity of bingo halls, as did the introduction of online bingo.

More recently, there has been an upswing in the popularity of bingo, especially among students seeking an affordable night out. Bingo halls have had to find new and interesting ways to bring in customers, with events such as drag queen bingo, to make it more fun and on trend.

This type of event has led to close-knit connections within the communities who take part, for example, if a regular member misses a couple of nights of bingo, another member will often check in on them (BBC News, 2023).

Planet

Environmental sustainability is now a major issue around the world. The poor management of natural resources (often associated with their overuse) has been identified as one of the main reasons why the planet is in great danger. Some of the most pressing environmental issues are described below (Dawson and Andriopoulos, 2017; and see Earth Org, 2025).

- *Climate change and global warming*: temperature rise is breaking records in many parts of the world and leading to an increase in natural hazards such as hurricanes, flooding, bushfires, earthquakes and heatwaves, including in parts of the world which should be very cold, for example Antarctica. This is due to greenhouse gas emissions blanketing the Earth and trapping the sun's heat. The use of fossil fuels (burning of coal, natural gas and oil) is the starting point of global warming and its related impacts.
- *Biodiversity loss*: the exponential growth of the world's population in addition to urbanisation and other factors has led humanity to over consume at a faster rate than the Earth can cope with. As a result, some species are now facing a decline in population, causing some to be considered as endangered.
- *Plastic pollution*: every year around 14 million tonnes of plastic end up in the ocean, endangering marine species and habitats. It is estimated that in 2040, the amount of plastic in the ocean will reach 29 million tonnes.
- *Deforestation*: it is suggested that if deforestation is not stopped, the Earth might only have 10 per cent of its forests left by 2030. Despite this pressing issue, deforestation remains legal in some parts of the world.
- *Air pollution*: this is caused mainly by industrialization and an increase in human mobility due to different modes of transport. Every year between 4.2 and 7 million people die from air pollution globally.
- *Fast fashion and textile waste*: the fashion industry plays a major role in environmental issues faced by the planet as it accounts for 10 per cent of global carbon emissions. The global production of textiles is expected to reach 134 million tonnes a year by 2030.

To address these environmental issues, summits such as the Conferences of the Parties, also known as COP, are organized. The first COP took place in Germany in 1995. At the time of writing, the most recent was COP 29 held in Baku in November 2024. The focus of these conferences is climate change.

The current situation has also led to the emergence of youth-led movements such as Fridays for Future (fridaysforfuture.org/), which was begun by Greta Thunberg, and who protest at what they see as a lack of action regarding climate crisis. Extinction Rebellion is a similar movement, which is 'demanding fair and transparent change to ensure the future of all life on Earth' (Extinction Rebellion.uk, n.d.).

Education and particularly the higher education sector also moved towards supporting sustainability through the development of the Principles for Responsible Management Education (PRME). This is a 'United Nations-supported initiative founded in 2007 that aims to raise the profile of sustainability in business and management education through Seven Principles focused on serving society and safeguarding our planet' (PRME, n.d.).

The events industry is contributing toward a better protection of the environment through a greening of its activities through the implementation of standards such as International Organization for Standardization (ISO), organizations such as A Greener Festival and through the development of new concepts such as 'Formula E' (London e-prix) which promotes mobility using electric vehicles. Venues are also getting involved through the development of their own environmental policies (Séraphin and Nolan, 2018). For example, as a venue for events, The Cavendish London hotel has developed a comprehensive environmental policy including reducing energy consumption, managing waste, using eco-friendly chemicals and purchasing recycled goods where possible.

Sustainability in events management is considered as a good selling point, and therefore contributes to the competitive advantage of the industry (Henderson, 2011). The following section discusses the 'profit' dimension of the TBL from an events management perspective.

Profit

Money is the backbone of many activities including events. The cost of attending an event plays a significant role in the level of attendance. On average in the UK, people spend £187 (Massive, 2025); however, the cost of attending an event such as a festival is likely to be much higher, while the cost of a conference may also vary according to its duration, location, calibre of speakers, etc. Worldwide the events industry is important in terms of generating income. Indeed, in 2021, globally the events industry was worth £800 billion (Jenkins, 2022). The profit from income is not just economic or financial; it can also be psychic. Indeed, for Delaney (2025): 'The psychic income refers to the positive psychological and emotional benefits that residents believe they receive from an event taking place nearby.' For sustainability reasons it could be argued that event managers should ensure that events should deliver both economic and psychic incomes and profits. Take the example of Winchester, a UK city which hosts many events (Table 2.1) and is located relatively close to other popular visitor destinations such as London, Oxford, and Cambridge. Winchester's events contribute to the quality of life and level of happiness of its residents, as the events support their culture, local economy and contribute to job creation (Séraphin et al, 2018). Equally important, events are positively perceived by Winchester residents because the benefits of running events are higher than the cost (Séraphin et al, 2018). On that basis, we could conclude that if attendees perceive the psychic incomes of events as being higher than their financial cost, they will be happy to be involved. For event organizers this means ensuring the events they plan, design and deliver create perceived value for attendees.

Table 2.1 List of events happening in Winchester

	EVENT	TYPE	WHEN
1	Taste of Wickham	Food and drink	September
2	Winchester Guitar Festival	Music	October
3	Hyde900	History and arts	October
4	Winchester Film Festival	Film	November
5	The Cheese and Chilli Festival	Food and drink	August
6	Winchester Poetry Festival	Literature	October
7	Winchester Bonfire and Fireworks	Entertainment	November
8	Wine Festival Winchester	Food and drink	November
9	Winchester Heritage open days	History and arts	September
10	Harvest Festival	Food and drink	October
11	Winchester Comedy Festival	Comedy	September
12	Winchester Design Festival	Arts	October
13	Winchester Christmas lights switch on	Christmas in Winchester	November
14	Christmas market	Christmas in Winchester	November
15	Christmas ice rink	Christmas in Winchester	November
16	Christmas lantern parade	Christmas in Winchester	November
17	Film screening for LGBT month	Film	February
18	Winchester Comedy Gala	Comedy	March
19	Children of Winchester Festival	Children	February
20	Winchester Beer and Cider Festival	Food and drink	March
21	Winchester Fashion Week	Fashion	April
22	Hampshire Pride	Entertainment	April
23	The Grange Festival	Music	June
24	Winchester Chamber Music Festival	Music	April
25	Stone Festival	Arts	June
26	Winchester and Country Music Festival	Music	May
27	Alresford Music Festival	Music	June
28	Winchester Mayfest	Arts	May
29	Winchester Ukelele Festival	Music	May
30	Winchester Cocktail week	Food and drink	June
31	Winchestival	Music and comedy	June
32	Hampshire Festival	Food and drink	June
33	Winchester Criterium and Cyclefest	Sports	June
34	Hat Fair	Arts	July

(continued)

Table 2.1 (Continued)

	EVENT	TYPE	WHEN
35	Winchester School of Art degree show	Arts	June
36	Wickham Festival	Music	August
37	Writers' Weekend Winchester	Literature	July
38	Boomtown	Music	August

Planning and designing sustainable events

When the 'why' of sustainable events are understood, the next step is the implementation of the principles of sustainability. The will of the event manager (and all other stakeholders involved in the planning, designing and delivery of the event) to deliver a sustainable event is central, and can happen if the conditions below are met (Visser, 2015):

- 'Unlocking change through transformational leadership': All stakeholders involved in the delivery of the event must have a sustainable mindset and truly believe that everyone has a role to play in the delivery of a sustainable event. This positioning implies that profitability cannot be the main driver, even if it remains an important aspect for the long-term sustainability of the event.
- 'Unlocking change through enterprise reform': This point is in line with the previous one. It emphasizes the fact that on top of making a profit, organizations (and in this case, event organizations) also have a social responsibility. As seen in the previous section, the events industry is aware of its societal role and duties towards ensuring sustainability. Enterprise reform could be implemented by constantly innovating in terms of what can be done to increase sustainability. This should be a key focus, alongside other aspects of the delivery of events.
- 'Unlocking change through technology innovation': The reforms discussed in the previous section could happen through technology innovation. Questions that stakeholders involved in events should ask themselves are: How can we use existing technology to improve the sustainability of the industry? What are the limitations of current technological tools? These two questions should be a driving force that maintains the momentum of events management sustainability through technology.

- 'Unlocking change through corporate transparency': This dimension can happen through reporting of strategies towards sustainability and outcomes of strategies put in place. Indeed, reporting could help with the wider spread of good practice in the event industry. However, since research and innovation is expensive and allows organizations to gain a competitive advantage, it is likely that not all will be willing to be transparent.
- 'Unlocking change through stakeholders' engagement': This section to some extent encompasses the previous one. Social media now plays a major role in how information is shared today. This form of communication could be used by events management organizations to campaign for better sustainability of the industry and to gather a wide range of stakeholders around this cause.
- 'Unlocking change through social responsibility': Once every stakeholder in the events industry has embraced the fact they have a role to play in the sustainability of the industry, stakeholder engagement, transformational leadership, enterprise reform, corporate transparency and technology innovation (particularly in larger organizations) will become more effective.
- 'Unlocking change through integrated value': Sustainability as a social responsibility is a value that needs to be embraced by all stakeholders of the industry for it to be effective (Figure 2.1).

A practical example of the above is provided by speed dating events. Yallop et al (2025) developed the partner ecosystem strategy model for a more effective collaboration between the dating industry (events organization and delivery) and hospitality industry (food/beverage and venues). This suggests that such a collaboration could result in a better experience for attendees ('people') and therefore a better performance (brand image, repeat customers) for the stakeholders involved in the organization and delivery of the event ('profit'). Because speed dating events often use physical and digital tools also referred as 'phygitalisation' (Séraphin and Abou Hamdan, 2023), this helps with the reduction of paper (booking and confirmation letters) being printed ('planet'). Activity 2.1 below provides an opportunity to apply the principles of sustainability to a specific type of event.

Figure 2.1 Sustainability as a value

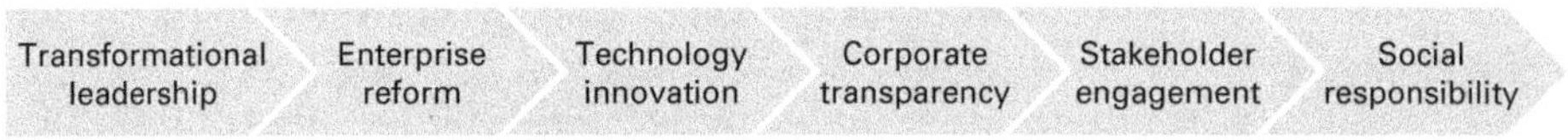

Transformational leadership → Enterprise reform → Technology innovation → Corporate transparency → Stakeholder engagement → Social responsibility

ACTIVITY 2.1

Event proposal

Client brief

We are launching a new concept of speed dating called 'Dinner Date'. As part of our marketing strategy, we would like you to plan and design a creative and sustainable two-hour event at a high-end restaurant. The purpose of this free event is twofold: First, to create a relaxing and memorable experience for the attendees. Second, to have 50 per cent of the attendees sign up for our next (fee paying) event.

You will have 15 minutes to present your proposal and you should use visual aids such as PowerPoint slides. Your proposal should include:

- the theme of the event
- the event's USP
- day/time of the event
- programme/schedule
- choice of venue
- target market
- marketing plans
- health and safety
- costings.

1 Provide a clear rationale for each of the above bullet points, which is closely linked with sustainability (both TBL and SDG) measures. You should ensure you consider the pre-event, event and post-event stages.

Identifying and responding to the needs of stakeholders

Ambidextrous management is an approach which involves combining strategies that are perceived to be in opposition to each other. This approach is widely used in management, and has often been associated with innovation, sustainability, improvement of performance, etc. (Mihalache and Mihalache, 2016; Vo Thanh et al, 2020). One of the conditions for this management approach is the ability of stakeholders in charge of the planning, design and delivery of an event to adopt a Janusian way of thinking, i.e. a way of thinking that is flexible enough to see how so-called or perceived opposites can work together.

Adopting an ambidextrous management approach or Janusian thinking approach is particularly suitable for the events industry due to the large number of stakeholders involved, all of which have different needs, expectations and objectives that nevertheless still need to be met. Examples of these stakeholders include buyers, suppliers, attendees, workers, event organizers, government, sponsors, client, venue staff, etc. The expected outcomes from an event will also vary between stakeholders, and might be economic, intrinsic satisfaction, development of social capital, job creation, promotion of an area, enforcement of policies or practices or enhanced reputation. Because of these different needs, expectations and objectives, the behaviour of stakeholders may vary during the planning, design and delivery of an event. Edger and Oddy (2018) have categorized these behaviours into *whiners*, constantly asking questions about how situations will be dealt with; *complicators*, who will ask unnecessary questions, and subsequently make the task of others more complicated; *prima donnas*, who are attention seekers always trying to bring the light on them; *controllers*, who constantly check what other stakeholders involved are doing; and finally, *toxic* stakeholders, who impact negatively on group dynamics due to a tendency to misinform and a desire to manipulate others.

Often the needs, expectations and objectives of stakeholders are perceived as opposing, or incompatible, when in fact they are very compatible. The Janusian thinking or ambidextrous approach could translate in real life into the following:

- Step 1 – Identifying the high compatibilities among the stakeholders involved.
- Step 2 – Identifying the low commitment and trust among the stakeholders involved.
- Step 3 – Identifying the intrinsic and extrinsic cues of the stakeholders involved to see how they can be combined to address step 2. This is often effective when a joint project is possible. It could be for instance the development of a new concept such as 'Dinner Date' between the hospitality and the dating industry (Yallop et al, 2025).

Loneliness as a societal issue

Academic research on loneliness is growing (Altinay et al, 2023; Séraphin, 2023; Tubadji, 2023). Loneliness is a major societal issue related to depression (Van As et al, 2022), which affects many different groups of people, including older people (Domènech-Abella et al, 2017), young adults (Matthews et al, 2016), people experiencing illness (Gallagher et al, 2020), etc. Loneliness affects 11 million adults in the UK, and is particularly common in women (Champion Health, 2023). In most cases loneliness is investigated in terms of isolation, particularly when it comes to older people (Feng et al, 2022; Fessman and Lester, 2000; Van As et al, 2022).

Romantic loneliness is very rarely investigated in academic literature regardless of the field of study (Adamczyk, 2017; Seeparsad et al, 2008; Séraphin, 2023). The limited existing research explains that individuals who are involuntarily single, and who want to be in a romantic relationship but are not, sometimes experience mental health issues (Adamczyk, 2017; Seeparsad et al, 2008). Thus, similar to other forms of loneliness, romantic loneliness presents a societal issue which deserves attention (Adamczyk, 2017; Van As et al, 2022). The following activity provides an opportunity to apply the topic discussed in this section.

> **ACTIVITY 2.2**
>
> Stakeholders and events
>
> The aim of this task is to investigate the contribution of speed dating events, and more specifically, the 'Dinner Date' concept to tackling issues of loneliness and depression, while also contributing to our understanding of meeting the needs of different stakeholders, all while bearing in mind the need to be sustainable (TBL and SDGs).
>
> 1. Identify and investigate the various stakeholders that could be involved in the delivery of the 'Dinner Date' event.
> 2. Once you have identified these stakeholders, make notes on their needs and expectations in terms of products, services, atmosphere and encounters
> 3. How will you meet these needs through the planning, design and delivery of the event?

Post-event evaluation of sustainability strategies

After an event has taken place, it is a common and even expected practice to evaluate the performance of the delivered product and/or service. This evaluation can enable the events organizer to gauge whether the event they planned, designed and delivered was a success or a failure. This process is also very important as it helps event organizers to improve their performance and attract repeat customers, which in turn plays a role in the economic sustainability of their organization. This process also benefits future attendees as they will be able to experience an event which is more likely to meet their needs. However, the gap between expectations and perception of what has been delivered makes customer satisfaction a challenging task (Bitner, 1995; Voorhees et al, 2017). There are different approaches to evaluate an event.

Evaluation of objectives

For Quinn (2013), evaluating an event involves assessing whether the objectives set at the pre-event stage (which would include the brief for the client, and the planning and designing stage) have been met at the post-event stage. From a sustainable perspective (TBL) this evaluation would also consider the economic, social and environmental impacts of the event, as shown in Figure 2.2 (Quinn, 2013).

Figure 2.2 Events objectives and sustainability (Quinn, 2013)

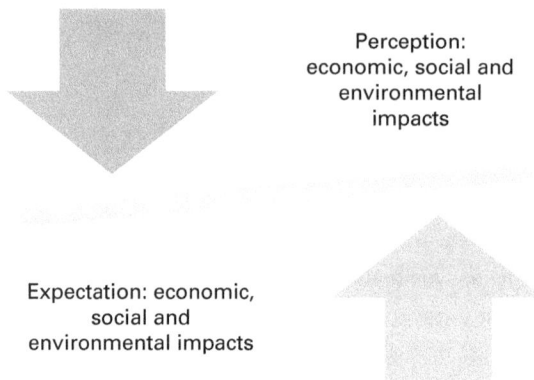

Evaluation of experiences

For Shone and Parry (2004) the evaluation of an event should consider the experience of all parties involved at one stage or another of the event (Figure 2.3). The key purpose of the task should be to identify what went well (and therefore should remained unchanged and/or strengthened) and what did not, in order to improve future delivery of the event. Shone and Parry (2004) also pointed out that the types of data to be collected during the evaluation process could be both qualitative (social impacts, perceptions of stakeholders involved, etc.) and quantitative (financial report, attendance statistics, economic impacts, etc). This data can come from different sources, including:

- questionnaires given to attendees to collect information about their experience
- security staff/police to understand challenges related to traffic, crowd management and incidents
- city council and local communities to understand how they have been impacted by the event
- mystery guests (participants' observation)
- staff and volunteers' log books
- sponsors or clients.

Questions to ask yourself

Powell (2013) pointed out that after an event, organizers should evaluate the different aspects of the event (Figure 2.4) by asking themselves the following questions:

- Cost effectiveness – did we make smart purchasing decisions?
- Attendance – were there any mitigating factors (weather, etc.)?

Figure 2.3 Events objectives and sustainability (Shone and Parry, 2004)

- Exhibitor/sponsor/partner – was the event a success for them? Why?
- Use of resources – did we use everything at our disposal in the best possible way?
- Deadlines – how many deadlines did we meet/miss? Why?
- Social inclusion – did we attract the audience we expected? Was anybody excluded because of how we set up the event?
- Venue – how did the venue's facilities stand up to the task? How did the venue cope on event day?
- Revenue – Did we make a loss, a profit or break even?

The above aspects of evaluation could be classified into hard criteria (tangible and quantitative and are about outputs) and soft criteria (intangible and qualitative and are about the process) (Powell, 2013; Watt, 1998) (Figure 2.5).

Sustainability in Events Management

Figure 2.4 Areas for evaluation

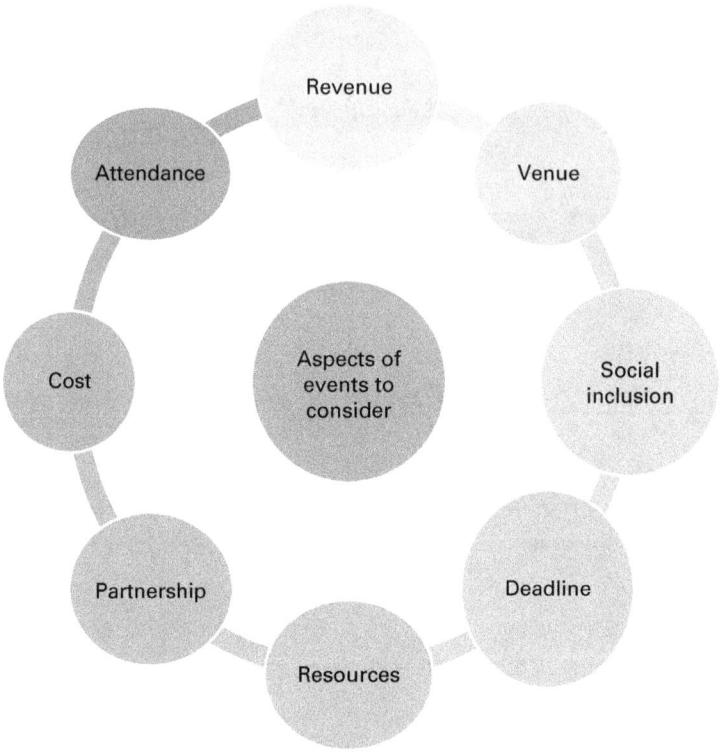

Figure 2.5 Evaluating an event

Hard criteria of evaluation	Soft criteria of evaluation
Deadlines	Social inclusion
Costs	Attendance
Resources	Experience of stakeholders

What matters most to individuals who attend events?

Four elements are particularly important for individuals attending events (Séraphin and Chaney, 2024):

1 The atmosphere is what matters the most for attendees. This includes meeting and interacting with others, having fun and approachable event organizers.
2 Customer service is equally important for attendees, for example, being able to contact the organizers (via email or another medium), knowing the process to cancel their attendance or obtain a refund in case they cannot attend and receiving a fast response to queries.
3 Food and beverages, the attitude and professionalism of the catering team, the quality of the service, the appearance of the venue, etc.
4 Finally, the calibre of participants, and the types of activities they will be involved in

Self-evaluation

Event organizers could also conduct a self-evaluation (Table 2.2) of their experience. Self-evaluation tools such as Kolb's Reflective Cycle or Gibbs' Reflective Cycle would be useful here (Brown, n.d.).

In summary, this section suggests that the evaluation of an event could be conducted through the consideration of five aspects (Figure 2.6), which also play a role in sustainability.

The following task provides an opportunity to evaluate a very specific type of event and suggest strategies to improve the event.

ACTIVITY 2.3

Post-event evaluation

Client brief

The launch of 'Dinner Date', a new concept of speed dating event, went well. You are now required to provide a detailed evaluation report of the event.

1 Provide evidence that the event you delivered met the needs of stakeholders. Structure your report using the following headings:
   - Theme of the event
   - USP
   - Day/time of the event

- Programme/schedule
- Choice of venue
- Target market
- Marketing
- Health and safety

2 As the objective of the company is to launch new concepts of dating events every other year, you also need to include in your report evidence that this type of event is sustainable (considering the triple bottom line and SDGs). Explain what could be done in the future to make the event even more sustainable (and therefore successful).

Table 2.2 Self-reflection

Kolb's reflective cycle (1984)	Gibbs' reflective cycle (1988)
- Concrete experience - Reflective observation - Abstract conceptualization - Active experimentation	- Description - Feelings - Evaluation - Conclusions - Action

Figure 2.6 The five dimensions of sustainability

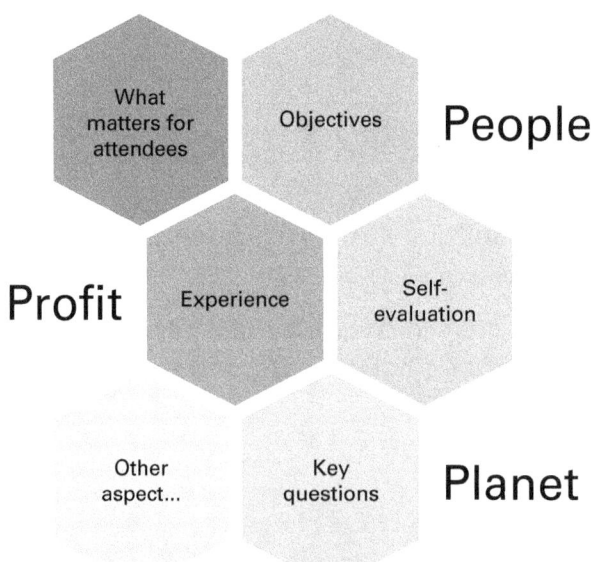

Future staging of sustainable events: recommendations

After collecting feedback from the different stakeholders involved in the planning, design and delivery of events, recommendations for improvement can be formulated by any of the stakeholders for the next delivery of the event. The formulation of recommendations could be part of the management of changes, creativity and innovation within an organization landscape (Dawson and Andriopoulos, 2017). This management of change process could include the factors shown in Figure 2.7 (Dawson and Andriopoulos, 2017).

Figure 2.7   The five dimensions of change, innovation and creativity

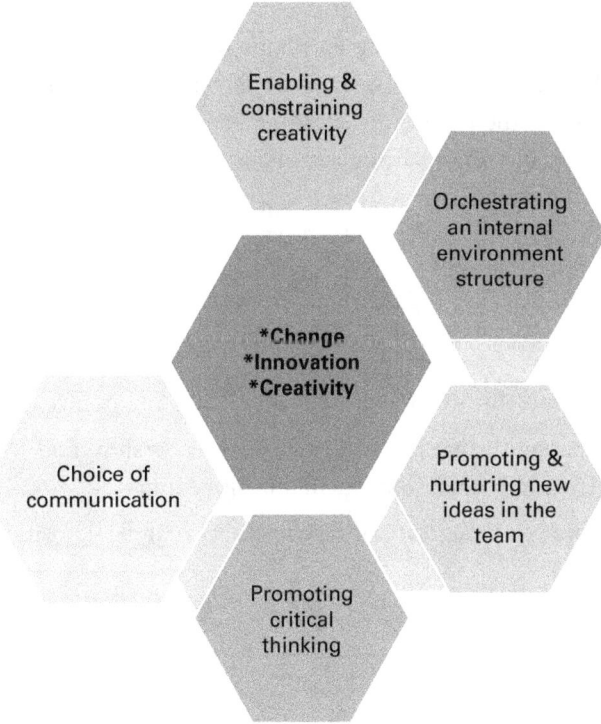

The application of the factors summarized in Figure 2.7 can lead to the development of sustainability strategies such as the development of policies towards zero waste; innovative ideas involving technology to reduce the use of natural resources; network planning to connect local suppliers and event organizers; and the development of partnerships (on a win-win basis) with eco-friendly venues.

People

Events of the future will have to be more considerate of the needs of individuals and subsequently be more inclusive in relation to the type of speakers, attendees, subjects covered, themes, etc. Promoting wellness and wellbeing should be one of the main priorities of events (Dawson and Andriopoulos, 2017; Dowson et al, 2022), which implies that event organizers will need to be keen observers of society. Beyond promoting wellness and wellbeing, events should play a role in the happiness of individuals and the society they take place in, meaning that the main priority of the organizers should not be profit (even if money remains the backbone of the organization of events). Visser (2015: 1–4) asks, 'How can we – as individuals, businesses, communities and policy-makers – prepare for the future? How can we maximize our chances of success, not only by being ready, but also by helping to shape the future that we desire?'

Figure 2.8 provides examples of key societal challenges to be addressed by the events industry. The main challenge for event managers will be to identify the type and theme of events to address these fundamental societal challenges. Such events could be articulated around four of Visser's (2015) seven steps of unlocking changes strategy, namely:

- 'Unlocking change through integrated value' (Starting point)
- 'Unlocking change through transformational leadership' and Unlocking change through enterprise reform' (Incremental positive impacts)
- 'Unlocking change through social responsibility' (Radical positive impacts).

Figure 2.8 Societal changes to be addressed by events

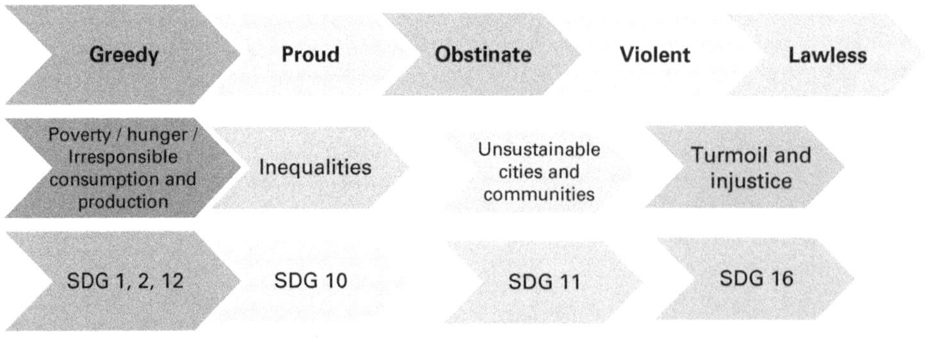

Greedy	Proud	Obstinate	Violent	Lawless
Poverty / hunger / Irresponsible consumption and production	Inequalities	Unsustainable cities and communities	Turmoil and injustice	
SDG 1, 2, 12	SDG 10	SDG 11	SDG 16	

Planet

To address the most pressing sustainability issues faced by the planet (Dawson and Andriopoulos, 2017; Robinson and Igini, 2025), the event industry could adapt and apply strategies adopted by similar industries such as the hospitality industry (Dawson and Andriopoulos, 2017), namely:

- food and beverage criteria for waste and net zero ambitions
- incentivizing stakeholders to save resources
- zero plastic in events
- unlocking the events management team's collective intelligence to encourage the emergence of innovative and new ideas
- marketing, communicating and engaging stakeholders in sustainability experiences
- incorporating nature in events.

It is important to involve the younger generation (children and young people) in the above strategies as they are the future of the events industry (Séraphin, 2023).

Although the achievement of sustainability (people, planet, profit) in the events industry is a priority, it still has not been achieved. Indeed, many events, particularly mega-events have been singled out for their poor sustainability performance. The Qatar World Cup was for instance considered a human and environmental disaster (NBC News, 2022). In contrast, at the Paris Olympics in 2024 much was done to make the event sustainable, such as reusing existing facilities, providing cardboard beds and other sustainable bedroom equipment to athletes, doubling the provision of plant-based foods and turning Paris into a cycling city (BBC Sport, 2024).

These two examples raise the question of the achievement of sustainability in the live events industry. Equally important, this situation highlights the fact that the events industry finds itself in a situation of 'doublethink', where it is publicly expressing its support to sustainability while engaging in activities displaying the opposite of this (Castro, 2013; El-Sawad et al, 2004; Wals and Jickling, 2002). Doublethinking is leading to 'Newspeak', which implies that a language is tightening around a limited number of words, making opposite thoughts and behaviour impossible (Borman, 1998; Napolitano et al, 2020). This means that once sustainability has reached the level of being the central word around which any language is articulated, stakeholders of the events industry will need to have an attitude and language that reflects this Newspeak. In Orwell's novel *1984* this became possible through the Thought Police of the Record Department of the Ministry of Truth (Borman, 1998).

Sustainability as a newspeak in events management will be perfected once all stakeholders of the event industry, and more broadly speaking, when all the members of a society will have the same approach towards sustainability. Such a societal change will take time and is likely to happen with a generation which will be well

Figure 2.9 Sequencing of the triple bottom line (Alberts and Niendorf, 2021)

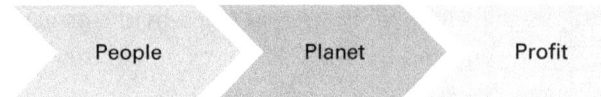

versed in sustainability matters, having grown up with these views. For the future generation to be fully versed in sustainability, education is very important, and this must come from the combined efforts of all stakeholders of the events industry and society, and not just be the duty of educational institutions.

Beyond this incremental strategy, this chapter suggests a more radical approach, namely letting go of the industrial system that is no longer fit for purpose, and instead, embracing a more value based (religious or other) system. Finally, based on the arguments raised in this chapter, Figure 2.9 shows the most appropriate sequencing of the triple bottom line.

ACTIVITY 2.4

Recommendations

In Activity 2.3 you developed a sustainable strategy for 'Dinner Date', a new concept of a speed dating event and were asked to provide evidence that your event was sustainable in terms of the TBL and SDGs. How does your strategy compare against the strategies suggested in this section?

CHECKLIST

The questions below assess your understanding of sustainability in events management.

Understanding of discussions around sustainable practices and their application in events management

- For an event you have been involved in, describe the commitment of the event towards sustainability.
- What strategies were put in place to minimize the negative impacts of the event, and maximize its positive impacts?

Plan and design a proposal for a staged event which conforms to current sustainability industry standards

- How do you keep up to date with current affairs in the industry?
- What good practice from the industry are you implementing?

Evaluating (post-event) the outcomes of the sustainability strategies

- What evaluation techniques do you use?
- What have you learnt from your latest experience of running an event?

Summary

The first take away from this chapter is that when sustainable practices are successfully applied to events management, they can play a significant role in the quality of life, wellbeing and happiness of some stakeholders, such as attendees and locals. The second take away from this chapter is the importance of the psychic income. By adding value to an event, organizers are more likely to get the support of stakeholders and particularly attendees. The third take away is that the planning and designing stage is very important in maintaining endeavours towards sustainability. Finally, an evaluation of sustainability strategies and recommendations as part of the post-event evaluation is central.

Further reading

Cheded, M, Hutton, M, Steinfield, L, Bettany, S, Burchiellaro, O and Venkatraman, R (2024) Moving gender across, between and beyond the binaries: In conversation with Shona Bettany, Olimpia Burchiellaro and Rohan Venkatraman, *Journal of Consumer Affairs*, 58 (1), 209–22

Korstanje, M E (2018) *The Mobilities Paradox: A critical analysis*, Edward Elgar Publishing, Cheltenham

Lestar, T and Böhm, S (2020) Eco-spirituality and sustainability transitions: Agency towards degrowth, *Religion, State & Society*, 48 (1), 56–73

Lestar T and Pellegrini-Masini, G (2023) The agency of children and young people in sustainability transitions: Eco-spiritual events on Hare Krishna eco-farms in Europe. In *Events Management for the Infant and Youth Market*, 85–99), Emerald Publishing, Leeds

References

Adamczyk, K (2017) Voluntary and involuntary singlehood and young adults' mental health: An investigation of mediating role of romantic loneliness, *Current Psychology*, 36 (4), 888–904

Alberts, H C and Niendorf, B D (2021) Interdisciplinary learning about people, planet, and profit in Germany, *The Geography Teacher*, 18 (3–4), 158–63

Altinay, L, Alrawadieh, Z, Tulucu, F and Arici, H E (2023) The effect of hospitableness on positive emotions, experience, and well-being of hospital patients, International Journal of Hospitality Management, 110, 103431

BBC News (2023) Bingo: 'Generational' game gets reinvented for new crowd, www.bbc.co.uk/news/uk-england-humber-65615206

BBC Sport (2024) Recycled bottle tops and tables made from shuttlecocks – the greenest Olympics? www.bbc.co.uk/sport/articles/cm52drr0lp1o

Bitner, M J (1995) Building service relationships: It's all about promises, *Journal of the Academy of Marketing Science*, 23 (4), 246–251

Borman, G (1998) *Cliffs Notes on Orwell's 1984*, CliffsNotes, Lincoln, Nebraska

Brown, N (n.d.) Reflective model according to Gibbs www.nicole-brown.co.uk/reflective-model-according-to-gibbs/?tag=reflective%20model

Brown, N (n.d.) Reflective model according to Kolb www.nicole-brown.co.uk/reflective-model-according-to-kolb/?tag=reflective%20model

Calver, J, Dashper, K, Finkel, R, Fletcher, T, Lamond, I R, May, E, Ormerod, N, Platt, L and Sharp, B (2025) The (in) visibility of equality, diversity, and inclusion research in events management journals, *Journal of Policy Research in Tourism, Leisure and Events*, 17 (2), 424-48

Castro, R (2013) Inconsistent respondents and sensitive questions, *Field Methods*, 25 (3), 283-98

Champion Health (2023) Depression statistics UK https://championhealth.co.uk/insights/depression-statistics/

Congress.gov (2021) Equity and Inclusion Enforcement Act of 2021, www.congress.gov/bill/117th-congress/house-bill/730

Dawson, P and Andriopoulos, C (2017) *Managing Change, Creativity and Innovation*, SAGE, London

Delaney, E (2025) Applying the psychic income paradigm to business events, *Event Management*, 29 (4), 627–31

Domènech-Abella, J, Lara, E, Rubio-Valera, M, Olaya, B, Moneta, M V, Rico-Uribe, L A, Ayuso-Mateos, J L, Mundó, J and Haro, J M (2017) Loneliness and depression in the elderly: the role of social network, *Social Psychiatry and Psychiatric Epidemiology*, 52 (4), 381–390

Dowson, R, Albert, B and Lomax, D (2022) *Event Planning and Management: Principles, planning and practice*, Kogan Page, London

Edger, C and Oddy, R E. (2018) *Events Management. 87 key models for event, venue and experience (EVE) managers*, Libri Publishing, Faringdon

El-Sawad, A, Arnold, J and Cohen, L (2004) 'Doublethink': The prevalence and function of contradiction in accounts of organizational life, *Human Relations*, 57 (9), 1179–203

Extinction Rebellion (n.d.) extinctionrebellion.uk/

Feng, K, Altinay, L and Alrawadieh, Z (2023) Social connectedness and well-being of elderly customers: Do employee-to-customer interactions matter? *Journal of Hospitality Marketing & Management*, 32 (2), 174–95

Fessman, N and Lester, D (2000) Loneliness and depression among elderly nursing home patients, *The International Journal of Aging and Human Development*, 51 (2), 137–41

Gallagher, M W, Zvolensky, M J, Long, L J, Rogers, A H and Garey, L 2020) The impact of Covid-19 experiences and associated stress on anxiety, depression, and functional impairment in American adults, *Cognitive Therapy and Research*, 44 (6), 1043–51

Henderson, S (2011) The development of competitive advantage through sustainable event management, *Worldwide Hospitality and Tourism Themes*, 3 (3), 245–57

Jenkins, A (2022) The events industry key statistics, Quadrant2Design, 14 December www.quadrant2design.com/the-events-industry-key-statistics/

Massive (2025) The mass participation, Pulse 2025, www.frontrunnerevents.co.uk/resources/the-mass-participation-pulse-report-2025.pdf

Matthews, T, Danese, A, Wertz, J, Odgers, C L, Ambler, A, Moffitt, T E and Arseneault, L (2016) Social isolation, loneliness and depression in young adulthood: a behavioural genetic analysis, *Social Psychiatry and Psychiatric Epidemiology*, 51 (3), 339–48

Mihalache, M and Mihalache, O R (2016) Organizational ambidexterity and sustained performance in the tourism industry, *Annals of Tourism Research*, 56, 142–44.

Napolitano, C M, Hoff, K A, Ming, C W J, Tu, N and Rounds, J (2020) Great expectations: Adolescents' intentional self-regulation predicts career aspiration and expectation consistency, *Journal of Vocational Behavior*, 120, 103423

NBC News (2022) Qatar World Cup lays bare the huge environmental cost of tournament www.nbcnews.com/news/world/qatar-world-cup-environmental-climate-change-cost-desert-rcna57632

Powell, C (2013) *How to Deliver Outstanding Corporate Events*, Lulu Press Inc., Durham, NC, www.lulu.com

Principles for Responsible Management Education (PRME) www.unprme.org/about/

Purple Guide (2015) www.thepurpleguide.co.uk/index.php/19-front-page/144-about-the-purple-guide

Quinn, B (2013) *Key Concepts in Event Management*, SAGE, London

Robinson, D and Igini, M (2025) 15 Biggest Environmental Problems of 2025, Earth.Org, 9 January https://earth.org/the-biggest-environmental-problems-of-our-lifetime/

Seepersad, S, Choi, M K and Shin, N (2008) How does culture influence the degree of romantic loneliness and closeness? *The Journal of Psychology*, 142 (2), 209–20

Séraphin, H (ed) (2023) *Events Management for the Infant and Youth Market*, Emerald Publishing, Leeds.

Séraphin, H (2024) Speed dating events: Introducing 'Special interest and meso-adultainment events' as a new type of event to existing literature, *Journal of Convention & Event Tourism*, 25 (1), 1–9

Séraphin, H and Abou Hamdan, O (2023) The 'Dinner Date' concept: Reconciliating the dating and hospitality industries, *Journal of Tourism, Heritage & Services Marketing*, 9 (2), 73–77

Séraphin, H and Chaney, D (2024) Identifying and understanding the intersectional cues that matter for customers in speed dating events, *Event Management*, 28 (6), 933–48

Séraphin, H and Korstanje, M E (2024) *Solo Travel, Tourism and Loneliness: A critical sociology*, Routledge, Abingdon

Séraphin, H and Nolan, E (eds) (2019) *Green Events and Green Tourism: An international guide to good practice*, Routledge, Abingdon

Séraphin, H, Platania, M, Spencer, P and Modica, G (2018) Events and tourism development within a local community: The case of Winchester (UK), *Sustainability*, 10 (10), 3728

Shone, A and Parry, B (2004) *Successful Event Management: A practical handbook*, 2nd edn, Thomson, London

Tubadji, A (2023) You'll never walk alone: Loneliness, religion, and politico-economic transformation, *Politics & Policy*, 51 (4), 661–95

UK Event Report (2024) https://cdn.asp.events/CLIENT_AEV_30A5AAAF_5056_B740_1746BDBB4A667186/sites/aev2022/media/pdfs/UK-EVENTS-Report-2024.pdf

UN DESA (n.d.) Sustainable Development Goals https://sdgs.un.org/goals

Van As, B A L, Imbimbo, E, Franceschi, A, Menesini, E and Nocentini, A (2022) The longitudinal association between loneliness and depressive symptoms in the elderly: a systematic review, International Psychogeriatrics, 34 (7), 657–669

Visser, W (2015) *Sustainable Frontiers: Unlocking change through business, leadership and innovation*, Routledge, Abingdon

Voorhees, C M, Fombelle, P W, Gregoire, Y, Bone, S, Gustafsson, A, Sousa, R and Walkowiak, T (2017) Service encounters, experiences and the customer journey: Defining the field and a call to expand our lens, *Journal of Business Research*, 79, 269–80

Vo Thanh, T, Seraphin, H, Okumus, F and Koseoglu, M A (2020) Organizational ambidexterity in tourism research: A systematic review, *Tourism Analysis*, 25 (1), 137–52

Wals, A E J and Jickling, B (2002) Sustainability in higher education: From Doublethink and Newspeak to critical thinking and meaningful learning, *International Journal of Sustainability in Higher Education*, 3 (3), 221–32

Watt, D C (1998) *Event Management in Leisure and Tourism*, Longman, London

Yallop, A C, Séraphin, H and Hamdan, O A (2025) Rethinking the relationship between dating services and the hospitality industry through speed dating events: A partner ecosystem strategy, *Event Management*, 29 (4), 565–83

03 | The targets of sustainable events

LEARNING OUTCOMES

By the end of Chapter 3, students will be able to:
- define sustainable events and articulate their importance within the broader framework of sustainable tourism
- recognize and analyse the key definitions, principles and characteristics of sustainable events in the tourism industry
- identify and evaluate critical environmental, social and economic sustainability targets relevant to event planning and management
- develop a comprehensive understanding of the factors that influence the achievement of sustainability goals in events, including policy, technology and stakeholder engagement
- gain insight into the roles and responsibilities of primary stakeholders in driving sustainable event practices and achieving long-term sustainability objectives.

Introduction

Sustainability is a fundamental dimension of development for tourist destinations (Mair, 2015). Events, as an integral part of the tourism offering, inevitably become part of the sustainability discourse due to their economic, social and environmental impacts (Lu, 2021; Mair and Smith, 2021). The concept of sustainable events is therefore not new; rather, it is deeply embedded in the broader discourse of sustainable tourism, which seeks to balance the needs of present and future generations while safeguarding ecological integrity, cultural authenticity and socio-economic equity (Séraphin et al, 2024; Séraphin and Gowreesunkar, 2020a).

As awareness of sustainability grows, it has become a critical consideration in the event industry. Events, regardless of their scale, location or purpose, can generate both positive and negative consequences. Achieving sustainability in events requires a strategic and holistic approach that considers multiple factors, including environmental responsibility, cultural and social impacts, economic viability and stakeholder engagement. Given these complexities, sustainability in events is a dynamic and context-dependent concept that must align with diverse objectives and constraints.

Against this backdrop, this chapter explores the key targets of sustainable event planning by integrating perspectives from environmental, social and economic sustainability. It outlines practical strategies for achieving these targets while shedding light on the core characteristics of sustainable events. Additionally, the chapter examines the role of stakeholders in fostering sustainability and discusses the factors that influence the successful implementation of sustainable event practices.

Definitions of sustainable events

Scholars have proposed various definitions of sustainable events, emphasizing their multidimensional nature. Mair and Jago (2010) define sustainable events as those designed, organized and executed in a way that ensures economic, social and environmental considerations are balanced and integrated throughout the event lifecycle. Similarly, Laing and Frost (2010) stress the importance of long-term environmental responsibility, advocating for eco-friendly event planning, carbon-neutral strategies and community engagement. While both definitions acknowledge sustainability's holistic nature, Mair and Jago (2010) take a broader perspective by incorporating economic aspects, whereas Laing and Frost (2010) focus primarily on environmental sustainability. Regardless of whether the emphasis is on community engagement, environmental responsibility or economic viability, a truly sustainable event is one that minimizes negative impacts while maximizing positive contributions to the host community, economy and environment (Gowreesunkar and Séraphin, 2020). To understand sustainability in events, two key dimensions must be considered. First is the sustainability of the event itself, which includes financial and economic viability, social acceptance and ownership by the local community, and environmental responsibility undertaken by event organizers. This aligns with the widely recognized concept of the triple bottom line – economic, social and environmental sustainability.

Sustainability in events

Sustainability in the events context refers both to the sustainability of the event itself – its financial viability over time, as well as acceptance and ownership of the event by the local community, and the environmental sustainability measures undertaken by the event organizers – and to the role that events may play in the sustainability of their host destination over time (Mair, 2015). For tourism destinations, maintaining visitor numbers at an economically acceptable level, without exceeding the capacity of the local environment, nor the tolerance levels of the local community, can be a difficult task. Events, whether large or small, can play a role in finding the sustainable balance that destinations seek. For instance, events can bring visitors outside the traditional peak seasons and can contribute substantially to local economies. Events can create awareness of a destination and be the catalyst for repeat visitation by attendees. Finally, events can draw attention to the social and environmental impacts of tourism, contributing to the education of visitors.

Mair and Smith (2021) further observe that in the relationship between event and sustainability, making events more sustainable is no longer enough in the 21st century; rather the focus should be on how events might contribute to the wider sustainability agenda. This point is graphically represented in Figure 3.1. An event is considered to be sustainable if it contributes to the United Nations SDGs and minimizes triple bottom line negative impacts. Sustainable events management is not merely about reducing carbon footprint but also about fostering long-term benefits for stakeholders. As Mair (2019a) and Getz (2017) argue, we should no longer merely be trying to run 'sustainable events'; rather, we should focus on how events can contribute to the sustainable economic, social and environmental development of the places which host them. Likewise, in his paper on festivals, sustainability commitments in the field of events, Zifkos (2015) states that the ethics of minimizing negative environmental impacts is more important than producing greater good, as the principles of sustainability would suggest.

According to Mair and Smith (2021), the sustainability logic suggests that sociocultural, economic and environmental systems are intertwined in events and this is also well illustrated in several case studies, including Mair (2015). She examines sustainability at three events – Parkes Elvis Festival in Parkes, Australia; the Triple

Figure 3.1 Essence of sustainable events

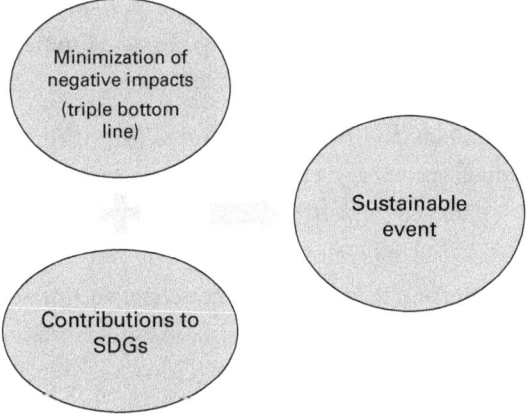

Crown Baseball Tournament in Steamboat Springs, USA; and Byron Bay Bluesfest, in Byron Bay (Australia). Mair (2015) further highlights the three pillars of sustainability, while showing the connections and overlaps. According to her observations, the fundamental pillars of sustainability in events are intertwined and overlap considerably, such that an economic boost to a tourist destination from an event can also have positive social impacts, while drawing attention to issues of environmental sustainability can have a positive economic impact on an event location.

Characteristics of sustainable events

Events, by their very nature, are temporary, whereas sustainability emphasizes long-term, resilient forms of development (Smith, 2012). This creates an inherent tension: while sustainability urges us to consider the well-being of future generations, events are often short-lived and vulnerable to cancellation or discontinuation (Getz, 2002). However, despite their transience, events can have lasting impacts – particularly if they deplete natural, built or socio-cultural resources in unsustainable ways. The challenge lies in demonstrating how such temporary occurrences can contribute positively to long-term sustainable development.

Sustainability has become a pressing concern across various industries, including events management. Increasingly, research highlights the need for an integrated approach to sustainability – one that balances environmental, social and economic dimensions rather than treating them in isolation. Mair and Smith (2021) reinforce this perspective through the concept of 'doughnut economics', which advocates building strong social and economic foundations to support quality of life while ensuring that ecological limits are not exceeded (Raworth, 2017). This signals the need to move beyond fragmented, 'siloed' thinking. Events management can take inspiration from the evolution of tourism studies, which has progressively embraced social sustainability alongside economic and environmental considerations. A similar shift in the event sector could pave the way for more meaningful contributions to sustainable development.

Sustainable events exhibit several key characteristics:

- *Environmental responsibility*: sustainable events prioritize eco-friendly practices such as waste reduction, energy efficiency and carbon offsetting. This includes using recyclable materials, promoting public transportation and ensuring responsible sourcing of products and services (Jones, 2014).
- *Economic viability*: beyond environmental concerns, sustainable events contribute to local economies by generating employment opportunities, supporting local businesses and fostering economic resilience (Gowreesunkar and Seraphin, 2020).

- *Social inclusion and community engagement*: events that promote sustainability often engage local communities, encourage diversity and inclusion and provide educational opportunities related to sustainability (Raj and Musgrave, 2009).
- *Governance and compliance*: sustainable events management involves adherence to national and international sustainability standards and guidelines, such as ISO 20121, which provides a systematic approach to event sustainability (Mair, 2019a).

Variability in sustainability

Event hosting has become one of the niche and popular tourism products in many countries and despite its growing importance in stimulating and enhancing economic growth, event hosting has a tremendous effect on sustainable development (Wee et al, 2017). Sustainability in events is not a one-size-fits-all approach; it varies significantly depending on the nature of the event, its location, stakeholder engagement and socio-economic conditions. Various factors, including cultural context, economic stability, political environment and event size, shape the sustainability framework for each event (Mair and Laing, 2012). As explained in Chapter 1, events and the evolution of society are entwined in the sense that as society evolves, the role, purpose and impacts of events also evolved.

Depending on who the event is for, the design and delivery of the event will be different. Indeed, the perception, understanding and importance of sustainability varies according to the demography. Subsequently, these variations need to be taken into consideration when designing, communicating and delivering the event as the expectations of attendees and other stakeholders involved will be different. The information provided will connect with the social aspects of sustainability and will include a range of perspectives of attendees. For instance, those who are mobility impaired, of different ethnicity or from different socioeconomic groups.

As an example, the sustainability considerations for mega-events such as the Olympics differ significantly from those for small-scale community festivals. Mega-events often require extensive infrastructure investments, contribute to environmental degradation and create concerns regarding displacement of local communities (Gaffney, 2013). However, they also present opportunities for global visibility, economic stimulation and long-term sustainability legacies if managed effectively (Smith, 2012). For instance, the London 2012 Olympics emphasized sustainability through green building initiatives, public transportation enhancements and waste management policies (Jones, 2018). In contrast, smaller community events focus on local engagement, heritage preservation and economic sustainability through supporting local vendors and artisans (Bolter and Seraphin, 2018, pp. 75–92).

Another critical determinant of sustainability variability is geographical location. Urban events face different challenges compared to rural or nature-based events. Urban settings often struggle with air pollution, congestion and excessive energy consumption, requiring event organizers to prioritize carbon footprint reduction strategies (Collins and Cooper, 2017). In contrast, rural or eco-tourism events are concerned with biodiversity conservation, local community involvement and minimizing ecological disruption (Gössling and Peeters, 2015). The Glastonbury Festival, for instance, has been lauded for its sustainability efforts, including banning single-use plastics, using composting toilets and supporting local environmental initiatives (Mair, 2019b).

Cultural and socio-economic factors also influence sustainability strategies. In developing countries, events are often driven by economic considerations, such as job creation and tourism revenue generation, sometimes at the expense of environmental and social sustainability (Scheyvens and Hughes, 2019). The Rio 2016 Olympics highlighted this issue, as it led to infrastructure development and job opportunities but also contributed to economic disparities and forced evictions in marginalized communities (Smith and Fox, 2019). Conversely, in developed nations with stringent environmental regulations, sustainability initiatives are often prioritized, with event organizers adopting stricter environmental and social governance frameworks (Laing and Frost, 2010).

Stakeholder involvement further determines the extent and effectiveness of sustainability initiatives. Events that integrate local communities, government bodies and private enterprises into planning processes tend to achieve better sustainability outcomes (Gowreesunkar and Seraphin, 2020). Collaborative governance, participatory decision-making and inclusive event policies ensure that sustainability goals align with the interests of all stakeholders (Richards, 2020). For example, community-driven cultural festivals such as the Notting Hill Carnival have succeeded in promoting both social sustainability and economic benefits by ensuring local people participate in event organization and revenue distribution (Mansfield and Seraphin, 2023).

The targets of sustainable events

Creating sustainability targets for an event from a tourism triple bottom line perspective involves considering the environmental, social and economic impacts of the event. This approach ensures that the event not only minimizes its negative effects on the environment but also promotes social equity and economic viability. Figure 3.2 visually represents the three core sustainability targets of events – environmental, social and economic. Each pillar is interconnected and contributes to a holistic sustainability approach in events management.

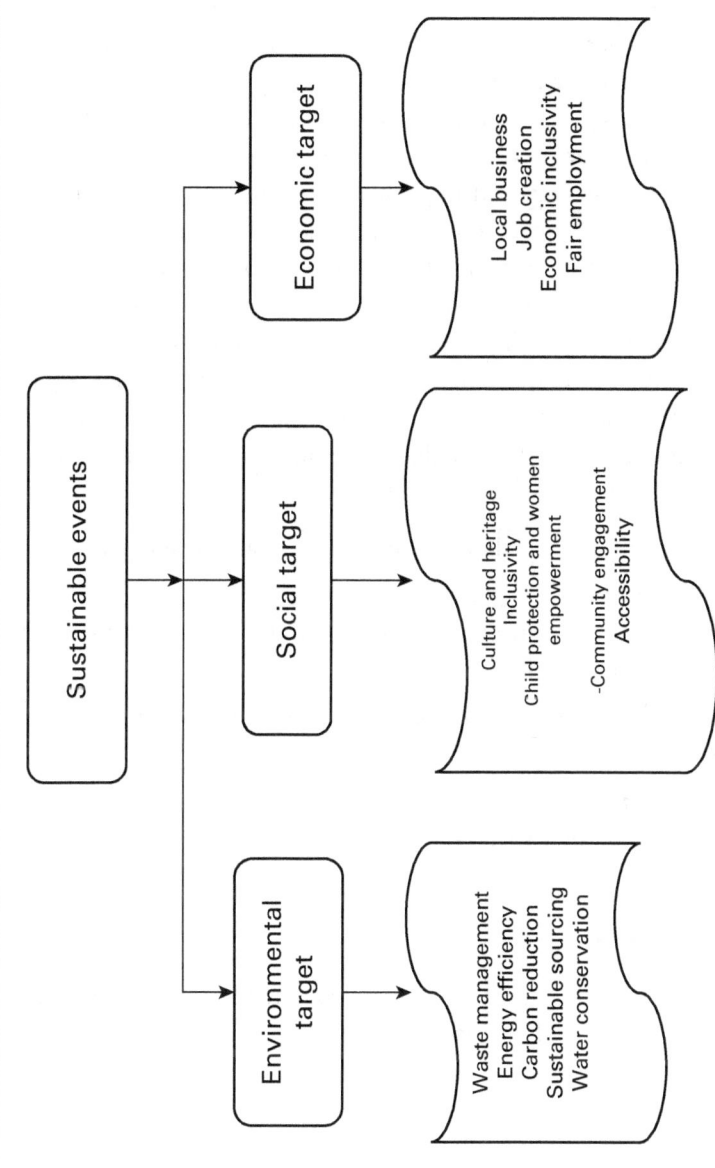

Figure 3.2 Sustainability targets

Environmental targets

The environmental footprint of events is substantial, as they generate significant amounts of waste, energy consumption and carbon emissions. Scholars such as Collins and Cooper (2017) have argued that event sustainability must prioritize waste management, energy efficiency and responsible sourcing of materials. For instance, waste generation is a major environmental concern in events management. Large-scale events often result in excessive food waste and non-recyclable materials. Events consume significant energy through lighting, sound systems and electronic equipment. Sustainable events adopt strategies such as carbon offset programmes, use of renewable energy and implementation of zero-waste initiatives to mitigate their environmental impact. For example, the 2012 London Olympics was heralded for its commitment to sustainability, incorporating green building designs, efficient transportation networks and a comprehensive waste diversion strategy (Jones, 2018). Additionally, sustainable events management includes promoting biodiversity conservation by preventing damage to local ecosystems, particularly in nature-based events. Water is a vital resource in events management as it is used for catering, sanitation and cleaning. Sustainable sourcing is crucial for reducing environmental impact. Best practices include the following:

- *Ethical procurement*: choosing environmentally responsible suppliers ensures sustainability.
- *Local and seasonal products*: sourcing locally reduces transportation emissions and supports regional economies.
- *Eco-friendly packaging*: using biodegradable and recyclable materials minimizes waste.
- *Fair Trade and ethical labour practices*: ensuring fair wages and humane working conditions promotes social sustainability.

Social targets

Events are a powerful means of fostering community engagement, cultural expression and social development. However, they also pose significant social challenges, particularly when they fail to respect the traditions, values and structures of the host community. Achieving social sustainability in events management is critical, as it ensures that events contribute positively to the well-being of local communities while avoiding potential negative consequences. Sustainable events can only be truly sustainable if they respect and integrate the socio-cultural aspects of the hosting country.

Events, by their nature, generate both positive and negative socio-cultural impacts on host communities. These impacts extend beyond economic benefits and entertainment value, influencing social structures, cultural identities and community well-being

(Mair and Laing, 2012). Social and cultural sustainability in events includes concepts such as equity, democratic participation, community empowerment, cultural integrity and quality of life (Ooi, 2013).

Positive socio-cultural impacts often arise when events provide opportunities for community bonding, revitalization of traditions and promotion of diversity. Events can enhance local pride, validate cultural identities and foster intercultural dialogue. Allen et al (2011) highlight that events can introduce new perspectives and increase tolerance within communities. For example, festivals celebrating minority cultures or marginalized groups can promote social inclusion and appreciation of diversity.

On the other hand, events can also bring about negative socio-cultural consequences, especially when they disregard the values and needs of the host community. Large-scale events often lead to disruptions such as overcrowding, noise pollution and increased crime rates (Allen et al, 2011). When an event fails to align with local socio-cultural norms, it can polarize the community, leading to conflicts between those who support and those who oppose the event. Such events can also commercialize cultural elements, stripping them of authenticity and commodifying traditions for profit (Mair and Laing, 2012).

One of the fundamental aspects of socio-cultural sustainability is ensuring that events are inclusive and participatory. Community engagement allows local populations to have a say in how events are planned, implemented and evaluated. Democratic participation ensures that events align with local values and needs, rather than being imposed upon communities for purely economic or political reasons (Ooi, 2013).

The role of events in fostering social capital has been widely recognized. Fredline et al (2005) argue that events influence people's quality of life, providing avenues for social interaction, shared experiences and identity formation. Events such as sports tournaments and cultural festivals help create shared values and social identities, fostering a sense of belonging among participants. This aligns with the idea that events are powerful modes of communication, engagement and affiliation (Warner and Dixon, 2011).

Additionally, social sustainability in events requires ensuring accessibility for all demographic groups, including marginalized populations. Gowreesunkar et al (2022) emphasize that sustainable events should prioritize inclusivity by promoting cultural heritage, providing educational opportunities and ensuring equitable participation. This means designing events that accommodate individuals with disabilities, offering affordable ticketing options and creating family-friendly environments. A key aspect of social sustainability is protecting vulnerable groups, such as children, within event settings. Research by Seraphin (2024)) highlights the need for child-friendly policies in event planning to prevent exploitation and exclusion. Child engagement in cultural events fosters early appreciation for heritage and promotes intergenerational participation. The Notting Hill Carnival, for example, integrates youth engagement programmes to ensure that children and adolescents actively participate in cultural celebrations (Seraphin, 2018).

Cultural integrity is a critical component of socio-cultural sustainability. Events should celebrate and respect local traditions rather than exploit or appropriate them. Hosting an event in a culturally sensitive manner ensures that local heritage is preserved while also promoting cultural exchange and appreciation.

Raworth (2017) introduces the concept of 'doughnut economics', advocating for building strong social and economic foundations while respecting ecological and cultural limits. Sustainable events should avoid overshooting these boundaries by prioritizing ethical cultural representation and ensuring that traditional practices are honoured. Mair (2019a) argues for a shift away from a 'siloed' approach to sustainability, emphasizing the importance of integrating social sustainability with economic and environmental considerations.

When events fail to respect cultural integrity, they risk alienating local communities and damaging the cultural fabric of the host destination. Large music festivals, for instance, often bring subcultures that clash with local values, leading to tensions and reputational harm (Allen et al, 2011). Additionally, the commodification of indigenous or traditional practices for commercial gain can erode cultural authenticity, reducing traditions to mere tourist attractions.

A compelling example of an event that aligns with socio-cultural sustainability principles is the Edinburgh Festival Fringe. As one of the world's largest arts festivals, it has been recognized for its commitment to promoting diversity, inclusion and cultural expression. The festival operates on an open-access model, allowing artists from diverse backgrounds to participate freely, fostering intercultural dialogue and artistic exchange (Richards, 2020).

The Edinburgh Festival Fringe also prioritizes accessibility by offering affordable ticketing options and inclusive programming, ensuring that people from different socio-economic backgrounds can engage with the arts. Moreover, the festival supports marginalized voices by providing a platform for underrepresented artists and performers. By respecting the cultural fabric of the host city while embracing global artistic influences, the festival demonstrates how large-scale events can achieve socio-cultural sustainability.

To achieve socio-cultural sustainability, the events industry must adopt more responsible practices that prioritize community engagement, inclusivity and cultural integrity. Sustainable business practices should involve local populations in decision-making processes and recognize the contributions of traditions and culture to the event experience (Wee et al, 2017). Events should foster mutually beneficial relationships between event organizers, employees, attendees and the local community.

Additionally, ensuring fair labour practices within the event industry is a crucial aspect of social sustainability. Many event workers and volunteers face precarious working conditions, with little job security or fair compensation. Implementing ethical labour policies and providing adequate support for event staff can contribute to a more sustainable and equitable industry.

Economic targets

The economic impact of an event is crucial to its sustainability, both in financial terms and in its broader contributions to the local economy. Events, particularly large-scale ones, offer opportunities for direct and indirect economic benefits through visitor spending, organizer expenditures and supply chain activities (Allen et al, 2011). However, for an event to be truly sustainable, it must go beyond short-term financial gains and contribute to long-term economic growth and stability for the host community. This discussion critically examines the key economic targets that an event should achieve in order to be considered sustainable.

One of the fundamental economic targets for a sustainable event is fostering economic growth by generating employment opportunities and stimulating local businesses. Events can create temporary jobs in various sectors, including hospitality, transportation and retail, as well as long-term positions in infrastructure and tourism management. For example, the Rio 2016 Olympics contributed significantly to Brazil's economy by creating employment opportunities and boosting tourism, though concerns about post-event sustainability persisted (Smith and Fox, 2019). However, critics argue that many jobs created by mega-events are often temporary and low-paying, which limits their long-term benefits. Therefore, sustainable events should aim to provide stable employment opportunities and skill development programmes to enhance workforce capabilities beyond the event period.

A sustainable event should ensure that its economic benefits are distributed equitably within the local community. This means prioritizing local suppliers and businesses rather than outsourcing to national or multinational corporations. Economic leakage, where financial benefits disproportionately flow to large corporations rather than remaining in the local economy, is a significant issue (Gowreesunkar et al, 2024, pp. 310–323). To mitigate this, event organizers should implement policies that favour local businesses in procurement processes. This approach not only supports local enterprises but also fosters community engagement and investment in regional economic development.

Beyond immediate economic benefits, sustainable events should contribute to long-term tourism growth and enhance the reputation of the host destination. Events serve as marketing tools that can attract future visitors by showcasing local attractions and culture. The Australian Tennis Open exemplifies this strategy; its televised coverage consistently includes picturesque views of Melbourne and its beaches, reinforcing the city's image as a desirable tourist destination (Allen et al, 2011). However, while such marketing efforts can boost tourism, the economic sustainability of this approach depends on whether the increased visitor numbers translate into sustained economic activity post-event. Thus, destination promotion should be paired with strategic investments in tourism infrastructure to accommodate and maintain long-term visitor interest.

Financial sustainability is a critical factor in determining an event's overall economic success. A sustainable event should not overly depend on public funding but should instead attract private sector investment through sponsorships, ticket sales and partnerships with sustainable enterprises. According to the UNEP report, economic responsibilities in the event industry include promoting profitability, increasing efficiency and ensuring responsible accounting (UN Environment Programme, n.d.). Many major events, however, struggle with financial sustainability. For instance, Olympic bids and preparations often rely heavily on taxpayer money, which can lead to public discontent, as seen in Toronto's failed 2008 Olympic bid. The 'Bread not Circuses' coalition argued that public funds should be directed toward social welfare rather than financing a costly Olympic bid (Carmichael, 2009)). This highlights the need for events organizers to balance economic ambitions with fiscal responsibility, ensuring that public funds are spent wisely and with long-term economic returns in mind.

A sustainable event should leave a lasting positive legacy in terms of infrastructure and community development. Mega-events often require substantial investment in transportation, accommodation and event venues. While these projects can boost the local economy during construction and operation, there is a risk of 'white elephant' facilities that become underutilized post-event. This issue was evident in the case of the Rio 2016 Olympics, where several stadiums and infrastructure developments fell into disuse after the games. To ensure sustainability, event planners must adopt a long-term vision that aligns event-related investments with broader urban development goals. For instance, temporary or multi-use facilities can be designed to ensure continued utility after the event concludes.

Economic sustainability in events also depends on ethical financial practices, including transparency and accountability in budgeting and procurement. The UNEP report emphasizes the importance of avoiding corruption, implementing transparent public procurement processes, and ensuring responsible accounting. Corruption and financial mismanagement have plagued many large-scale events, leading to budget overruns and public distrust. Sustainable events management requires rigorous financial oversight, clear reporting mechanisms and stakeholder engagement to ensure that economic benefits are equitably distributed and that financial resources are managed responsibly.

While economic success is a crucial component of sustainability, it should not come at the expense of social and environmental considerations. Sustainable events should strive to balance profitability with broader social and environmental objectives. For instance, job creation should prioritize fair wages and good working conditions, while investments in infrastructure should align with environmental sustainability principles, such as energy efficiency and reduced waste. Economic sustainability should be integrated with other pillars of sustainability to ensure that the event generates holistic and long-lasting benefits.

The Rio 2016 Olympics provide an instructive example of both the potential benefits and challenges associated with hosting a major event. The games generated significant short-term economic activity, including job creation and increased tourism. However, the long-term sustainability of these economic benefits has been questioned. Many Olympic venues became abandoned or underutilized, and the financial burden of hosting the games contributed to Brazil's economic struggles. This case illustrates the importance of strategic planning to ensure that the economic benefits of an event extend beyond its immediate duration and contribute to long-term financial sustainability.

Key stakeholders in sustainable events targets

There are a number of key stakeholders that are seen as a driving force behind sustainable events management. These include event organizers, government bodies, sponsors, suppliers, attendees, local communities and non-governmental organizations (NGOs). They act as catalysts in achieving environmental, social and economic targets. Sustainable events management requires collaboration among multiple stakeholders to minimize environmental impacts, promote social responsibility and ensure economic viability. Together, these key stakeholders create a synergistic framework that minimizes ecological footprints, promotes social responsibility and enhances economic viability, making sustainable events management a collective success (Mair, 2019a). The roles and involvement of these stakeholders in achieving sustainability targets in events are explained below.

Event organizers

Event organizers play a crucial role in driving sustainability in tourism events by making strategic decisions regarding venue selection, resource management, waste reduction and carbon footprint mitigation (Jones, 2014). As the primary coordinators of events, organizers must integrate sustainability into every stage of event planning, from concept development to post-event evaluation, ensuring that environmental, social and economic sustainability goals are met. Several major events worldwide showcase how organizers influence sustainable practices. Glastonbury Festival in the UK, for instance, has implemented a comprehensive sustainability strategy, including a ban on single-use plastics, a 'love the farm, leave no trace' policy, and a solar-powered Pyramid Stage to minimize carbon emissions (Jones, 2018). Similarly, the Super Bowl LVIII in the United States adopted sustainability measures such as zero-waste initiatives, food redistribution programmes and the use of renewable energy to power event facilities, setting a new standard for large-scale sports events (Alshikhy et al, 2025). Another significant example is Tomorrowland in Belgium, which has introduced sustainable campsite initiatives, water conservation measures and a global reforestation project as part of its commitment to reducing the festival's environmental impact (Chele et al, 2024)). Despite these advancements, event organizers often face challenges in balancing sustainability efforts with budget constraints and stakeholder expectations. Implementing sustainable solutions – such as renewable energy sources, eco-friendly catering and carbon offset programs – can require higher initial investments. However, research highlights that sustainable events management leads to long-term benefits, including cost savings, enhanced reputation and increased attendee engagement (Mair and Laing, 2012). For example, the Berlin International Film Festival has gained international recognition for its commitment to climate-neutral operations, attracting environmentally-conscious sponsors and attendees (Frank, 2011)).

To successfully integrate sustainability, event organizers must adopt innovative planning approaches, such as green procurement policies, digital ticketing systems to reduce paper waste and collaborations with sustainable suppliers. Additionally, organizers can leverage carbon offset programmes, public transport incentives and circular economy principles to ensure that events contribute positively to environmental and social sustainability goals. By taking a proactive leadership role, event organizers have the power to influence industry standards and inspire global action towards sustainable tourism events.

Government bodies and regulatory agencies

Governments and regulatory bodies play a pivotal role in ensuring sustainability in tourism events by enforcing environmental policies, setting industry standards and providing financial incentives for green initiatives. Regulations concerning waste management, carbon emissions, labour rights and energy efficiency shape how events are planned and executed (Raj and Musgrave, 2009). By implementing sustainability-focused policies, governments not only minimize the environmental footprint of events but also encourage innovation in sustainable events management. One significant example is the European Union's Green Deal, which promotes circular economy principles and sets strict sustainability guidelines for large-scale events, including waste reduction and carbon neutrality targets (Silander, 2019, pp. 2–35). Under this framework, events across Europe are required to adopt eco-friendly practices such as banning single-use plastics, increasing renewable energy use and implementing green mobility plans. Similarly, the Paris 2024 Olympics was set to become the most sustainable Olympic Games in history by utilizing 100 per cent renewable energy, constructing venues with low-carbon materials, and enforcing stringent emissions reduction policies as part of France's national sustainability strategy (Bellotto, 2024). Governments also play a crucial role in supporting sustainability efforts through funding and infrastructure development. The Tokyo 2020 Olympics, for example, incorporated sustainable construction, carbon offset programmes and resource efficiency measures, aligning with Japan's broader environmental policies and commitment to the UN Sustainable Development Goals (UNEP, 2021).

Another prominent example is Singapore's Green Plan 2030, which influences the sustainability framework for major events such as the Singapore Grand Prix, requiring organizers to implement green energy solutions and promote waste minimization strategies (De Marchi, 2022).

However, challenges remain in ensuring compliance with sustainability regulations, particularly when balancing economic priorities with environmental goals. Bureaucratic hurdles, slow policy implementation and resistance from industry stakeholders can delay sustainable projects. To address this, some governments have introduced financial incentives, grants and tax breaks for event organizers that prioritize eco-friendly initiatives. For example, the UK Government's Net Zero Strategy provides funding for festivals and sports events that commit to carbon reduction goals and green innovations (Koenig-Lewis et al, 2025, pp. 331–345).

Ultimately, governments and regulatory bodies act as key enablers of sustainability in the events industry. Through a combination of legislation, financial support and infrastructure investment, they can drive systemic change and ensure that large-scale tourism events contribute positively to environmental and social sustainability goals.

Sponsors and corporate partners

Sponsors play a crucial role in achieving sustainability targets in tourism events by influencing funding decisions, branding requirements and the overall sustainability agenda. As corporate social responsibility (CSR) and environmental, social and governance initiatives gain prominence, companies increasingly seek to align their sponsorships with sustainable events to enhance their brand image and demonstrate environmental commitment (Gowreesunkar and Seraphin, 2020). By supporting green initiatives, sustainable infrastructure and eco-friendly event practices, sponsors can significantly impact the industry's transition toward sustainability. Several recent high-profile events illustrate the role of sponsors in driving sustainability. For instance, Adidas partnered with the Boston Marathon, manufacturing event merchandise using recycled ocean plastics, reinforcing its commitment to sustainability (Laukkanen, 2021). Similarly, Heineken sponsored the Heineken Greener Bar initiative at events like the Formula 1 Dutch Grand Prix, implementing carbon-neutral bars that use renewable energy and reduce waste through circular economy principles (Heineken, 2023). Another notable example is Visa's sponsorship of the FIFA Women's World Cup 2023, where the company promoted carbon-neutral payment systems and supported sustainable tourism initiatives to offset event-related emissions (de Sá Ribas Guebert, 2024).

However, ensuring sponsorship agreements align with genuine sustainability efforts remains a challenge. Some companies engage in greenwashing – making misleading claims about their sustainability efforts without real action – which can damage an event's credibility and undermine public trust (Mair, 2019a). To mitigate this, event organizers must establish rigorous sustainability criteria when selecting sponsors, requiring tangible commitments such as carbon offset programmes, sustainable product offerings or transparent ESG reporting. For example, Glastonbury Festival only partners with sponsors that meet strict environmental guidelines, such as banning single-use plastics and contributing to reforestation projects. By leveraging sponsorship agreements to fund sustainable initiatives, promote responsible consumption and set industry-wide sustainability standards, sponsors can be powerful drivers of positive change. However, their role must be carefully managed to ensure their contributions align with genuine sustainability commitments rather than superficial branding exercises.

Suppliers and vendors

Suppliers and vendors play a critical role in achieving sustainability targets in tourism events by providing essential goods and services such as catering, logistics and event materials. Their commitment to sustainable procurement practices, such as sourcing local and organic food, using biodegradable packaging and minimizing transportation emissions, significantly reduces the environmental impact of events (Jones, 2014). By adopting green supply chain practices, suppliers can help event organizers meet sustainability goals while also influencing industry-wide standards. Several global events showcase how suppliers and vendors contribute to sustainability initiatives. For example, the Melbourne Food and Wine Festival partners with local farmers to source fresh, organic ingredients, reducing the carbon footprint associated with food transportation and supporting the regional economy (Laing and Frost, 2010). Similarly, at the COP26 Climate Summit in Glasgow, vendors were required to adhere to strict sustainability criteria, including providing plant-based food options, using compostable utensils and minimizing food waste through redistribution programmes (Alabrese and Saba, 2023). Another notable example is the Olympic Games, where organizers have increasingly prioritized eco-friendly suppliers. The Tokyo 2020 Olympics implemented a circular economy approach, sourcing recyclable materials for event infrastructure and ensuring that vendors followed sustainability guidelines to minimize waste and energy consumption (Bellotto, 2024).

Despite these efforts, challenges remain in implementing sustainable procurement in events management. The availability and cost of eco-friendly alternatives can be a barrier for suppliers, particularly small businesses that may struggle to meet sustainability requirements due to financial constraints (Mair and Jago, 2010). Additionally, some vendors may lack the knowledge or resources to adopt sustainable practices effectively. To address these challenges, event organizers can set clear sustainability requirements in contracts, provide incentives for green procurement, and collaborate with vendors to develop innovative solutions. For instance, some festivals have introduced vendor sustainability certification programmes, rewarding suppliers who meet specific environmental criteria. By integrating sustainable practices into procurement policies and fostering strong collaborations with suppliers, event organizers can drive long-term industry transformation. Suppliers and vendors are not just service providers; they are key sustainability partners whose choices directly impact an event's environmental, social and economic footprint.

Attendees and participants

Attendees and participants play a crucial role in achieving sustainability targets at events through their behaviours, choices and engagement with eco-friendly initiatives. Their willingness to adopt sustainable practices, such as waste segregation, responsible consumption and the use of green transportation, can significantly reduce the environmental impact of large-scale gatherings (Raj and Musgrave, 2009). Event organizers increasingly recognize attendees as active stakeholders whose participation is essential for the success of sustainability efforts.

Several events around the world have successfully integrated attendee-driven sustainability initiatives. For example, the Roskilde Festival in Denmark incentivizes attendees to return waste for recycling by offering discounts on future tickets, which has led to increased recycling rates and waste reduction (Mair and Laing, 2012). Similarly, Glastonbury Festival in the UK encourages participants to bring reusable water bottles and bans single-use plastics, significantly reducing landfill waste. The festival also promotes public transport and carpooling to lower carbon emissions from attendee travel (Jones, 2014). In the Tokyo Marathon, runners are provided with biodegradable cups and water stations to minimize plastic waste, demonstrating how large-scale sporting events can integrate sustainable practices with attendee participation (Kellison, 2024, pp. 362–372).

To enhance attendee involvement, events employ various engagement strategies such as sustainability pledges, awareness campaigns and gamification techniques that reward responsible behaviour. For instance, some music festivals use mobile apps to encourage attendees to track their carbon footprint and participate in eco-friendly activities in exchange for rewards. However, changing attendee habits remains a challenge, particularly when convenience conflicts with sustainability principles (Jones, 2014).

Ultimately, attendees' collective actions have a profound impact on an event's overall sustainability. By actively participating in green initiatives, making responsible choices and embracing eco-conscious behaviours, attendees become essential contributors to sustainable events management. Ensuring their engagement through incentives, education and innovative strategies is key to achieving long-term sustainability goals in the event industry.

Local communities

Local communities play a vital role in achieving sustainability targets in events by actively participating in planning, implementation and monitoring processes. Their involvement ensures that events align with environmental, social and economic sustainability goals. Community-led initiatives can help reduce the environmental impact of events through waste management programmes, local sourcing of goods and sustainable transport solutions. Additionally, fostering community engagement enhances cultural preservation, economic inclusion and long-term sustainability. For instance, the Rio Carnival in Brazil demonstrates the power of local involvement by integrating community-led sustainability projects, such as waste collection cooperatives, which create economic opportunities for marginalized groups while reducing environmental harm (Laing and Frost, 2010). Similarly, at the Edinburgh Festival Fringe, local businesses, artists and residents collaborate to implement waste reduction strategies and promote eco-friendly tourism. These efforts not only help meet sustainability targets but also ensure that the benefits of events are distributed within the community. Empowering local residents through education, dialogue and decision-making opportunities fosters a sense of ownership and responsibility toward sustainable event practices. When communities are engaged, they become key drivers of eco-friendly initiatives, ensuring that events are both successful and aligned with long-term sustainability goals. By leveraging local knowledge, resources and commitment, events can become powerful catalysts for sustainable development.

Non-governmental organizations (NGOs) and advocacy groups

NGOs and advocacy groups play a crucial role in advancing sustainability targets by driving awareness, enforcing accountability and implementing practical solutions within the events industry. They influence event sustainability by promoting best practices, conducting environmental audits and pressuring organizers to adopt greener alternatives. Organizations like the Sustainable Event Alliance (SEA) (which closed in 2023) provided certification and training programmes to encourage sustainable events management and ensure industry-wide adherence to eco-friendly standards (Sustainable Event Alliance, 2011). NGOs also engage in activism, advocating for policy reforms and pushing corporations to adopt more responsible environmental practices. For instance, Greenpeace has actively campaigned against high-carbon-impact events, urging major festivals to transition to renewable energy sources while promoting waste reduction initiatives (Jones, 2014). Another notable example is A Greener Festival (AGF), an international NGO that collaborates with music and cultural festivals to implement carbon footprint assessments, introduce reusable infrastructure and educate attendees on sustainable practices. Their work has influenced major events like Glastonbury Festival to significantly cut down on single-use plastics and adopt solar-powered energy solutions. Despite their impact, NGOs face challenges such as securing funding, navigating complex regulatory environments, and overcoming resistance from event stakeholders who often prioritize profitability over sustainability. However, their persistent efforts continue to shape the future of sustainable events management, making them indispensable in the global push toward environmentally responsible gatherings.

Children

Children can play an active role in achieving sustainability targets, as evidenced by numerous real-world examples. As highlighted in Chapter 5, children are significant stakeholders in the events industry, with many events dedicated to them for purposes such as fun, competition, education and entertainment. A growing body of research shows that children are no longer silent stakeholders in society but are increasingly participating in sustainability initiatives (Séraphin and Gowreesunkar, 2020b; Lugosi et al, 2020; Spyrou, 2020). The study by Hill et al (2014) on sustainability practices among Australian children illustrates their pivotal role in sustainability principles, leading the Australian government to integrate sustainability topics into childhood education policies. Similarly, Indian companies actively involve children as ambassadors for sustainability messages, as children in India are often regarded as representing the voice of God. As a result, child-led activism for environmental sustainability is widespread across Indian cities (Gowreesunkar and Maingi, 2023, pp. 197–207).

By taking on the role of sustainability transformers, children have the power to influence their peers, encouraging responsible behaviours toward the environment. Louv (2008) emphasizes that children need opportunities to engage with nature firsthand, as this fosters a sense of connection and care for the environment. Moreover, when children are actively involved in sustainability efforts, parents also become interested and even take time off work to participate. Children, as agents of change, can significantly impact sustainability targets if they are intentionally included in such initiatives (Séraphin and Gowreesunkar, 2020b). Given that children are the leaders of tomorrow and sustainability remains one of the most pressing concerns of the 21st century (Gowreesunkar and Maingi, 2023), it is crucial to engage them in sustainable civic actions and instil moral, social and environmental values to ensure a sustainable future.

The influence of children on sustainability goals has been extensively discussed by Séraphin and Gowreesunkar, as illustrated in Figure 3.3. A child-centred rights approach to sustainable tourism emphasizes integrating child rights within tourism systems and value chains. This approach prioritizes the best interests of children, including their family and social relationships (White, 2002; Kratcoski et al, 2019) and their protection in business settings (Séraphin et al, 2023). Promoting child-centred economic policies within national and tourism economies is a crucial step in securing sustainable development. The Slovene child benefit programme serves as an exemplary model of a family-centred economy, where children receive financial support for education, subsistence and overall well-being, effectively addressing child poverty and ensuring dignity

Figure 3.3 Children in sustainability targets

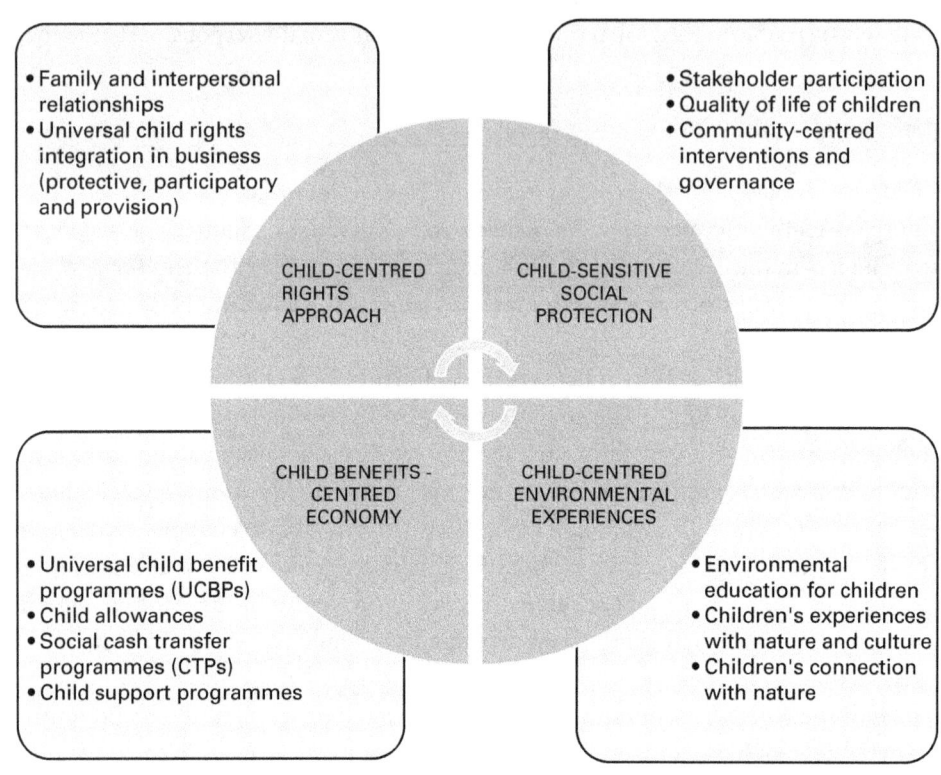

SOURCE Séraphin et al (2023)

for all children (Svetina et al, 2013). According to Donnell and Rinkoff (2015), children's direct environmental experiences play a critical role in fostering ecological awareness and cultural appreciation. Lastly, implementing child-sensitive social protection policies and programmes is essential to addressing the needs of poor households and vulnerable children (OVCs), reinforcing the idea that children are not just passive beneficiaries but active contributors to a more sustainable and equitable society.

ACTIVITY 3.1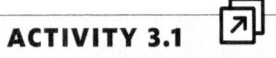

Designing a sustainable event – 'Mission: GreenFest'

Objective

You are required to work as part of a team from a fictious events management consultancy to design a concept for a tourism-related event that meets environmental, social and economic sustainability targets. You should apply the principles covered in this chapter to propose realistic, creative and measurable solutions.

1. Form teams of five to six people – each team represents an events management consultancy hired to plan a sustainable event for a tourism destination.
2. Choose your event theme, for example, an eco-friendly cultural festival, sustainable food and craft fair, responsible adventure tourism weekend, community-based heritage celebration. You must ensure your event meets the three pillars of sustainability: environmental, social and economic (10 minutes).
3. Set sustainability targets (20 minutes). Using what you learned in this chapter, identify at least two measurable targets in each pillar:
- Environmental, for example, zero plastic use, carbon offset, renewable energy.
- Social, for example, local job creation, cultural preservation and inclusivity.
- Economic, for example, support local suppliers, fair pricing and revenue for community projects.
4. Create a stakeholder engagement plan (15 minutes). As a team, list the key stakeholders (local government, vendors, NGOs, tourists, local communities) and describe their role in achieving your targets.
5. Present your sustainable event plan (5 minutes per team).

Summary

This chapter considered the importance of sustainable events within the broader framework of sustainable tourism. Sustainability within events refers both to the sustainability of the event – for instance, the viability of the event financially over time – and the environmental measures taken by the event organizers. While events by their very nature are temporary, they can have lasting impacts and contribute positively to long-term sustainable development.

This chapter also recognized the key stakeholders involved in ensuring an event's sustainable goals, including the event organizers, as well as sponsors, suppliers and vendors, government bodies, NGOs and advocacy groups, local communities and attendees and participants. Each stakeholder plays a role in achieving environmental, social and economic targets.

Further reading

Jones, M (2025) *Sustainable Events management: A practical guide*, Routledge, Abingdon

The book covers environmental, social and economic targets, stakeholder engagement, policy compliance and innovations in event sustainability. The case studies offer valuable examples that can be adapted to tourism contexts.

Goodwin, H (2016) *Responsible Tourism: Using tourism for sustainable development*, Goodfellow Publishers Limited, Oxford

This book explores how tourism – including events – can contribute to sustainable development when planned and managed responsibly. It addresses key stakeholder roles, policy implications and ethical considerations, offering a global perspective backed by research and field experience.

References

Alabrese, M and Saba, A (Eds) (2023) *EU Law on Sustainable and Climate Resilient Agriculture after the European Green Deal*, Rurinnova, Pula

Allen, J, O'Toole, W, Harris, R and McDonnell, I (2011) *Festival and Special Event Management*, Routledge, Abingdon

Alshikhy, T, O'Sullivan, H, Polkinghorne, M and Gennings, E (2025) The role and impact of sporting mega-events in the context of soft power, *Encyclopedia*, 5 (1), 31

Bellotto, G (2024) Sustainability in Mega Sports Events: Between Tokyo 2020 and Paris 2024 (Master's thesis), Ca' Foscari University of Venice, Venice

Bolter, F and Seraphin, G (2018) Child protection in France, In: *National Systems of Child Protection: Understanding the international variability and context for developing policy and practice*, Springer International Publishing, Cham

Carmichael, R (2009) *Hidden Costs of the Olympics: Preparation, politics and control*, Simon Fraser University, Burnaby

Chele, A C, Podaru, G and Strătilă, V (2024) The role of special events in tourism, *Cactus – The Tourism Journal for Research, Education, Culture and Soul*, 6 (2), 93–106

Collins, A and Cooper, C (2017) Measuring the environmental sustainability of events, *Event Management*, 21 (3), 231–50

De Marchi, E (2022) *Green Cities and the Challenge Towards Climate Change: An analysis of Singapore's sustainable urbanism*, (Master's thesis), Ca' Foscari University of Venice, Venice

de Sá Ribas Guebert, L (2024) *Beyond the Scoreboard: Examining media activism related to the FIFA World Cup Qatar 2022 to the 2023 FIFA Women's World Cup* (Master's thesis), Charles University, Prague

Donnell, A and Rinkoff, R (2015) The influence of culture on children's relationships with nature, *Children, Youth and Environments*, (25 (3), 62–89

Frank, A E (2011) Berlin International Film Festival – Berlinale 2011, *Film Philosophy*, 15 (1), 234–39

Fredline, L, Deery, M and Jago, L (2005) *Host community perceptions of the impact of events. A comparison of different event themes in urban and regional communities*, https://sustain.pata.org/wp-content/uploads/2015/02/Fredline_compareVICevents.pdf

Gaffney, C (2013) Mega-events and socio-spatial dynamics in Rio de Janeiro, *Journal of Latin American Geography*, 12 (3), 7–29

Getz, D (2002) Why festivals fail, Event Management, 7 (4), 209–19, doi.org/10.3727/152599502108751604

Getz, D (2017) Developing a framework for sustainable event cities, *Event Management*, 21 (5), 575–91

Gössling, S and Peeters, P (2015) Assessing tourism's global environmental impact, *Journal of Sustainable Tourism*, 23 (3), 401–16

Gowreesunkar, V and Maingi, S W (2023) Organising events with children with disabilities at ANPRAS (Mauritius): Insights and implications. In: *Events Management for the Infant and Youth Market*, Emerald Publishing Limited, Leeds

Gowreesunkar, V and Séraphin, H (2020) *Sustainable Tourism and Events Planning*, Routledge, Abingdon

Gowreesunkar, V, Maingi, S W and Ming'ate, F L M (Eds) (2022) *Management of Tourism Ecosystems in a Post-Pandemic Context: Global perspectives*, Routledge, Abingdon

Heineken (2023) theheinekencompany.com/sites/heineken-corp/files/heineken-corp/investors/results-reports-webcasts-presentations/2014/heineken-nv-sustainability-report-2013.pdf

Hill, A, Emery, S, Nailon, D, Dyment, J, Getenet, S, McCrea, N and Davis, J M (2014) Exploring how adults who work with young children conceptualise sustainability and describe their practice initiatives. *Australasian Journal of Early Childhood*, 39(3), 14–22

Jones, M (2014) *Sustainable Event Management: A Practical Guide*, Routledge, Abingdon.

Jones, M (2018) *Sustainable Event Management: A Practical Guide*, Routledge, Abingdon

Kellison, T (2024) Sporting infrastructure and urban environmental planning. In: *Research Handbook on Major Sporting Events*, Edward Elgar Publishing, Cheltenham

Koenig-Lewis, N, Collins, A and McCullough, B (2025). The game is on!–Sports (Events) as a Driving Force for Sustainability. In: *The Routledge Companion to Marketing and Sustainability*, Routledge, Abingdon

Kratcoski, P C, Dunn Kratcoski, L and Kratcoski, P C (2019) Laws and court cases pertaining to children: Offenders and victims. In: *Juvenile Delinquency: Theory, Research and the Juvenile Justice Process*, Springer International Publishing, Cham

Laing, J and Frost, W (2010) How green was my festival: Exploring challenges and opportunities of staging green events, *International Journal of Hospitality Management*, 29 (2), 261–67

Laukkanen, J (2021) *Sustainability Marketing in Sporting Goods Industry* (Master's thesis), Lappeenranta-Lahti University of Technology LUT School of Business and Management, Finland

Louv, R (2008) Paul F Brandwein Lecture 2007, A Brief History of the Children & Nature Movement: Presentation at the NSTA 2007 Annual Conference, *Journal of Science Education and Technology*, 17 (3), 217–18

Lu, H F (2021) Hallmark sporting events as a vehicle for promoting the sustainable development of regional tourism: Strategic perspectives from stakeholders, *Sustainability*, 13 (6), 3460

Lugosi, P, Golubovskaya, M, Robinson, R N, Quinton, S and Konz, J (2020) Creating family-friendly pub experiences: A composite data study, *International Journal of Hospitality Management*, 91, 102690

Mair, J (2015) The role of events in creating sustainable tourism destinations. In: *The Practice of Sustainable Tourism*, 247–62, Routledge, Abingdon

Mair, J. (2019a) *The Routledge Handbook of Festivals*, Routledge, Abingdon

Mair, J (2019b) The greening of music festivals: Motivations, barriers, and outcomes, *Journal of Sustainable Tourism*, 27 (5), 683–700

Mair, J and Jago, L (2010) The development of a conceptual model of greening in the business events sector, *Journal of Sustainable Tourism*, 18 (1), 77–94

Mair, J and Laing, J (2012) The role of sustainability in event management, *Event Management*, 16 (1), 1–8

Mair, J and Smith, A (2021) Events and sustainability: why making events more sustainable is not enough, *Journal of Sustainable Tourism*, 29 (11–12), 1739–55 https://doi.org/10.1080/09669582.2021.1942480

Mansfield, C and Seraphin, H (2023) Turning Winchester (UK) Into an eventful children city: investigating the creation of a Webtoon Festival, In: *Events Management for the Infant and Youth Market* (101-118), Emerald Publishing Limited, Leeds

Ooi, N K S (2013) Social capital and socio-cultural sustainability: Mountain resort tourism and the community of Steamboat Springs (Doctoral dissertation), Monash University, Melbourne

Raj, R and Musgrave, J (2009) *Event Management and Sustainability*, CABI, Wallingford

Raworth, K (2017) *Doughnut Economics: Seven ways to think like a 21st-century economist*, Penguin, London

Richards, G (2020) Designing creative places: The role of creative tourism, *Annals of Tourism Research*, 85, 102922

Scheyvens, R and Hughes, E (2019) Can tourism be inclusive? *Tourism Geographies*, 21 (1), 129–50

Séraphin, H (2018) The role of community-based events in sustainable tourism, *Journal of Hospitality and Tourism Management*, 37 (4), 223–34

Séraphin, H (2024) Understanding the traits of tourism sustainability activists through a life course framework, *Journal of Policy Research in Tourism, Leisure and Events*, 16 (14), 749–67

Séraphin, H, Fotiadis, A and Gowreesunkar, V (2024) Editorial: Liveable cities for locals and visitors: challenges and opportunities for destinations, *International Journal of Tourism Cities*, 10 (4), 1185-91, https://doi.org/10.1108/IJTC-12-2024-305

Séraphin, H and Gowreesunkar, V G (2020a) Unlocking changes for sport tourism products using the Blakeley-Visser model: An application to sports events in small islands: The case of Martinique. In: *Post-Disaster and Post-Conflict Tourism*, 143–62, Apple Academic Press, Palm Beach, FL

Séraphin, H and Gowreesunkar, V (eds) (2020b) *Children in Hospitality and Tourism: Marketing and Managing Experiences* (Vol 4), Walter de Gruyter GmbH & Co, Berlin

Seraphin, H, Gowreesunkar, V and Canosa, A (2023) Destination marketing organizations: The need for a child-centred approach to diaspora tourism, *Tourism Planning & Development*, 20 (3), 468–80

Silander, D (2019) The European Commission and Europe 2020: Smart, sustainable and inclusive growth, In: *Smart, Sustainable and Inclusive Growth*, Edward Elgar Publishing, Cheltenham

Smith, A (2012) *Events and Urban Regeneration: The strategic use of events to revitalize cities*, Routledge, Abingdon

Smith, A and Fox, T (2019) Assessing the economic impact of mega-events, *Tourism Economics*, 25 (3), 409–28

Spyrou, S (2020) Children as future-makers, *Childhood*, 27 (1), 3–7

Sustainable Event Alliance (2011) (Unpublished)

Svetina, M, Istenič-Starčič, A, Juvančič, M, Novljan, T, Šubic-Kovač, M, Verovšek, Š and Zupančič, T (2013) How children come to understand sustainable development: A contribution to educational agenda, *Sustainable Development*, 21 (4), 260– 269

UN Environment Programme (n.d.) Sustainable Development Goals. www.unep.org/topics/sustainable-development-goals

Warner, S and Dixon, M A (2011) Understanding sense of community from the athlete's perspective, *Journal of Sport Management*, 25 (3), 257–71

Wee, H, Mahdzar, M, Hamid, Z A, Shariff, F M, Chang, F and Ismail, W N H M (2017) Sustainable event tourism: Evidence of practices and outcomes among festival organizers, *Advanced Science Letters*, 23 (8), 7719–22

White, S C (2002) Being, becoming and relationship: Conceptual challenges of a child rights approach in development, *Journal of International Development*, 14 (8), 1095–104

Zifkos, G (2015) Sustainability everywhere: problematising the 'sustainable festival' phenomenon, *Tourism Planning & Development*, 12 (1), 6–19

04 | Choosing a sustainable venue

LEARNING OUTCOMES

By the end of Chapter 4, you should be able to:
- recognize the different types of event venues
- assess the significant role of the venue in event design and delivery
- compare venues based on indicators of their sustainability
- identify the contribution of the venue to sustainable supply chain management
- evaluate venue sustainability accreditation and certification schemes, including ISO 20121.

Introduction

The choice of venue for any event is a major decision that will influence the design and delivery of the event programme and the experience of attendees. The venue itself will become one of the main assets of the event and the venue management team will become key event stakeholders. In recent years, venues that have adopted sustainable practices have become more important to event planners in the venue selection process (An et al, 2021) and this chapter will illustrate the ways in which the novice event manager can appraise event venues in terms of their commitment to sustainability. One such technique is through venue grading and certification schemes and this chapter will discuss how these are tools for identifying and measuring sustainable venue management.

When designing events, it may be prudent to choose a venue that has the principles of sustainability at its core and is both strategically and operationally focused on responsibly hosting events. Choosing a venue with such values and processes will help to ensure a synthesis between the venue and the event. Incorporating sustainable practices into the management of event venues is an ongoing, important and still emerging trend, but many venues have invested much time and effort in developing and implementing sustainability policies and can be considered to be more advanced than event planners (Nolan, 2018). As such, this chapter will explore sustainability from a venue perspective, and it will illustrate how event managers can draw on the information and guidance available to them from venue managers. This chapter explores the importance of assessing supply chain management when choosing and working with an event venue, as ultimately, working closely with the venue will complement and advance the goal of planning and delivering a sustainable event.

Types of event venues

As selecting the right venue for any event is an important task, as it will become critical to the event's success. As the backdrop to all activities, the venue will make a notable contribution to the theme and ambience of the event and as many of its facilities will be used by attendees, it will have a significant impact on their experience. The number of event venues has increased in recent years as visitor attractions, religious buildings and sporting complexes, among others, have diversified to make their venues available for events (Delaney, 2023, pp. 139–51). Thus, event managers now have an increasing list of viable spaces to use as the location for each of their events which may be categorized as shown in Figure 4.1.

Figure 4.1   Categories of types of venues

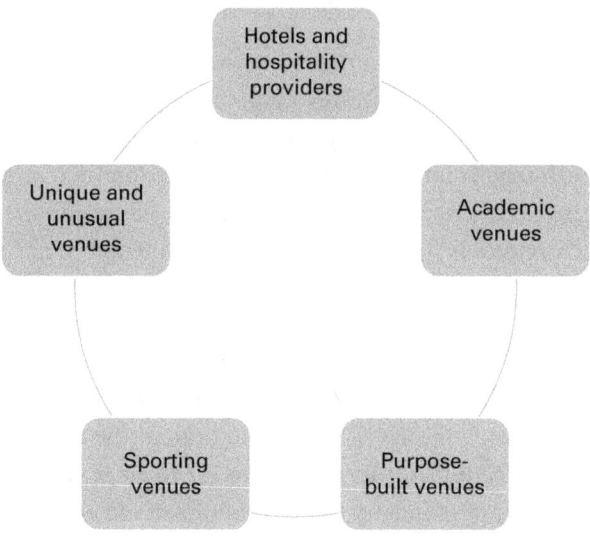

Hotels

Hotels can make excellent event venues as they will have a fully operational catering facility on site and plenty of accommodation. Many hotels have separate rooms for functions taking place within the venue and, for fully catered events, these spaces can often be hired for free. However, there is sometimes a disparity between the capacity of the function space and the number of bedrooms at the venue. This means that some hotels, for example, can accommodate large events but can only provide bedrooms for some of the attendees. The reverse can also be true, where bed stock is greater than the capacity of the principal function room, which means that as an event planner, it is important to compare the capacities of both. A number of hotels will have additional facilities such as a pool, spa and golf course, which may be useful in attracting people to the event. However, they can sometimes provide an unwanted distraction. Similarly, although many hotels are located in city centres, some are to be found in rural locations that may limit transport options to the site. Hotels can offer very competitive rates to event managers for both function space and bedroom accommodation and will often negotiate charges, particularly for regular users. Larger establishments are more likely to be a part of a national or international chain although frequently they operate as franchises. A franchised hotel will be run by an individual or a group of individuals but it will operate under a well-known name or brand and in accordance with their policies. Chains and franchised hotels can sometimes offer appealing rates to event managers who will provide them with a regular income but at times they can be restricted as to how far they are able to negotiate hire charges.

Unusual venues

There has been a noticeable trend in the rise of unique or unusual venues offering up hireable space to event organizers. This can include visitor attractions, museums, music venues, theatres and cinemas. Such venues can often be quirky, full of original features with a real wow factor and the careful integration of an unusual venue into the event experience can result in a truly unique and outstanding event. The drawback of using such venues is that they can be quite limited in terms of when they are available and visitor attractions, for example, may only be available for evening hire and for short periods of time; conversely theatres and cinemas can generally only be hired for daytime use. Furthermore, historical venues can sometimes have very poor access, narrow stairways and strict rules against the use of decorations. Frequently they are listed buildings, which means that they cannot be altered without special permission which can be difficult to obtain. Access to such venues may be very restricted, with limited entry points for equipment or staging and this problem will be compounded by a short get in period. Historical venues and museums may also have very strict rules to protect their artefacts and exhibits. As many unusual venues do not have a regular need for AV equipment or staging, such equipment would need to be hired in at an extra cost and this will increase the transportation of goods to the venue, and as such, it will increase the carbon footprint of the event.

Sporting venues

As with hotels, there are a great number of sporting venues around the globe that can also be used for other types of events. Although the main function of these venues is to support sports training and sporting competitions, many are run as commercial ventures and they are increasingly marketed to event managers. In fact, in the last decade new stadia have been designed with flexibility of use in mind to facilitate the generation of additional and regular income to insure their long-term economic viability (Bladen et al, 2022). Although major sporting events such as the Olympics, are often criticized for how they require the construction of new venues that will have a limited use post-event, some cities have very carefully strategized for the long-term sustainability of new venues. Barcelona is one such example, as much of the infrastructure built for the 1992 Olympics continues to serve the flourishing Spanish tourism and events industry. In general, sporting venues have much to offer the events industry. The outdoor seating and pitch area of a stadium combine to create a generous capacity for large-scale music concerts, while some of the smaller rooms used for match day hospitality are suitable for meetings, parties and more intimate events. Typically sporting venues have strong transport links which will encourage event guests to travel to the venue by public transport.

Academic venues

Academic venues are also a very viable category of venue for many types of events and many universities for example, employ a specialist events team dedicated to promoting the use of their campuses and extensive choice of rooms to event planners. Most university campuses will be made up of a large number of lecture halls and seminar rooms, all equipped with lecterns, microphones, projectors and screens which may suit a range of events and many will have extensive sporting facilities too, such as gyms, tennis courts and pools as well as student accommodation, which may be available for event guests outside of semester time.

Purpose-built venues

Davidson and Rogers (2016) affirm that the US was the first country to embrace the concept of building purpose-built event space and in most developed countries, purpose-built venues have been built to serve and attract events such as conferences and exhibitions. Such modern venues will often have excellent green credentials and they can make suitable spaces for a range of events as they have been specifically designed to suit the needs of the events industry.

> **REAL-WORLD EXAMPLE**   The Convention Centre Dublin
>
> The Convention Centre Dublin (CCD, 2025) is the first carbon-neutral constructed convention centre and it aims to become the Republic of Ireland's most sustainable venue and a leading expert in sustainable events management (Figure 4.2). The venue has a comprehensive waste management policy in place to help manage the generation and segregation of waste and the its recycling figures are consistently above 95 per cent. The venue will assess how to best manage the creation, segregation and recycling of waste, not only within the building, but also for every event, and to achieve this, it has custom-built recycle-friendly bins to help event guests in this mission to reduce, reuse and recycle.
>
> The venue uses 100 per cent recycled napkins and wooden stir sticks and all chocolate, tea and coffee supplies are fair trade. Most of the food, including all beef and chicken supplies, are locally sourced, which ensures meals are fresh and in season and local farmers are supported. In terms of venue cleaning, the CCD uses reusable microfibre cloths and mops made from recyclable materials that are laundered on site, as well as recycled paper products and re-fillable soap dispensers. To ensure minimum water usage, sensor taps are in all wash hand basins and sensor flushes in all urinals. The venue uses a sustainable energy supplier and has installed a thermal wheel heat recovery system and an Ice Storage Thermal Unit (ISTU), which chills water overnight to form large ice blocks that melt during the day to provide air conditioning for the entire building. The building design makes use of natural light in all foyer spaces and small meeting rooms and most of the meeting spaces are fitted with motion sensors, which automatically turn off lights when the room is empty. All the CCD's exterior lights use energy-saving LED bulbs and all computers and office equipment on site has an automatically activated sleep-mode.
>
> The CCD is committed to long-term sustainable excellence sustainability continues to be an integral part of the venue's core values, strategic initiatives and day-to-day operations. The venue strives to engage and influence service partners, contractors and suppliers seeks to specialize in hosting sustainable events.
>
> **SOURCE** The CCD, 2025.

Venue selection in events management

Given the complexity of venue selection, many event managers will use an intermediary to either choose, or shortlist, suitable venues. Intermediaries can include venue finding agencies, convention bureaus and other destination management organizations that are specialists and often provide their service free of charge to the event planner, although sometimes they will take a commission from the venue when a booking is made (Nadda et al, 2022). Destination management agencies can make excellent intermediaries as they have unparalleled knowledge of their geographical area and can support event managers in a number of ways, very often for little or no charge. They can provide a venue finding service as well as secure accommodation fovr event attendees and connect event planners with local suppliers.

When using an intermediary, it is important for the event manager to be clear about what venue factors are most important to them and typically, the choice of venue will be based on a range of factors as illustrated in Figure 4.3.

Figure 4.2 The Convention Centre Dublin © The CCD

Figure 4.3 Factors influencing the choice of venue

Price	Rooms & capacities	Location
Accessibility	Facilities	Experience
Availability	Residential options	Restrictions

Often, the cost of hiring the venue will be the most important consideration for the event manager, alongside the number of rooms within the venue and their individual and overall capacities. The event manager will often prioritize the geographic location of the venue as well as its accessibility, in terms of how event guests will get to the venue. It remains a challenge to organize sustainable face-to-face events, if attendees are dependent on CO_2 emitting means of transport, such as aeroplanes (Hagen, 2021, pp. 259–75). Thus there is a strong argument for planners to choose venues that are easily reachable by public transport and, for overnight events, to choose a residential venue (i.e. one with accommodation on site) or a venue that is close to local accommodation to minimize the requirement for transport between sites. Some venues, such as hotels and academic institutions, have residential options, meaning that they have bedrooms onsite that may be made available to event guests. For events lasting more than one day, this can be a particularly important consideration when choosing a venue. Creating a transport plan for the event, is one technique that may help the event manager compare viable venues with the potential transport requirements of everyone involved in the event. This may include looking at public transport options, the number and proximity of bus stops, stations and drop off/pick up points in relation to the venue as well as car parks and park-and-ride schemes. A transport plan may also put in place a one-way system or timed loading and unloading schedule for supplier vehicles.

When comparing event venues, what facilities are available free of charge or for a small cost, may become a deciding factor and this can include furniture, audio-visual equipment, staging and electricity. Whether the venue has previously hosted similar events may also be a factor in choosing one venue over another. It can be a distinct advantage when planning events, to draw on the experience of the venue manager who has first-hand knowledge of how different types of events will work in a given space.

Many venues will have limited availability for event hires, such as sporting venues that are primarily used for hosting competitions and providing athletes with a training ground. Similarly, some unique venues, such as visitor attractions, will only be available for private events outside of their standard opening times (or at great expense). Most venues will have restrictions in place for events, which means that they may prohibit certain activities taking place, limit what existing infrastructure can be removed or moved and what décor can and cannot be installed. Assessing the limitations of using event spaces is an important element of identifying and choosing an appropriate event venue. Given this non-exhaustive list of variables that influence the choice of venue, it is already clear that choosing a venue can be a difficult challenge. Adding in the sustainability of the venue potentially complicates this decision further, and the following sections of this chapter will provide event managers with tools and resources to help make that decision.

What is a sustainable venue?

In terms of event venues, a sustainable venue is a space or a building that has been designed or has evolved into an environmentally friendly site that operates without damaging the environment. Broadly speaking, a sustainable venue practices energy efficiency, recycling and implements sustainable practices (Hagen, 2021, pp. 259–75). Some of the ways in which a sustainable venue can be identified are illustrated in Figure 4.4, while Table 4.1 provides a checklist for event managers to use to assess the sustainability of an event venue.

> **ACTIVITY 4.1**
>
> Using the indicators of venue sustainability in Table 4.1, choose an events venue from each of the categories shown in Figure 4.1 and compare and contrast them to identify which you believe to be the most sustainable venue.

Figure 4.4 Indicators of venue sustainability

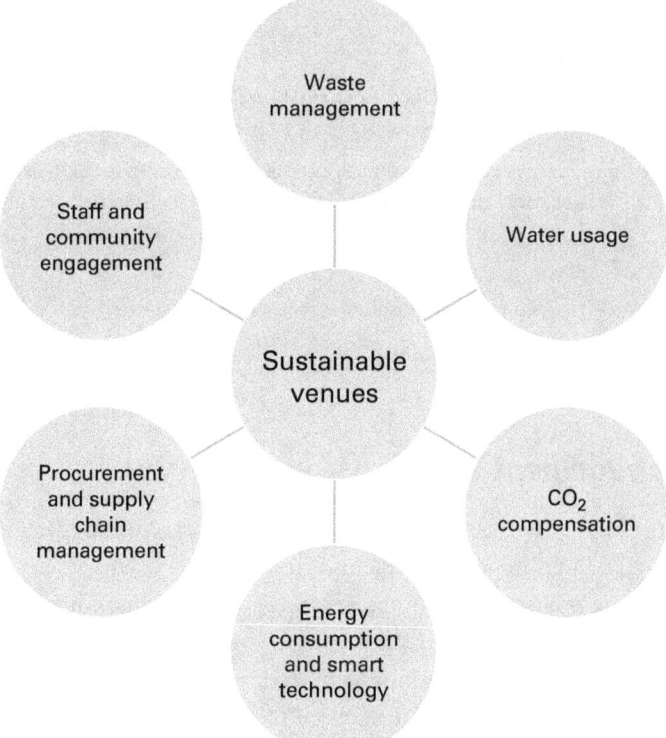

Table 4.1 Checklist of indicators of venue sustainability

Indicator	Questions to ask the venue	√
Waste management	• How much recycling does the venue undertake? • What recycling bins are available at the venues for event attendees to use? • Do you have a composting programme?	
Water usage	• What measures do you have in place to monitor water usage? • How does the venue minimize water consumption? • Does the venue have refilling water stations?	
CO_2 compensation	• What is the venue's carbon footprint? • Do you operate at net zero or is this a goal? • If not, how do you offset the venue's greenhouse gases emissions? • What support do you offer event planners in calculating the carbon footprint of their event?	
Energy consumption and smart technology	• Does the venue use any renewable energies? • What other systems or processes does the venue have in place to minimize energy usage?	
Supply chain management	• How do you choose suppliers? • Do you use local suppliers? • How do you ensure the sustainability credentials of your suppliers? • What environmental and quality standards do you expect your suppliers to adhere to? • Does your in-house or appointed caterer use local, fresh, seasonal produce and offer vegan and organic options?	
Staff and community engagement	• How do you encourage staff and the local community to adopt green practices? • Do you train staff on your sustainability initiatives? • How do you support the local community?	

Waste management

Waste management involves implementing processes to reduce waste production within a venue, to encourage recycling and to repurpose waste where possible. This means that a basic requirement for venues is to have recycling bins widely available across the premises to allow for different types of waste (e.g. plastic, glass, paper) to be regularly recycled. These should be placed in appropriate locations within the venue and signage and/or colour coding used to help event guests to make good use of them. However, as event venues produce substantial amounts of waste (Santos et al, 2023), further efforts must be made to limit the environmental impact of waste generation. This may include a waste management system that includes a composting programme to transform waste into a new resource as part of a sustainable circular economy (Dolf and Teehan, 2015).

REAL-WORLD EXAMPLE   Excel London

Excel London (Figure 4.5) has established itself as one of the UK's leading event venues as its flexible, multi-purpose spaces, state-of-the-art conference facilities, smaller meeting rooms and blank canvas event halls, can be tailored to a range of small and large events. In terms of the venue's commitment to sustainability, 100 per cent of its electricity comes from renewable sources and the venue has operated a zero waste-to-landfill policy since 2012, with 71 per cent of waste recycled in 2021 and the remaining 29 per cent used to create refuse-derived fuels.

The venue's waterless urinals save enough water to fill six Olympic-size swimming pools each year and used cooking oil is collected for recycling into biofuel. The venue has water fountains installed throughout the site which results in 200,000 fewer plastic bottles used every year and a living wall along its promenade which is home to more than 9,000 plants which help to remove air pollutants. The venue is also home to one of the largest commercial wormeries in the world. Vegetable leftovers are broken down in a macerator so that they can be fed to the 300,000 worms who live in the wormery at Excel. The compost generated at the wormery is then collected and used to fertilize the green spaces around the site in a continuous cycle.

SOURCE Excel London, 2025

Water usage

Venues can consume a lot of water, particularly via the provision of potable water to their customers, through catering operations at the venue, and in the management of bathrooms or restrooms. As such, some event venues now have water meters installed on site, which help to monitor water consumption and put in place efforts to conserve water. Some venues now have efficient fixtures or flow restrictors on existing fixtures, electronic sensors or touchless water taps, urinals and toilets which all help to reduce the use of water on site (Santos et al, 2023). Some venues provide water refilling stations that can be used by event attendees, and signage encouraging guests to bring a bottle and refill it, rather than purchase a plastic bottle of water, can also contribute to reducing waste.

Figure 4.5 Excel London © Excel London

CO_2 compensation

Many venues are now focused on reducing the amount of greenhouse gases that they release into the atmosphere as these trap heat and contribute to global warming. In particular, permanent venue equipment such as boilers and generators can release significant amounts of carbon dioxide. For many venues, the goal is to operate at carbon neutral or net zero, which is when no harmful emissions are created or when emissions are offset (which means compensating for what is emitted by making reductions elsewhere). For venues to be able to achieve this, they must first calculate their current emissions and use this information to create a carbon footprint. The footprint can then be offset in different ways, such as through the planting of trees which will naturally absorb carbon dioxide from the atmosphere.

Many venues now extend this process to event planners and they will use a carbon calculator to calculate the emissions generated by an event. This includes assessing various event factors such as the number of attendees, how they have travelled to the venue, where they have stayed and what catering has been provided at the venue for the event.

Energy consumption and smart technology

Perhaps the best indicator of how seriously a venue is taking its commitment to sustainability is through the venue's use of renewable energy, as around 75 per cent of the carbon footprint of a venue is linked to energy use (The Company of Biologists, 2023).

Renewable energies include solar or wind power, and many venues have invested in these as their primary source of energy. Installing timed or motion sensor lights and ensuring equipment is switched off when not in use are other ways that venues are limiting their energy as well as minimizing the use of air conditioning and switching from halogen to LED lightbulbs. The use of intelligent systems and software within venues, helps them to monitor and reduce or optimize the use of electrical equipment within the venue, thus limiting the amount of electrical energy that is created at events (Ke, 2021). Technology now supports the use of digital signage within venues which can also limit the amount of plastic or paper waste created through temporary event signage and other event essentials such as table plans.

Procurement and supply chain management

Venues will be reliant on a number of suppliers of goods and services as part of their daily operations and one of the most important ways in which they can demonstrate their commitment to ethical and sustainable practices is through the management of their supply chain. Figure 4.6 illustrates some of the ways in which the supply chain can be managed.

Venues can manage their supply chain by ensuring that only products that are required are ordered and they are delivered only when needed. Costs of products and services can be achieved through a bidding process and event venues can often use their relationships with event planners to leverage competitive rates, such as through a preferred supplier agreement (see below). Quality control of products and services can be achieved through inspecting goods and ensuring that suppliers have relevant credentials and meet professional standards. Working with local suppliers ensures that the community around the venue also benefit from this arrangement and it also limits the travel involved in products reaching the venue. Essentially, venues that strive to be sustainable will work with suppliers that align with their own environmental and social values and have similar sustainability practices in place.

Figure 4.6 Supply chain management

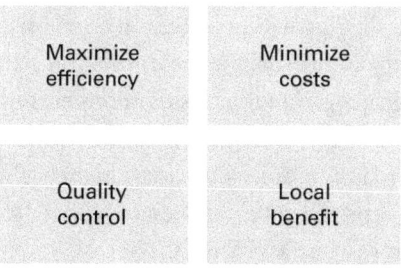

When assessing event venues, it will become evident that venues will often have their own extensive teams of professionals to provide specific services to event planners. This can include technicians to oversee the stage management or production elements of an event and caterers to fulfil any hospitality requirements. If the venue has staff based permanently on site they will either form part of an in-house department or they will be there as a separate company but an appointed supplier. Such a supplier will have a contractual agreement with the venue and will retain sole rights to providing a specific service or product. Many hotels and other venues, whose primary function is to offer hospitality, will have an in-house catering team, as providing a regular food service will be central to their day-to-day operations. The team may include chefs and waiting staff and be led by a banqueting co-ordinator or a food and beverage manager (often abbreviated to F&B manager).

If a venue has an in-house or appointed supplier, event managers and other users of the venue will be obliged to work with them. As most venues are cautious about allowing third-party contractors into their facilities to provide key event requirements such as catering venues without an in-house or appointed caterer will usually provide event planners with a list of preferred suppliers (Nolan, 2018). In other words, a list of acceptable, and vetted organizations that the venue are happy to allow on site to cater the event. Preferred suppliers are usually well-known to the venue, often locally based, and will have worked with them in the past, giving the venue confidence in their ability and professionalism. Usually there will be several companies listed as preferred suppliers, so event managers will have a choice of provider. Typically, appointed or preferred suppliers will have values that align with the venue and using them will minimize the transporting of goods to the venue. However, implementing and executing sustainability policies at an operational level across a large organization can be very challenging, while, managers of small organizations must also prioritize aspects of sustainable management. Some venues find there is a limited number of suitable local suppliers for them to work with and a limited number of green products; both of these have been identified as a key barrier to the success of sustainability initiatives in some venues (Event Decision, 2023).

Despite the challenges that venues may face, as a hirer of the building it is important to assess the sustainability credentials of venue suppliers, particularly if there is limited choice or no choice at all over which suppliers must be used. Indicators include the use of local, fresh, seasonal produce, an emphasis on plant-based food and high welfare standards for items such as meat, fish and dairy products. Event catering should account for dietary and religious requirements but also include vegan and organic options, which are less damaging to the environment. Research indicates that attendee satisfaction at events is sometimes higher where local foods are available for consumption and that event attendees are willing to pay a premium price for locally sourced food items (Mair and Smith, 2021).

Staff and community engagement

Another strong indication of a venue's commitment to sustainability is how it encourages its staff and the local community to adopt green practices. Indicators of this include the venue promoting the concept of combatting climate change through a joint effort. Venue staff should have access to the venue's sustainability goals and policies and regular training to ensure that they understand and can implement them into their work and homelife practices. Indicators of a venue's commitment to staff and community engagement may be evident in a clear environmental policy which encompasses all their activities that relate to communication with and involvement of staff, guests and the local community. There are many ways in which venues can work with and support their local community, such as using local suppliers, donating to foodbanks and supporting local environmental charities and initiatives.

In some parts of the world, large or important venues are used by the state or business leaders to promote sustainability initiatives. For example, the naming rights to the Key Arena in Seattle were purchased by the Chief Executive of Amazon, Jeff Bezos, in 2020 and the venue was renamed 'Climate Pledge Arena' thus using the venue as 'a regular reminder of the importance of fighting climate change' (Kellison, 2022, p. 269).

Venue grading and sustainability certification

One of the simplest ways to understand a venue's commitment to sustainability is by checking if the venue has been awarded any green certification or sustainability grading that has been undertaken by a third party. This is when an independent organization assesses the venue's documentation and operations in relation to specific sustainability criteria. Based on the outcome of the assessment, the venue may be awarded a certificate, membership or endorsement.

The development of sustainability certification

The first attempt at creating a framework to measure event or venue sustainability was the Hannover Principles, which was the name given to a set of guidelines for the design of buildings and objects (Nolan, 2018). The Hannover Principles aim to provide a platform upon which designers can consider how to adapt their work toward sustainable ends and it was formulated as part of the planning process for the Expo 2000 World Fair, which was held in Hanover. The Hannover Principles focused on the elements and included consideration of water (minimizing usage), air (minimizing pollution), earth (encouraging recycling) as well as spirit (encouraging feelings of belonging) (Ferdinand and Kitchin, 2017).

Another important milestone in the development of sustainable events management practices in the UK was the introduction of British Standard 8901. The British

Standards Institution produces standards for a range of services and products and it certifies compliance with these standards within the UK:

- BS8901 was developed specifically for the events industry and one of the key drivers of the introduction of the standard was the 2012 London Olympic Games and the desire to prove that the Olympics, as a mega-event, could be delivered in a sustainable manner.
- BS8901 covers three key areas of events: environmental responsibility, economic activity and social progress, thereby mirroring the triple bottom line.
- BS8901 has since developed into a new international standard ISO20121. which was launched at the same time as the London Olympic Games in 2012.

International Organization for Standardization

ISO, the International Organization for Standardization, is an independent organization based in Switzerland that publishes standards and specifications for products, services and systems to uphold quality, safety and efficiency. International standards are a mark of quality assurance and thereby a basis for enhanced client or customer satisfaction (Davidson and Rogers, 2016). ISO20121 is a standard that indicates a development towards more sustainable events management practices. In Europe this has led to larger companies being asked to produce a CSR report which may include how they are promoting the use of sustainable events (Hagen, 2021, pp. 259–75). The ISO 20121 standard involves measuring the full life cycle of an event, and it has been developed so that it can be used not just by mega-events such as the Olympics but can be applied to a range of events, including smaller, local or community-level events (McCullough et al, 2022).

One of the challenges of identifying suitable venues is the lack of any standardized grading criteria for venues. Any venue can market itself as a space that can be used for events, and in most countries, there is no regulatory or quality control framework in place for event venues. This presents the event manager with the challenge of how to select the best quality venue for their event and matching venue brand with client brand.

For an event manager, ISO20121 will also provide confirmation that an event supplier (such as a venue) is meeting sustainability standards. There are additional international standards that apply to elements of venue management, including ISO 9001 which is a management system that demonstrates quality in all areas of a business (including facilities, training, people, services and equipment). It is being adopted by many venues as a means of providing quality assurance to clients as well as motivating staff and demonstrating a commitment to ongoing development. Similarly, ISO 14000 applies to environmentally sustainable operations and aims to reduce an organization's environmental footprint, particularly through reducing waste and pollution. This standard is also being adopted by venues who use it not only through operational management of the building but also as a marketing tool to promote a positive image of the business.

Alternative routes to accreditation or grading

There are now many other ways for venues to receive a green accreditation, often from their local destination management organization or local or state authority. There are independent certifiers too, such as Green Globe, an affiliate member of the UNWTO, which offers certification in sustainable operations to venues such as hotels and conference centres. Green Globe (2025a) assess venues in relation to 44 criteria including their purchasing policy, how many local residents they employ and what relevant training they provide to their staff. Green Globe (2025a) accreditation has been developed over three decades and demonstrates a high level of sustainable venue operations and management. Another example is the British Association for Sustainable Sport (BASIS), which offers accreditation to sporting venues in the UK through assessing the sustainability performance of venues against twelve principles which are categorized into the three related pillars of environmental responsibility, social progress and economic activity (BASIS, 2025). Some of their accredited members include the All England Lawn Tennis Club (Wimbledon), Ascot Racecourse and Arsenal Football Club (Emirates Stadium). Some would argue that event planners should only choose venues with an environmental certification issued by an internationally-recognized system or organization (Santos et al, 2023).

Another potential way for event planners to evaluate a venue, via third-party accreditation, is through venue grading schemes, and in many parts of the world it is commonplace for the national or local destination marketing organization (DMO) to inspect and grade accommodation according to specific criteria. This then provides event planners with standardized benchmarks to use in order to compare venues and some schemes extend to venues other than hotels, as illustrated in the Real-world example. Additionally, there are many organizations that also offer such schemes, such as the Association of Event Venues (AEV), who represent venues of all sizes and types and aim to share best practice and showcase venues that demonstrate a commitment to sustainability (AEV, 2022).

Meeting the expectations of clients and event attendees

For event planners, as well as looking at green certification or accreditation of a venue, the views, needs and expectations of event guests should be taken into consideration when choosing a venue. For example, worldwide, many people now have very strong views on the importance of sustainability and engage in activities to limit the destruction of the environment (Salimi et al, 2023). Consequently, it is extremely important to choose a venue that matches these values and goals. Additionally, there is growing evidence that event attendees are more considerate of organization's commitment to sustainability and are more willing to pay a premium to attend a green event (Santos et al, 2023). Event guests may have prior experience of or preconceived ideas about venues (good or bad). They may live near to or far away from the venue, and this, as well as how easy it is for them to travel to the venue, is likely to contribute to their decision to attend. As such, it will be essential to choose a venue that clearly demonstrates its commitment to sustainability and whose operations go beyond providing recycling bins, which attendees will consider routine (Santos et al, 2023). Furthermore, there is evidence to suggest that some event attendees will consider venues with particularly strong environmental credentials to be of a higher overall quality than others (Teng et al, 2015).

However, not everyone who attends an event will notice the sustainability policies of the event or the venue and they may even feel frustrated by what they perceive to be inconvenience caused by sustainability practices (Teng et al, 2015). In such circumstances, it may be important to use the event to encourage responsible behaviour and the venue may offer advice on how this can be achieved, such as through signage and messaging on site that encourages guests to support sustainability initiatives. For example, the Green Globe accredited hotel, Pullman Jakarta Central Park in Indonesia, encourages people to calculate their own carbon footprint created through attending an event at the venue and to take part in an offsetting programme. The hotel also launched the first electric vehicle charging station in the area, partly to mitigate the environmental impact of travel but also to raise awareness of eco-friendly practices (Green Globe, 2025b). As Mair and Smith (2021) confirm, events can play a very valuable role in the environmental education of their participants and can be used as a means to promote important green messages. Furthermore, although a venue may be designed and operated in accordance with sustainability standards, it takes the cooperation of the event manager to drive forward change, so event planners must follow guidelines suggested by the venue manager.

The role of the venue in event planning

Once the event planner has selected a venue, the process of events management will start to move from the event design phase into event production as the programme develops, suppliers are secured and the event is marketed to its target audience. Matthews (2016, p.176) suggests that effective event production rests on becoming completely familiar with the venue's limitations to 'prepare for additional support or to change the production accordingly.' Working closely with the venue manager is therefore essential as they can provide advice and suggestions throughout the project management of the event. They should be seen as a useful resource and therefore involved in event production.

Venue staff will be able to oversee event plans to ensure that all the activities are viable within the space that has been booked. They can offer advice on what has previously worked well as well as what has not. The venue will usually be able to provide scaled floorplans of each room which can help to ensure event plans maximize the use of space and resources available. Venue staff can also advise on how long it will take them to set up rooms (in terms of the layout of the furniture) and whether they have enough furniture and equipment for everything that is planned to take place in each room or area. They can confirm the availability of facilities such as a cloakroom (for the storage of bags and coats) and the availability of rooms which have been approved for use as a crèche, for example. The venue will normally have an excellent network of local contacts that they have worked with before and who therefore know the venue well.

For some events it may be helpful to put a traffic and transport plan into operation throughout the event to facilitate parking and unloading and dropping off at the venue. This will need the input of the venue manager and potentially the local authorities (highways, police, etc.) to ensure that a suitable system is in place, giving suppliers a designated time slot for dropping off and setting up their equipment and for marshalling traffic to maintain the safety of pedestrians and access for emergency vehicles and venue staff.

As part of managing the event, consideration must be given to how the venue's commitment to sustainability can be embedded into all phases of event design. The venue itself will be a significant contributor to the event programme as it is indeed part of the whole attraction of the event. The architecture, layout, furniture and décor of the venue may complement the event programme and as the event plans move from design to delivery, it can be useful to reflect on how the event might be shaped around the space that has been hired. Further, as the production and consumption of energy will occur during the event set up, during the event, and during the event dismantle, the event planner must take into account the onsite activities of all types of people involved, including attendees, sponsors, the media, suppliers, contractors and staff. It is prudent to involve the venue in the ongoing development of event plans to ensure that sustainability is embedded into all elements of the event, and as Matthews (2016) indicates, the creative process must be built upon extensive knowledge of the resources available, which will come from forming a close working relationship with the venue manager.

ACTIVITY 4.2

Undertake research to identify a purpose-built event venue that has been constructed in the last five years. Explore the venue's website and media coverage of the opening of the venue to determine how the venue is using technology to achieve sustainability goals.

The future of sustainable venues

The creation of new venues to support the growing events industry is an ongoing trend and governments around the globe are investing in the construction of regional and city convention centres in particular, specifically to support business events (An et al, 2021). Venues can become significant edifices that contribute to the branding of a destination and may be used to promote the preservation of a city or region's cultural heritage (McCullough et al, 2022). However, the act of constructing a new venue can be very environmentally damaging as it may involve the reduction or disturbance of wildlife, trees, grasses, plant life and other vegetation. The process of building a venue will involve the large consumption of natural resources including energy, water, and non-renewable resources and this therefore creates an increased threat to the environment (Teng et al, 2015). Approximately 10–20 per cent of the energy used during the lifetime of a venue will actually derive from its original construction rather than from the day-to-day running of the building (The Company of Biologists, 2023). Additionally, the creation of infrastructure can have significant negative sociocultural impacts, such as the displacement of people and businesses or disruption to their relationships. Therefore the development of any new venue must be carefully and strategically planned and must be designed to protect natural and biological resources, improve the use of energy and reduce water consumption (Salimi et al, 2023). New venues should be built with locally available and responsibly sourced building materials as this will also help to limit the negative environmental impact that comes with erecting and maintaining a venue (McCullough et al, 2022).

Advances in scientific technology now allow developers to control and prevent environmental problems when building new venues, and to comply with sustainability standards. The development of venues as a form of urbanization can be done in an environmentally friendly way by careful surveying the land and planning the carrying capacity of the environment, the optimal use of space, fresh water, energy and other vital resources and the use of green building materials (Salimi et al, 2023). Venues should be designed to use building materials with a lower carbon footprint, such as timber from sustainable sources or recycled steel, walls and roofs should be insulated, and where possible natural ventilation should be used to reduce the need for mechanical cooling systems. In fact, sustainably-designed venues can reduce local demand on a city's energy and water resources and can improve the quality of life for local residents they are 'the foundations of cities and communities' (McCullough and Murfee, 2022, p.8); as such, venues contribute to the long-term sustainability of communities.

Of course, a much greener alternative to building a new venue may be to refurbish or update an existing building (McCullough et al, 2022). Renovation is arguably a better option than creating new infrastructure in order to lower energy consumption (Ke, 2021). However, the feasibility of refurbishment may be dependent on factors such as the age of the building and its existing infrastructure since, for example, the cost of a retrofit on existing equipment may make this prohibitive. Additionally, despite the obvious efforts of many venues to put sustainability at the heart of their operations, many cannot meet the high costs involved in remodelling and renovating buildings in order to conform to environmental standards (Teng et al, 2015). However, as consumers are placing increased importance on how businesses demonstrate a commitment to CSR and sustainability, venues are realizing that meeting these expectations is essential if they are to compete for events (An et al, 2021).

Potentially, the success of a venue or even its ability to survive in what is now a very competitive environment, may depend on its ability to use new technologies to create competitive advantages (Salimi et al, 2023). Now, more than ever, it is apparent that given the huge choice of available venues for events, the best choice will be a venue that can demonstrate that it is environmentally conscious (The Company of Biologists, 2023).

Summary

Choosing a venue is a significant step in the management of any event. The venue will become a key stakeholder in the planning and delivery of the event and will shape the guest experience. Purpose-built event spaces now compete with a range of hotels, sporting, academic and unusual venues and a venue's attitude towards sustainability can be part of its competitive advantage.

Venues may claim to have strong green credentials, but a third-party accreditation, such as ISO20121, provides event planners with confirmation of a venue's commitment to sustainability. Other ways in which the sustainability of venues can be compared is through their waste management processes, water usage, net zero target and their use of smart technology and renewable energy. How venues interact with their suppliers and the local community will also indicate their level of commitment to their own sustainability goals and ambitions. Venues that source products and services from local businesses and engage with local residents and authorities are also furthering their green practices and positive influence on others.

As a key stakeholder in the delivery of an event, it is prudent to work closely with the venue on the design as well as the delivery of the event and to draw on the venue manager's knowledge and experience. This helps to ensure that the sustainability of the event itself is maximized and that the event can become a vehicle for the promotion of green practices.

Further reading

For information on sustainability certification and criteria, see:

www.greenglobe.com/criteria-indicators

For further tips on planning a sustainable event, see:

www.visitbritain.org/bring-your-event-britain

References

An, J, Kim, H and Hur, D (2021) 'Keeping the competitive edge of a convention and exhibition center in MICE environment: identification of event attributes for long-run success', *Sustainability*, 13 (9) doi.org/10.3390/su13095030

Association of Event Venues (AEV) (2022), Cross association sustainability commitments, www.aev.org.uk/member-zone-login/cross-association-sustainability-commitment-guides

Bladen, C, Kennell, J, Abson, E and Wilde, N (2022) *Events Management: An introduction*, (3rd ed.), Routledge, Abingdon

British Association for Sustainable Sport (BASIS) (2025) '12 Principles', https://basis.org.uk/about/12-principles/#

Company of Biologists, The (2023) Choosing sustainable venues: a guide, www.biologists.com/stories/choosing-sustainable-venues-a-guide/

Convention Centre Dublin (CCD), The (2025) Sustainable Events Venue, www.theccd.ie/event-venue/sustainability/

Davidson, R and Rogers, T (2016) Marketing Destinations and Venues for Conferences, Conventions and Business Events (2nd edn), Routledge, Abingdon

Delaney, E (2023) Venue considerations when planning child centric events. In: H Séraphin, (Ed) *Events Management for the Infant and Youth Market*, Emerald Publishing Limited, Leeds, doi.org/10.1108/978-1-80455-690-020231017

Dolf, M and Teehan, P (2015) Reducing the carbon footprint of spectator and team travel at the University of British Columbia's varsity sports events, *Sport Management Review*, 18 (2), 244–55, doi.org/10.1016/j.smr.2014.06.003

Event Decision (2023) Why do UK Hotel Venues Lag in Sustainability? https://eventdecision.com/uk-hotel-venues-sustainability-gap/

Excel London (2025) Sustainability and Legacy, www.excel.london/visitor/sustainability-and-legacy

Ferdinand, N and Kitchin, P J (2017) Events Management, an international approach. (2nd edn.) SAGE, London

Green Globe (2025a) Green Globe International Standard for Sustainable Tourism, www.greenglobe.com/criteria-indicators

Green Globe (2025b) Take Steps with Pullman Jakarta Central Park to Reduce Carbon Footprint, www.greenglobe.com/green-globe-case-studies-blog/pullman-jakarta-central-park-encourages-guests-to-calculate-their-carbon-footprint

Hagen, D (2021) Sustainable events management: new perspectives for the meeting industry through innovation and digitalization? In: Leal Filho, W Krasnov, E V and Gaeva, D V (Eds) *Innovations and Traditions for Sustainable Development*, Springer, Cham doi.org/10.1007/978-3-030-78825-4

Ke, Y (2021) Research on energy-saving strategies of college stadiums and sports venues under the concept of low carbon development, E3S Web of Conferences, 275, doi.org/10.1051/e3sconf/202127502007

Kellison, T (2022) An overview of sustainable development goal 11'. In: B P McCullough, Kellison, T and Melton, E N (Eds) *The Routledge Handbook of Sport and Sustainable Development*, Routledge, Abingdon

Mair, J and Smith, A (2021) Events and sustainability: why making events more sustainable is not enough, *Journal of Sustainable Tourism*, 29 (11–12), 1739–55, doi.org/10.1080/09669582.2021.1942480

Matthews, D (2016) *Special Event Production: The process*, (2nd edn.), Routledge, Abingdon

McCullough, B P and Murfee, J R (2022) An overview of sustainable development goal 13. In: B P McCullough, Kellison, T and Melton, E N (Eds) *The Routledge Handbook of Sport and Sustainable Development*, Routledge, Abingdon

McCullough, B P, Kellison, T and Melton, E N (Eds) (2022) *The Routledge Handbook of Sport and Sustainable Development*, Routledge, Abingdon

Nadda, V, Arnott, A, Sealy, W and Delaney, E (2022) *Employability and Skills Development in the Sports, Events, and Hospitality Industry*, IGI Global, Pennsylvania, doi.org/10.4018/978-1-7998-7781-3

Nolan, E (2018) *Working with Venues on Events*, Routledge, Abingdon

Salimi, M., Dadgar, H and Taghavy, A (2023) Providing a sustainable green model for large sports venues, www.researchsquare.com/article/rs-2597720/v1

Santos, J A C, Fernandez-Gamez, M A, Guevara-Plaza, A, Santos, M C and Pestana, M H (2023) The sustainable transformation of business events: sociodemographic variables as determinants of attitudes towards sustainable academic conferences, *International Journal of Event and Festival Management*, 14 (1),1–22, doi.org/10.1108/IJEFM-05-2022-0041

Teng, C-C, Horng, J-S and Hu, I-C (2015) Hotel environmental management decision: the stakeholder perspective, *International Journal of Hospitality & Tourism Administration*, 16 (1), 78–98

05 | Stakeholders in sustainable events

LEARNING OUTCOMES

By the end of Chapter 5, students should be able to:

- appreciate the importance of stakeholder selection during event planning, regarding the event's sustainable goals
- recognize the challenges from previous events regarding sustainable planning decision-making
- understand the significance of stakeholder involvement in the wider event planning process.

Introduction

As with many other aspects of planning, designing and delivering events, the subject of stakeholder engagement remains central to achieving success in event objectives. Allen et al (2011) identify important stakeholders as 'key players.' Events can create magnificent life-changing experiences for audiences; this is not achieved alone but by working alongside other core groups to help succeed in this experience (Goldblatt, 2005, Berridge, 2011).

This has been shown within the industry even more so since the Covid-19 pandemic, where the wave of reopening events to audiences can be seen as part of a demand for a shared experience. Events may have always required us to work as a team, but arguably more than ever the role of these teams is at the heart of future proofing our industry. Authors such as Jones (2018) go into detail regarding sustainability, highlighting stakeholder identification as being core to successful planning, while Wrathall and Steriopoulos (2022) discuss post-pandemic the importance of embedding sustainable practices into stakeholder groups to create their own value. Sustainable events have a positive impact on people, the planet and profit margins and so help to meet the economic, socio-cultural and environmental needs of event stakeholders (Ferdinand and Kitchin, 2012). Consideration of the impact that stakeholders will have on events is not a simple topic of discussion; instead, a pragmatic approach is often needed by the events organizer to get the best out of relationships with them.

This chapter will consider the role that event organizers have regarding stakeholder planning to achieve sustainable goals as part of their wider events management plan (EMP). First we will describe the importance of stakeholder selection, where possible, relationship building and shared values that form the basis to achieving a successful outcome. We then discuss the challenges and impacts of working towards these outcomes, with examples of past events that may impact negatively on the sustainability of an event. Focusing on the negatives may seem a frustrating focus, but much can be learnt here. Finally, the chapter will examine the significance of stakeholder involvement in the core event strategy to help achieve sustainability for your event.

Alongside real-world examples to help illustrate this sometimes-overwhelming subject, there is also a practical checklist at the end of this chapter to support discussion and assist you in future planning of stakeholder engagement when it comes to your event's sustainable goals.

Types of stakeholders

Berridge (2007) cites research by Diller et al (2005) who identified the 15 most meaningful experiences that people value from any kind of engagement. While broad, they are all open to debate as relating to the process of stakeholder engagement with sustainable objectives. Stakeholders should be working alongside the event organizer to achieve these attendee experiences.

According to Diller et al (2005) the following are stand-out types in the research:

- Community – a sense of unity
- Duty – willingly responsible
- Justice – ensuring equitable and unbiased treatment
- Truth – committing to honesty and integrity
- Accomplishment – a sense of satisfaction

Bowdin et al (2024) suggests that stakeholders play a significant role in an event's life cycle, and for many events they remain long-lasting partners for future success. In sustainable planning, stakeholder analysis becomes even more crucial.

Internal stakeholders

Internal stakeholders, such as those contracted to work for or on behalf of the event, must all play their part in the event's sustainable strategy, and this must begin in the recruitment phase. As a hypothetical example, when recruiting a transport manager for an outdoor event, sustainable considerations in terms of their objectives may be:

- the event's carbon objectives and recording of carbon use
- managing the relationship with the travel company
- helping communicate to attendees the event's transport options.

However, if recruiting an artistic director for an event, then there may be some greater considerations when it comes to sustainable objectives that are perhaps more complicated, for example:

- sourcing artists aligned with the event's sustainable plan/strategy
- heritage and indigenous rights
- community involvement in the event's activities.

The role of sustainability covers a wide range of tasks for some event roles.

REAL-WORLD EXAMPLE   Arts by the Sea Festival

Arts by the Sea is a festival in Dorset, UK. It aims to bring together theatrical performances, diverse music, intriguing installations, dance, street theatre, participatory experiences and much more (Arts By the Sea Festival, 2025).

The festival is free and celebrates culture, arts and people through a series of performances and installations with the objective to engage audiences. Like many similar events, it is mainly funded by the local council and Arts Council funding for cultural events.

Since 2023, festivals such as this have faced uncertainty in terms of funding grants. Council spending on culture and leisure services in England has fallen by £2.3bn in real terms since 2010–11 according to research from the Local Government Association (LGA) (2024).

The festival recruits an artistic director to help deliver artistic content to the event and ensure this remains true to the festival's overall objectives. The festival's ongoing Sustainability Action Plan aims to tackle some of the core sustainability categories that mean the most to event organizers. They say that by using resources from Julie's Bicycle and toolkits like Seasons for Change, they are working towards a greater consideration of sustainability in event planning. One action is 'to ensure festival staff and volunteers are informed and engaged', keeping regular contact with local groups, sharing best practice and offering training to staff, freelancers and volunteers at the event (Arts By the Sea, 2025).

The festival also offers performers a 'Green Rider' asking them to reflect on their own practices, informing them of potential sustainable changes that they can make from environmental and ethical impacts that they may contribute towards by performing at the event.

Festivals such as this have a unique opportunity within local communities to share the message of sustainable living. Arts festivals often have the power to carry messaging and foster change in creative and engaging ways. Celebration is the way humans integrate change (Dunstan, 1994). This could include involvement with a range of groups to promote social sustainability and align with local council policy regarding net zero targets.

Other internal stakeholders in event planning should be extensions of event messaging. This should be central to an event's objective. For example, Shambala Festival in Northamptonshire, UK, created a 'Guide to Sustainable Creative Production' as part of its ambition to 'become profoundly regenerative, rather than just being sustainable' (shambalafestival.org, 2025).

The guide is one part of their tool kit to try and become a circular model by 2025, suggesting to the large number of suppliers at this 15,000-capacity festival how to use 'circular economy principles' when designing, creating and building the festival's infrastructure.

External stakeholders

External stakeholders, by their very definition, can be more challenging. According to Bowdin et al (2024: 339–40), 'It is no longer sufficient for an event to meet just the needs of its audience. It must also embrace a plethora of other requirements, including government objectives and regulations, media requirements, sponsors' needs and community expectations.' This signals the importance that an event has on a range of external stakeholders regardless of the event's size. Although written contracts should be in place with some stakeholders, this won't be the case for all. Event organizers should be switched on to changing environments and managing relationships in this area of event planning.

While stakeholders such as local authorities should be viewed as an essential part of any event plan, they can also be an asset regarding sustainability goals. Many local authorities will have their own strategies, objectives and recommendations for businesses, organizations and local events. More so, commitments by central governments to achieve net zero targets creates a knock-on effect when it comes to local plans and targets. The European Commission's long-term strategy is striving to become the world's first climate-neutral continent by 2050 (European Commission, 2020). Many local authorities create guidance and documentation, and event organizers should engage fully with local plans as this may open doors in terms of more sustainable practices at their event. Some local authorities will operate 'community based' committees, and it is here in which event organizers can discuss how their event's sustainability strategy can fit into core local authority objectives. This is discussed further within this chapter.

The role that sponsorship plays as an external stakeholder in the sustainability of an event has perhaps never been more important than it is now. In essence, sponsors hold much power to share values, communicate your message, and improve planning of the event (Jones, 2018). Building relationships with sponsors to achieve objectives must be carefully considered to ensure ethics align and goals are shared. Sponsors can have great influence, and this can be used to the event organizers' benefit and in turn the sustainability of the event.

The audience

The audience must remain a central part of stakeholder engagement in sustainable planning. While inevitably the goal is to have attendees return following a positive experience, the role that a customer has in the event's sustainable journey must begin well before the event takes place. Seraphin and Korstanje (2018) conducted research at Love Saves the Day music festival which takes place in Bristol, UK. Key issues suggested that there was a lack of knowledge of environmental impacts and sustainability measures. There was also a difference between attendee attitudes to environmental impacts and sustainability measures by organizers.

The post-Covid climate for events such as these can be one of contentment for attendees. The industry in many places had to rebuild, with economic growth remaining a key objective. Most large-scale annual events returned in 2022 and the focus understandably was on growth and in returning to some form of normal. Perhaps more than ever now, a sustainable approach to event planning must remain at the heart of the event's marketing strategy, including audiences, from the very beginning, well before they attend the event itself. Taking the audience with you is as important as the event's success itself, as this creates a more circular approach to the very definition of attending events. It also goes some way to create the popularized 'social capital', solving several social problems as stated by Foley et al (2012).

Managing the different types of stakeholders

No stakeholder is more important than any other when considering sustainable objectives; some may have more ability to effect decisions, but equality in the relationship is key. An event organizer should remain in control of decision making, using internal stakeholders to help manage the more difficult external stakeholders where required. Figure 5.1 shows the decision-making process and influence from stakeholders in event planning. Internal stakeholders remain a key link when it comes to effective communication.

In summary:

- The value of stakeholders should be considered in multiple ways to help achieve sustainable event planning at an event.
- Key stakeholders must remain at the heart of planning in the early stages of sustainable event design.
- Event organizers should remain in control while working closely with stakeholders.

Figure 5.1 Decision-making process and influence from stakeholders in event planning

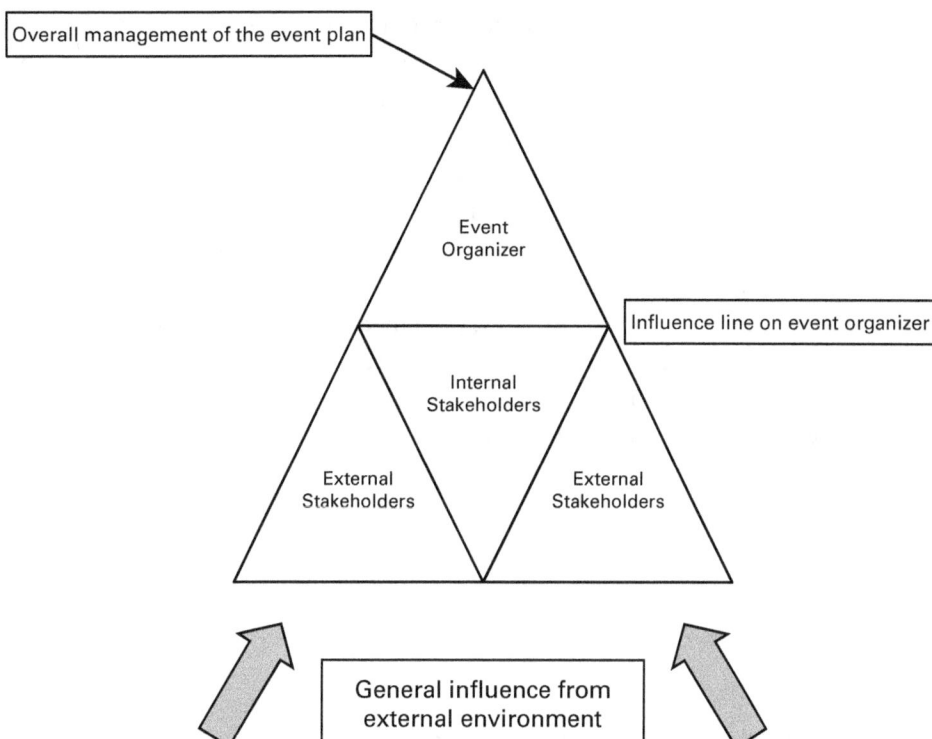

Considerations and challenges when working with stakeholders

Communication and expectations

For many stakeholders such as the media, communities, authorities, regional bodies and attendees, 'you' as the event organizer may not always have *input* into stakeholder choices and approaches to sustainable practice. The added 'noise' created when communicating with event attendees should also be considered. You can, however, have *influence*, and so when considering the relationship between you (as the event organizer) and them (an external stakeholder) you should be mindful of your own clear, transparent personal objective(s). This means having a clear statement of intent or similar early in the event plan – something that will not and should not change.

Identifying what existing roles stakeholders may already play in sustainable goals also helps relationship building. For example, while some forms of media may be helpful to get your message out or report on your event, opportunities should be taken to use media outlets more efficiently to tell your story and share your ambitions for sustainable growth, in exchange for your event doing the same for them. Waldron (2024) writes, 'Misinformation and disinformation on social media is confusing people. It is a distraction from the real conversation about sustainability and what people can do to make a difference.' Schramm and Roberts (1955) outlined being clear in communication messaging, and one solution here could be working with a media stakeholder that shares your statement of intent or values. Integrating the message better so that it is a trusted source, part of a consumer's routine is also key. Waldron (2024) goes on to say, 'I would like to see more smartphone apps that become mainstream, tracking not just the environmental impacts of events, but also calculating our carbon footprint, which will encourage us to do better and suggest how we do so.'

Managing external stakeholder expectations can be a challenge for any event given the diverse nature of the groups that could be involved. Todd et al (2017) breaks down stakeholder types which can help us consider this better:

- organizing
- participating
- attending
- supplying
- supporting

Identifying the needs of each stakeholder and working hard to manage this two-way relationship is often a fine balancing act for event planners, perhaps no more so than with mega-events. Masterman (2022) suggests that all event partners require the same long-term relationships to be nurtured. Mega-event objectives are often seen as long-term strategies which then by default naturally include longer-term relationships. Here, the importance of suppliers and services becomes essential to the sustainability of the event and its legacy.

REAL-WORLD EXAMPLE   FIFA World Cup Qatar 2022

One mega-event that captures the example of long-term stakeholders is the Men's FIFA World Cup in Qatar in 2022. As part of the host's aims to create a more sustainable approach to the use of mega venues at the tournament, the Stadium 974 was designed by Spanish architects Fenwick Iribarren Architects as a 40,000-seater venue built from salvaged shipping containers and modular steel.

After use for tournament games, the intention was for the stadium to be disassembled and rebuilt elsewhere, likely in Africa. It was seen as the first 100 per cent demountable stadium in the tournament's history. Three years after the event, the stadium has not yet moved. It has been used for some other sporting events, but the conversation suggests that although it will indeed move, its destination is yet to be decided.

In isolation, a large-scale project such as this is a positive approach to venue use at mega-events, but it is of course also a complex process regarding infrastructure removal and changing global conditions post-tournament. It has been widely reported from the region that the cost is also a huge factor in moving the stadium. It is a stark reminder of how important clear long-term strategy is to ensure sustainable practice, as well as a consideration of the effect of political and economic changes on stakeholders.

Where event destinations cannot make use of existing venues (such as the 2024 Paris Olympic Games), projects such as Stadium 974 produce a lower carbon impact to achieve sustainable objectives for an event and should therefore continue to be explored. It does also highlight the importance of strategy and working with other destinations who may benefit from a similar approach.

The wider context here for further research is that the stadium was also part of the wider sustainability strategy for the 2022 tournament managed by FIFA, where FIFA announced that the entire event would be carbon neutral. Carbon Market Watch, a climate activism organization, released a report suggesting that FIFA 'dramatically underestimated the tournament's emissions levels' (Dufrasne, 2022).

Collaboration

In the first instance, it is of course preferable during the event planning process to try and identify external stakeholders who share your values, beliefs and overall goals. It is a natural approach to want those people who can help contribute towards a solution. Outlining a process in which potential stakeholders can be included in your goals creates an easier environment in which to operate and plan. This is relevant only for those events in which 'you' as an organizer can have this type of control, but is helpful for a few reasons:

- It provides clear communication with the stakeholder about your overall vision, from the beginning of the event journey.
- It helps identify those stakeholders who want to contribute to your sustainable goals, as much as benefit from involvement in the event.
- It includes potential stakeholders in 'goal setting' and strategy to achieve these goals.

Examples of this are often seen either in tendering for contracts or in specification requirements. While the removal or reduction of single-use materials and clear messaging to achieve this is often standard practice for many outdoor festivals, measuring carbon footprint is a positive way to approach traders. Reviewing carbon use (see Chapter 7) can be the most effective approach to reducing carbon emissions. Data collection such as this will go a long way in understanding the impact an event may have, which in turn can help shape the strategy of carbon reduction when the event itself takes place.

Decision making

It is important to identify situations in which stakeholders can dictate aspects of your event. In the case of the meetings, incentive travel, conferences and exhibitions sector (also known as MICE) an event organizer may rely on a venue's decision when it comes to services such as food and beverage, while in the case of sporting events, existing sponsorship contracts may dictate. Nolan (2017) states that the venue is a good example of a high power and high interest stakeholder, because it can significantly shape the event. This is particularly important in our discussion on decision making, as the venue should help you achieve your event's sustainable goals. In essence, if using an indoor venue for an event, then a large proportion of your ecological sustainable goals will be facilitated and managed in some part by the venue (discussed in Chapter 4). This is notable because this two-way relationship can often be a little tricky to manage. For example, despite sustainable thinking being part of your event design, these objectives could be interrupted if some external stakeholders are not in your control, such as a venue contractor who then subcontracts some of its services to someone else.

Therefore, it is perhaps helpful to discuss the notion that not all stakeholders are required to achieve an event's sustainable objectives. Jones (2018) and Bowdin et al (2024) discuss outlining core event values to plan for sustainable practices, even though it is not always possible to control the decision making of many external stakeholders, and instead we can only influence. Being realistic and reminding yourself of where sustainable practices could be a 'work in progress' and not an 'immediate option' in your EMP is helpful here. So, while including these values in the decision-making of stakeholders (e.g. event sponsors) may be practical, some of your stakeholders' decisions may be defined by the effect that they could have on the overall sustainable plan and how this is communicated more broadly to other external stakeholders, notably event attendees.

Ethics and transparency

Event organizers and stakeholders can become somewhat lost in the discussion of sustainable practices. 'Greenwashing' (the conscious or subconscious claim(s) made to deceive consumers) and 'greenlighting' (used in this context to describe when attention is drawn away from potentially damaging activities elsewhere), are frequently-used terms (see Figure 5.2). The well-documented case of the London Olympic Games in 2012 and its gas sponsor BP showed that there are several angles to consider in terms of greenwashing in sponsorship. (Mhanna et al, 2018) suggested that BP adopted its strategy to counter negative perceptions from the Deepwater Horizon oil spill in 2010, thus, shifting perceptions by offering 'green' services to the games.

In some cases, the very conscious approach to make a greater effort with sustainable practices can be somewhat misguided. The ever-increasing occurrence of tree planting

Figure 5.2 Socially used terms in the context of a company/business

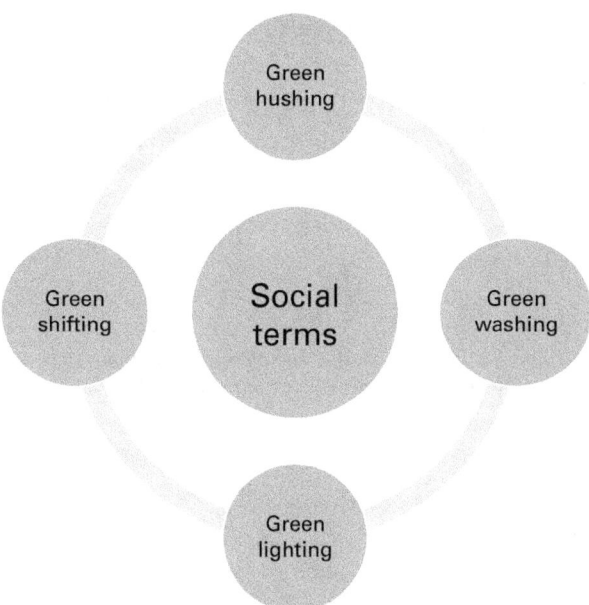

linked to tickets sold, merchandise purchased and other regenerative ideas as part of the consumer purchase transaction is perhaps a good example of this. While 'offsetting' should remain an important part of zero targets, event organizers must be cautious of how they approach this. As Dr Teresa Moore of A Greener Future explains,

> There's still a tendency to think that if you plant trees, your carbon emissions are balanced, job done, but that's not the case. It takes at least 10–20 years in some cases much longer for tree planting schemes to begin to sequester any meaningful amounts of carbon from the atmosphere.

This poses several questions to ask as part of a careful approach to offsetting, and notably the increasing number of organizations that offer it (see Figure 5.3). As well as the questionable carbon emissions versus those an event will create, the negative effect tree planting may have on local communities should also be considered.

> Tree planting has many benefits beyond carbon sequestration, trees combat air pollution and noise, help to cool our towns and cities and can help our mental well-being but we need to recognize that it is legacy not an immediate solution to carbon emissions.
>
> **SOURCE** Dr Teresa Moore, Director, A Greener Future (2024)

Other terms used in this context include 'greenhushing' – known for remaining 'quiet' publicly to customers about climate strategies, or 'green shifting' – when organizations suggest that the customer is at fault, shifting the blame away from themselves. Furthermore, event organizers are often seen to have little control over what external stakeholders (such as sponsors) do within their own organizations. So, to help in this delicate area event organizers could consider the five steps shown in Figure 5.4.

Figure 5.3 Example risk assessment questions when considering tree planting as part of offsetting emissions

- Where geographically will the tree planting take place, and what do you know about this local community?

- Can you collect reviews/feedback on how previous projects have been carried out?

- What risks are there to consider, such as the length of time/amount of carbon that is returned to the atmosphere versus what your event generates in emissions?

Figure 5.4 Five steps

1. Be consistently transparent with all your stakeholders in your sustainable goals by ensuring regular updates are given - through arranged meetings or sharing short reports

2. In the relationship between organizer and stakeholder, ask for updates from your stakeholders on their *own* sustainable policy. This allows transparency and builds trust while ensuring a clear line of communication remains

3. During the event life cycle, ask for feedback more broadly from stakeholders on how your event's sustainable goals messaging/marketing appears to be communicated

4. Always ensure that you take an honest and open approach to any mistakes that you make along the way, responding to them efficiently

5. Communicate all these points with internal stakeholders (e.g. direct staff working for you and the event)

In summary:

- To achieve sustainable objectives, clear and consistent messaging is central to good relationship building with stakeholders.
- As an event organizer, identify objectives with a realistic, not pessimistic approach.
- Being conscious of social terms such as greenwashing and others, helps in the ethical planning and communication to event attendees. Careful planning is required, rather than rushed decisions.

REAL-WORLD EXAMPLE Edinburgh Festival Fringe and Ballie Gifford

Edinburgh Festival Fringe (n.d.) is the world's largest performance arts festival. In 2024, it faced a significant public relations challenge after the festival's sponsor, Baillie Gifford, an independent investment firm founded in Edinburgh, was publicly attacked by climate campaigners following a statement from the campaign group Fossil Free Books (FFB) who reported that the firm invested in the fossil fuel industry.

Following the backlash, leading book festivals such as Hay Festival and Edinburgh International Book Festival both announced that they had removed ties with Baillie Gifford after much pressure. However, the Edinburgh Festival Fringe did not cut ties with Baillie Gifford after the charity's board members suggested they had discussions and voted in firm support of the sponsorship of the event (Brooks, 2024).

What is clear here is the complicated nature of sponsorship relationships and that those that invest money more widely can have greater consequences on a national or international stage. As event organizers, some decisions should be made based on values, but the needs of the event, which includes the wider context, are more complex than that; customer satisfaction, future event reputation and other stakeholder relationships must all be considered.

Vulnerable stakeholders

Vulnerable stakeholders are considered those individuals with a disability, mental disorders, older people, low-income earners, refugees, etc. Because of their vulnerability, these individuals face a high risk of exclusion and/or limited opportunities to participate in activities that other non-vulnerable individuals are involved in. These activities include attendance and/or involvement in events. In the same way that the tourism industry has the potential to become a tool for justice and not just leisure, it could be argued that the event industry has the same potential and even duty (Orea-Giner, 2025). Taking the case of children, a 'left behind' group according to Grande and Séraphin (2025), it is only recently that academic research in events has acknowledged them, and yet, children are important stakeholders of the events industry (Muller, 2020; Ng et al, 2022; Sadeghi et al, 2023).

Quite a significant number of festivals and events are dedicated to this group and happen to be calendar events (Sadeghi et al, 2023), with objectives such as fun, competition, challenge, entertain and educate (Alton, 1998; Martin et al, 2018). Examples of events that fall under this description include Street Child United (UK), the International Children's Games (held annually in a different country each year) and Children of Winchester Festival (UK), etc. These events have many benefits for children and their community. The Győr Kids Festival is the largest festival for children (primarily those aged 3–14) in Hungary. This event has significantly contributed to an improvement in the wellbeing of children (Ercsey, 2019). Others, such as the WeeFestival in Canada, have contributed to tightening the relationship between age groups of the same community (Frey, 2019). The Out of the Box Festival of Early Childhood in Australia, organized for 3–8 years, is designed to enhance the participation of children within their community (Tayler et al, 2006). Because of the many benefits of festivals for children, organizers and local communities are keen to have children and their carers more involved in these events.

Incorporating stakeholders into event planning

Strategy approach

As outlined so far in this chapter, the importance of stakeholders must always be considered and event organizers should remain cautious in their planning. Event organizers should aim to surround themselves with the right stakeholders; however, where this is not practical or possible, then it is important not to lose sight of the core sustainable objectives for the event as these will be fundamental to effective sustainable planning.

Ensuring that you continue to use industry frameworks and guidance can help achieve this and potentially help in ongoing discussions that you may have with your stakeholders. ISO 20121:2024 remains a significant event sustainability management system and should be used to help event organizers and stakeholders in the creation of an event plan (see Chapter 8).

Community

The host community impacts greatly on the success or failure of the event (Bowdin et al, 2024). Being involved in or contributing to an event should remain a necessity for the community. Co-production of events (where services are jointly designed, produced and used) provides benefits in terms of service outcomes and social capital formation (Miller and McTavish, 2013). This can also be appreciated within Elkington's triple bottom line (Figure 5.5) and is why co-produced events will always be more sustainable.

Figure 5.5 Elkington's triple bottom line

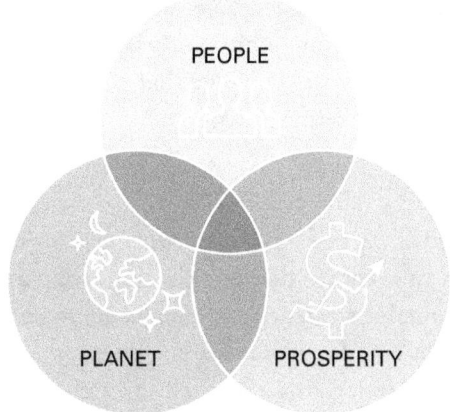

Bladen et al (2012) discusses the role that motivation plays in event volunteer recruitment and cites Bowdin et al (2011) when addressing the repeated process of event organizations who use larger numbers of volunteers than needed in order to overcompensate the event's needs. This has traditionally been an unsustainable model, but one we often see in large-scale event planning which brings several short- and long-term sustainable challenges to an event, such as retaining volunteers and ensuring that messaging issued to event volunteers is clear. One positive example is the charity Oxfam, who recruit a high number of volunteer stewards to work at various UK festivals annually. Roles include information giving, ticketing, signposting and fundraising. Volunteers for the charity are seen as an extension of its message on climate justice, poverty, etc. Campaigning therefore plays a core part in this type of event role, since most of Oxfam's end-user work is carried out in some of the most deprived communities globally.

The most circular of events are often seen as those which can continue to give back to others. Where geographically the event is giving back too, is a greater area of study. Sometimes giving back can be a complicated process in identifying who is most at need. Maslow (1943) outlines the basic needs of human beings, such as safety and stability. It is right and ethical that help goes to the poorest people in the world. A decision about where event profits go should be included in a clear discussion about what is fundamentally important to the event's values. However, the motivation to volunteer and raise awareness of various local causes is something we see in local communities and must be part of the circular approach to events. One example of how to use these stakeholders in achieving community engagement is by identifying ambassador-type roles for your event. This can be a rewarding way of improving community relations, while building on sustainable practices.

Boomtown Festival in Hampshire, UK, has won various awards at the UK Festival Awards for the last three years (UK Festival Awards, n.d.). It increased its capacity in

2025 from 65,999 to 76,999 and had its licence approved following a local council review (Needs, 2025). The festival employs a community engagement officer who solely works on building community relations and social capital. This not only forms a direct line between the host community and the event, it also creates space for building links to work with key stakeholders that share similar visions to the event and ensure the festival's longer term strategy.

Suppliers and services

A core group considered as part of stakeholder engagement must be those supplying products or services to an event. To discuss how this group of stakeholders can help shape your event's sustainable strategy, first it may help to consider the positives and challenges of achieving a circular economy. The concept of circular living is not a new one, but we are now seeing this approach through community-led events and customer-led demand. As Nolan (2017) and others suggest, the role of catering and available choice depending on the venue are core considerations for any event organizer. Many venues have procurement guidelines to ensure that suppliers are recruited within a set kilometre radius. The marketing aspect to this approach is just as effective as the sustainable one.

Farnborough International Exhibition Centre in the UK identifies the distance which food produce travels. They share this with customers who choose to use their catering services. It is part of carbon footprint capture, and important for the overall impact that the venue and its events have on the environment. This perhaps is an important aspect given that Farnborough International Exhibition Centre is widely recognized as operating one of Europe's largest air shows, which by definition is a challenging event in which to reduce carbon emissions.

As an event organizer, an important aspect to incorporating suppliers and services into your strategy is by understanding the total possible impact that a supplier may have on the event. Carbon calculators from industry bodies such as Julie's Bicycle are helpful tools to consider sustainable approaches, and should be part of early conversations with suppliers, if not already part of how they are procured.

Sponsorship

Getz (2020, p. 202; 2024) discusses numerous issues and risks associated with corporate sponsorship. While sponsorship in events has been widely written about due to its importance within the success of an event, it is never without its risks; it is considered here within sustainable planning and discussed in this chapter's case studies.

Income generation is almost always needed by an event, and sponsorship can hold this key within the long-term sustainability of your event plan. Masterman (2022) suggests that many sporting sponsorship agreements have a mixture of sponsorship in kind and paid fees, and it is unlikely that successful title sponsorship will not have some form of provision of products or services to the event. It is therefore significant to an event's sustainable objectives that as the event organizer, you consider how your sponsors can leverage your objectives through this balance.

While paid fees are crucial to the long-term success of the event, so could implementation of the sponsor's services. For example, International Confex takes place annually in London, UK. In 2025, one of its sponsors, emc3, a company who design and plan events, carried out some of its services on the event, helping Confex event organizers to measure and break down sustainable impacts of the event.

It is this topic of discussion where event values and statement of intent should not be ignored, and as discussed already in this chapter, shared with potential stakeholders such as sponsors at the earliest opportunity in the pre-planning process.

Jones (2018) outlines three angles in which brands and sponsors can positively influence an event's sustainability, and these should be considered in the early stages of an event:

- They can work with events they are aligned with.
- They can help support goals through event activations.
- They can align these activations with relevant sustainable issues (Jones 2018).

Working with sponsors is a two-way relationship with goals to be achieved on both sides. While it may be ideal to align your event with sponsors that share the same vision, working together to find common ground should always be central.

Local authorities

Local authorities play a vital role in your event logistics, however a core consideration of this is their own objectives. While there will be a main legislative role to ensure your event is safe, it should be part of an event organizer's thought process to engage with relevant officials from regulating authorities who may have the knowledge, tools and guidance to help make the event more sustainable. Some authorities may offer guidance through event checklists or considerations, such as Manchester City Council, UK, who continue to use templates created by Julie's Bicycle to give event organizers information on how to consider sustainability in their event planning. Some more active local authorities or where the agenda or local plan is part of policy, may take a stronger view here. Issuing an event licence or passing an event through a safety advisory group (SAG) may also require a level of commitment in relation to local sustainable objectives.

> We have ambitious Carbon Neutrality targets, and events and festivals are integral to achieving these goals – local authorities can advise and signpost to ensure that events meet everyone's standards and expectations.
>
> **SOURCE** Emalene Hickman, Culture and Creative Sector Development Officer, Winchester City Council (2025)

Event organizers should not shy away from discussions with local authorities and instead embrace and utilize the expectations of you and your event. Equally, where there is any uncertainty or questions within local government about an event, then the importance of sustainable events – socially, environmentally, economically – should be broken down so that they can see your clear approach. Table 5.1 helps break down some of these important dimensions regarding sustainability.

In summary:

- Stakeholder selection (where practical and/or possible) is key to positive outcomes for an event.
- Relationship building is always easier when shared values are agreed in advance.
- Engaging the community in your event is a core part of long-term sustainable planning.
- Identifying and supporting the potential of stakeholders can be beneficial to the event's life cycle.

Table 5.1 Issues related to sustainability in festivals and events tourism (adapted by Pinar, 2019)

Society	Ecologic	Economic
Community participation and involvement	Waste management	Local produce consumption
Social integration	Renewable energy consumption	Local entrepreneurship
Protection and exploration of cultural traditions	Responsible procurement and supply chain management	Fair trade
Authenticity	Green technology	Local employment
Local area identity	Environmental auditing and certifications	Repetitive business

REAL-WORLD EXAMPLE Conference of the Parties (COP) Summit

COP has operated since 1995. Held by the United Nations, it remains the biggest annual conference and trade fair on the global climate crisis. It is a good example of bringing together key global stakeholders to discuss, agree and outline initiatives to achieve global sustainable goals, running alongside a huge trade fair for green industries.

In more recent years the conference has been in discussion more broadly, notably as global political changes take place and global temperatures exceed thresholds outlined in the 2015 Paris Agreement.

What is perhaps most important with COP, given its purpose, is the outcomes. Some organizations believe decision making at high levels during these conferences are full of rhetoric, trade-offs and generally do not go far enough to solve world climate concerns. While progress has been made integrating non-governmental stakeholders, significant milestones remain to be achieved (Ramos, 2024).

ACTIVITY 5.1

1. State three reasons why it may be helpful to include stakeholders during the process of setting an event's sustainable goals.
2. In small groups, discuss what is meant by 'green shifting' and then research an example of this taking place within an event.
3. Do you think that the sustainability strategy for the FIFA World Cup Qatar 2022 can be seen as 'greenwashing'? Research and discuss your views in a small group.
4. Find two real-world job descriptions for a role in community/sustainable planning at an event venue or event planning organization.

CHECKLIST WITH STAKEHOLDER ENGAGEMENT

Below is a list of questions to ask yourself, that supports this chapter's discussion of stakeholder engagement in future plans when it comes to your event's sustainable goals.

Sustainable objectives

Internal stakeholders

- Are all stakeholders clear on your event's sustainable objectives?
- Who specifically is required to carry out duties to actively achieve these objectives?
- How can stakeholders contribute towards the sustainable strategy for the event?
- Are those who are leading teams clear and comfortable with this strategy?
- Are those who are responsible for sub-contracting clear and comfortable with this strategy?

- How will all stakeholders be part of your ongoing briefings and give feedback to you?
- What ongoing training can you/they suggest to ensure sustainable practices carry through the event's life cycle?

External stakeholders

- Do you need to vary the way in which you communicate your sustainable objectives, depending on the stakeholder?
- What are your expectations of each other (event organizer and stakeholder)? This may also be linked to a formal contract.
- How can stakeholders contribute towards the sustainable strategy for the event as well as achieve their own objectives?
- How can stakeholders contribute to the solution?
- How can stakeholders add to their own social capital?
- How will all these stakeholders be part of your ongoing briefings and give feedback to you?

Summary

This chapter considered the role that event organizers have regarding stakeholder planning. Sustainable goals can only be achieved by working with staff, volunteers, partners, sponsors, community groups and the many other stakeholders who help form the event that you are planning. Where practical, selection is key for some stakeholders. Relationship building is always easier when shared values are agreed.

There are various considerations to working with stakeholders to achieve your sustainable event goals, and challenges will always remain, regardless of how well you plan. However, transparency, open communication and taking an audience with you on the journey are all key factors to overcome obstacles. Overall, stakeholder involvement in core event strategy is fundamental to the sustainability of an event.

Further reading

Amato, A (2022) *The Circular Economy Challenge: Towards a sustainable development*, MDPI Books, Basel

Roberts, P (2022) *Simplifying Risk Management: An evidence-based approach to creating value for stakeholders*, Routledge, Abingdon

Staedler, R (2021) *Knowledge Management in Event Organisations: Theory and methods for events management and tourism*, Goodfellow Publishers Limited, Oxford

References

Allen, J, O'Toole, W, Harris, R and McDonnell, I (2011) *Festival and Special Events Management*, John Wiley & Sons, Hoboken, NJ

Alton, A H (1998) Bring the child in you out to play: Canadian Children's culture and the 1997 Calgary International Children's Festival, *Canadian Children Literature*, 90 (24), 17–27

Arts by The Sea Festival (2025) artsbythesea.co.uk

Berridge, G (2007) *Events Design and Experience*, Butterworth Heinemann, London

Berridge, G (2011) *Events Design and Experience*, Routledge, Abingdon

Bladen, C, Kennel, J, Abson, E and Wilde, N (2012) *Events Management: An introduction*, Routledge, Abingdon

Bowdin, G A J, Allen, J, O'Toole, W, Harris, R and McDonnell, I (2011) *Events Management*, Elsevier, London

Bowdin, G A J, Allen, J, Harris, R, McDonnell, I and O'Toole, W (2024) *Events Management*, Routledge, Abingdon

Brooks, L (2024) Edinburgh Festival Fringe Society CEO defends Baillie Gifford sponsorship, *The Guardian Online*, www.theguardian.com/culture/article/2024/jun/12/edinburgh-festival-fringe-society-ceo-defends-baillie-gifford-sponsorship

Diller, S, Shedroff, N and Rhea, D (2005) *Making Meaning: How successful businesses deliver meaningful customer experiences*, New Riders Publishing, Pearson Education, Hoboken, NJ

Dufrasne, G (2022) Poor tackling: Yellow card for 2022 FIFA World Cup's carbon neutrality claim, *Carbon Market Watch*, carbonmarketwatch.org/publications/poor-tackling-yellow-card-for-2022-fifa-world-cups-carbon-neutrality-claim/

Dunstan, G (1994) Becoming coastwise, the path of festivals and cultural tourism. In: *Landscape and Lifestyle Choices for the Northern Rivers of NSW*, Southern Cross University, Lismore, NSW

Edinburgh Fringe Festival (n.d.) edfringe.com

Ercsey, I (2019) A successful festival for kids in Győr. In: M M Galan-Ladero and H M Alves (eds) *Case Studies on Social Marketing. Management for Professionals*, Springer, Cham, doi.org/10.1007/978-3-030-04843-3_13

European Commission (2020) 2050 long-term strategy, climate.ec.europa.eu/eu-action/climate-strategies-targets/2050-long-term-strategy_en

Ferdinand, N and Kitchin, P J (2012) *Events Management: An international approach*, SAGE, London

Foley, M, McGillivray, D and McPherson, G (2012) *Event Policy: From theory to strategy*, Routledge, Abingdon

Frey, H F (2019) A small festival for small people: The WeeFestival as Advocacy, *Theatre Research in Canada*, 40 (1–2), 64–82

Getz, D (2020) *Event Studies: Theory, research and policy for planned events*, Routledge, Abingdon

Getz, D (2024) *Event Studies: Theory, research and policy for planned events*, Routledge, Abingdon

Goldblatt, J (2005) *Special Events*, John Wiley & Sons, Hoboken, NJ

Grande, K and Séraphin, H (2025) Children as a 'left behind' group by outdoor hospitality businesses (campsites): A human resources perspective, *International Journal of Hospitality Management*, 125, 104001

Hickman, E (2025) Culture and Creative Sector Development Officer, Winchester City Council, www.winchester.gov.uk

Jones, M (2018) *Sustainable Event Management: A practical guide*, Routledge, Abingdon

Local Government Association (2024) LGA infographics reveal fragmented culture funding needs reform, www.local.gov.uk/about/news/lga-infographics-reveal-fragmented-culture-funding-needs-reform

Martin, A J, Batty, R, Thompson, A, Kuchar, R and Pancoska, P (2018) An examination of children's motives for triathlon participation as a function of age, *Annals of Leisure Research*, 22 (2), 183–201

Maslow, A H (1943) A theory of human motivation, *Psychological Review*, 50 (4), 370–96

Masterman, G. (2022) *Strategic Sports Event Management*, Routledge, Abingdon

Mhanna, R, Balake, A and Jones, I (2018) In: H Séraphin and M Korstanje (eds), *International Event Management: Bridging the gap between theory and practice*, Nova, New York

Miller, K M and McTavish, D (2013) *Making and Managing Public Policy*, Routledge, Abingdon

Moore, T (2024) A Greener Future, www.agreenerfuture.com/

Muller, J (2020) The children of the revolution, the nation's future: Understanding the multigenerational audience of the rock in Rio Music Festival, *International Journal of Communication*, 14, 221–38

Needs, N (2025) Festival survives review following man's death, BBC News, 5 February www.bbc.co.uk/news/articles/c05lv3qqvjvo

Ng, S Y C, Bloom, A, Corcoran, S L, Fletcher, T and Sibley, J (2022) 'If you respect us … listen to us': How sporting event media reframes or reinforces representations of street-connected children, *Leisure Studies*, 41 (6), 757–74

Nolan, E (2017) *Working With Venues For Events: A practical guide*, Routledge, Abingdon

Orea-Giner, A (2025) Ecofeminism and food activism in transformative travel as a tool for change, *Journal of Sustainable Tourism*, 1–27, doi.org/10.1080/09669582.2025.2488962

Pinar, I, Kurtural, S and Tutuncuoglu, M (2019) Festivals and destination marketing: An application from Izmir City, *Journal of Tourism, Heritage & Services Marketing*, 5 (1), 9–14

Ramos, Y (2024) Inclusion and Influence: Examining stakeholders diversity in the Conference of Parties (Cops) of the United Nations Framework Convention on Climate Change (Unfccc), University of Lisbon, 21 December, papers.ssrn.com/sol3/papers.cfm?abstract_id=5066628

Sadeghi Shahdani, H, Torabi Farsani, N, Moslehi, M and Zahedi, M (2023) Designing an event calendar for children and teenagers: a tool for educational tourism, *Journal of Hospitality & Tourism Education*, 36 (2), 192–200, doi.org/10.1080/10963758.2023.2176312

Schramm, W and Roberts, D F (eds) (1955) *The Process and Effects of Mass Communication*, University of Illinois Press, Chicago

Séraphin, H and Korstanje, M (2018) *International Event Management: Bridging the gap between theory and practice*, Nova, New York

Shambala Festival (2025) Green Road Map, www.shambalafestival.org/essential-info/sustainability/green-road-map-2025/

Tayler, C, McCardle, F, Richer, S, Brennan, C and Weier, K (2006) Learning partnerships with parents of young children: Studying the impact of a major Festival of Early Childhood in Australia, *European Early Childhood Education Research Journal*, 14 (2), 7–19, doi.org/10.1080/13502930285209881

Todd, L, Leask, A and Ensor, J (2017) Understanding primary stakeholders' multiple roles in hallmark event tourism management, *Tourism Management*, 59, 494–509, www.researchgate.net/publication/308391931_Understanding_primary_stakeholders%27_multiple_roles_in_hallmark_event_tourism_management

UK Festival Awards (n.d.) www.festivalawards.com

Waldron, S (2024) Trends and best practices in sustainability, *A Greener Future*, www.agreenerfuture.com/blog-agf/agf-insider-trends-and-best-practices-in-sustainability

Wrathall, J and Steriopoulos, E (2022) *Reimagining and Reshaping Events: Theoretical and practical perspectives*, Goodfellow Publishers Limited, Oxford

06 | Designing the sustainable event

LEARNING OUTCOMES

By the end of Chapter 6, you should be able to:
- understand the concept of sustainable event design
- appreciate factors that contribute to the design of a sustainable event
- recognize the role of event psychology and biophilic design within events management
- design events that will deliver sustainability goals and educate attendees
- appreciate the importance of intersectionality in events management.

Introduction

Well-designed events can be impactful, memorable and eco-friendly while promoting wellness and supporting local communities. The process of designing events and how event planners can embed sustainability into this element of events management will be explored. This chapter provides tips for effective brainstorming to generate event ideas and looks at how event psychology and theming can be used to develop memorable event programmes. How planners can bring biophilia into event design and make green choices when planning for a specific event ambience is also discussed. The chapter includes advice on how to design events around technology, co-creation and intersectionality, and looks at how event design influences behaviour and can, for example, promote compliance with sustainable practices. As equality, diversity and inclusion (EDI) are important aspects of designing events and help to address the 'people' aspect of the triple bottom line, this chapter also discusses how carefully planned events can promote EDI.

Designing events is the process of creating an idea for a live event and developing the idea into a programme, or a detailed outline of components that make up the event as a whole. The event programme defines what the audience will take part in, watch, listen to, consume, etc., and some examples of programme elements are illustrated in Figure 6.1.

Figure 6.1 Elements of an event programme

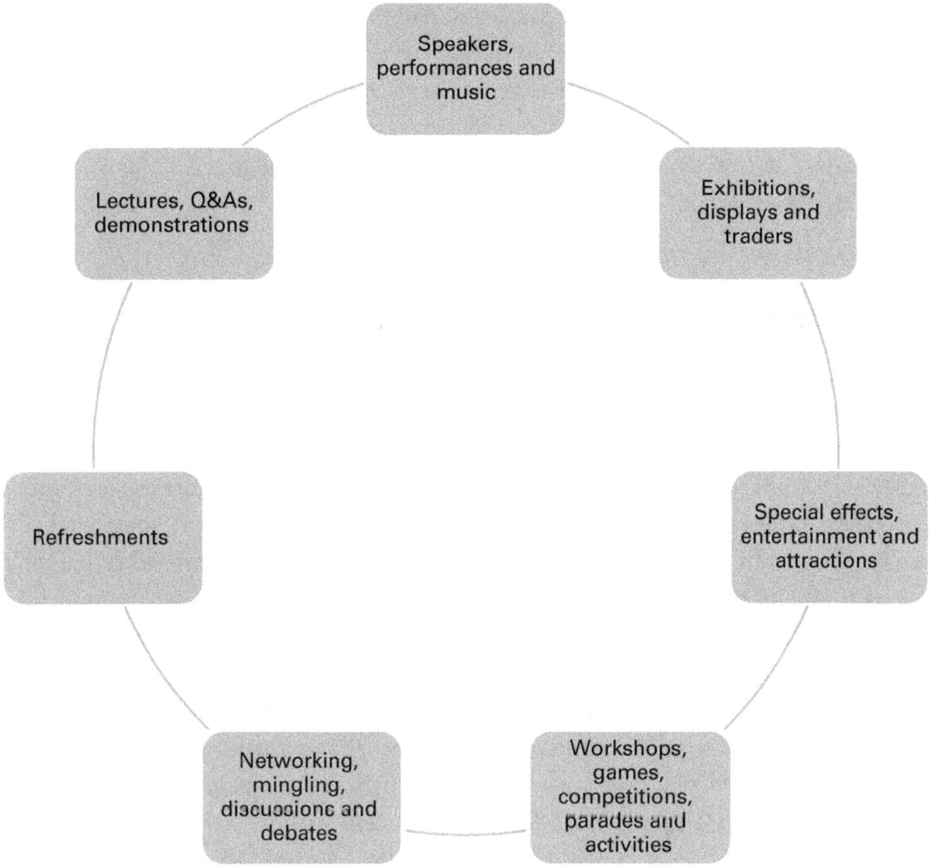

Attending a live event should give guests a unique experience that they cannot get elsewhere. Thus, the event planner can shape and influence that experience through a careful and purposeful event design process. Designing an event can be challenging as it requires a planner to conceptualize, visualize and plot a project that may be multifaceted, and often this must be done without all the necessary information (Dowson et al, 2023). Generally, event organizers are planning events for a client or third party, and some clients may have a clear idea of what they want to happen at an event in terms of activities, performers or a theme that they want to feature at the event. Other clients may leave this up to the events management team, thus giving over full responsibility for the creative development of the event programme.

There are differing views on how to creatively develop ideas for events, with some arguing that this process should be free from any constraints (e.g. budget). However, it may be prudent to consider why the event is being held and what the event aims to achieve, before the brainstorming process begins. It is also debatable as to where sustainability considerations should fit into the planning process. It can be argued that sustainability criteria are a type of constraint and therefore they may limit the creative process and should not be considered during the early stages of event design and development. However, given that the average event may generate up to 389 pounds of CO_2 equivalent emissions per day and will therefore contribute significantly to climate change and resource depletion (Jain, 2024), sustainable event design is not just desirable, it is essential.

What is a sustainably designed event and why design one?

A sustainably designed event is one that places environmental and social responsibility at the heart of the event concept so that these values permeate the entire event planning process. This means that event planners must integrate environmental, social and economic considerations into every aspect of event design. This will start with designing events to minimize their environmental impact, and event planners can be guided by the four principles of sustainable events: reduce, reuse, recycle and respect. However, event design must go further than simply limiting the impact of an event. Planners must ensure that their events will create positive social and economic outcomes, too, and a lasting legacy for the host community, sponsors and attendees (Fletcher, 2023).

Sustainable event planning means taking steps to minimize the ecological footprint of an event and to align the design of an event with global initiatives such as the UN Sustainable Development Goals (SDGs). Responsible event design is also an opportunity to contribute towards positive branding (of an event, a client, a venue or an organization) and to encourage the social engagement of event attendees. As the design of an event begins to develop into a fully formed plan or programme, it also opens up the possibility of partnering with environmentally conscious suppliers and developing ways to measure the achievements of the event in terms of meeting sustainability goals.

Sustainability may be seen as a limitation or a restriction on the creative process. For example, it could deter the creation of an event that featured heavy use of electrical equipment or a high use of non-recyclable materials. However, there are now so many ways in which event planners can make responsible choices, that this negates the need to see sustainability as restrictive. Furthermore, as sustainability is now a well understood and supported concept; year on year, there is a shift in consumer behaviour towards a demand for sustainable products and services and an acceptance that these may cost a little more. Thus, events that are designed to be green and socially responsible often result in higher attendance rates (Fletcher, 2023).

The benefits of designing sustainable events are now evident as not only will responsible events benefit the environment but it is also proved that such events can enhance a brand's reputation and inspire others to adopt sustainable practices (ICC Belfast, 2024). Additionally, it is a misconception that sustainable choices will incur expense, as reducing waste generation, encouraging recycling and using reusable materials will generate event efficiencies that will reduce operational costs. In fact, there is evidence to suggest that sustainable practices can lead to a 20–30 per cent cost saving in event expenses (Jain, 2024).

Of course, designing sustainable events is not just about saving money or promoting a responsible image (of the event or client or both), it is the responsible way forward. A well-designed event, that has core green values, will demonstrate a level of respect for the environment, all those involved in the event and for the local community in the area where the event is hosted. It demonstrates the integrity of those involved in planning and delivering the event and thus ensures the longevity and success of events management as a profession.

> **ACTIVITY 6.1**
>
> You have been tasked with designing a new book festival to take place in a deprived local area. Devise a range of ways in which you will encourage co-creation of the festival programme. In particular, decide how you will identify and then target traditionally underrepresented book festival attendees, to become co-creators.

Brainstorming ideas for events

Being creative is not always a natural trait and Matthews (2016) for example, suggests that creativity is inherent and is more prevalent in people with certain traits such as being independent, nonconformist and with wide interests. However, it is generally accepted that creativity can be stimulated through the use of triggers, such as observation, participation and reading. Therefore, when we read about or attend events we are likely to pick up ideas of how to create our own, memorable and engaging events. Brainstorming, or spending time with others discussing and developing event ideas, is a useful method for idea generation. For brainstorming to be most effective, it should take place in a relaxed and conducive environment, without distractions, interruptions or limitations (e.g. budget, pre-determined venue, etc.). Brainstorming can be stimulated through the use of images, random words or random objects that may be included in the discussion to generate ideas. Brainstorming generally works best when there is no judgement involved, in other

Table 6.1 A checklist for shortlisting event ideas (adapted from Powell, 2015)

Event objectives	How well does the idea match up with your original event purpose and the reason for organizing the event in the first place? Will this idea provide the solution to the audience's problems or current needs?
Target audience	Will people attend? Will the target audience like it, understand what they are coming to and value the experience? What will the event offer the audience that they will hear or see for the first time or which will make a difference to them?
Budget	Based on realistic estimates for how much this idea will cost to become a reality, can the budget cover this idea? Does the event need to break-even or raise a profit and will this idea do that?
Feasibility	Does the events management team have the skills to deliver this event or is there the budget to buy in and/or recruit some expert help?
Wildcards	This section is for the wildcard ideas. These ideas capture the imagination and, while they possibly do not meet all the assessment criteria above, they 'feel' right. Only one or two of these types of ideas should make the shortlist.

words, when no idea is disqualified for being too outrageous, expensive or unfeasible for example. Ultimately a feasibility process will be required to ensure that the idea for an event is plausible and this process will often involve refining or adapting the central idea. However, often the best and most innovative ideas for events are borne out of a limitless brainstorming activity.

Once a few event ideas have been generated through brainstorming, you may need to narrow down the list so that a final idea can be agreed upon and then progressed. Powell (2015) has developed a framework for shortlisting event ideas and this framework poses questions that will help to evalauate ideas in relation to the event's overall objectives, target audience, budget and feasibility, see Table 6.1. The framework allows for a certain amount of flexibility and for the inclusion of wildcards, or potentially innovative ideas that may need to be thought through carefully to ensure viability. The framework is the basis for this checklist which will aid in shortlisting event ideas.

Setting sustainability goals

The creative design process can be the most fun part of events management and the best event ideas may come from a brainstorming process that is free from restrictions or constraints. However, events are generally designed to meet specific goals, whether that be to raise money, raise awareness, celebrate a milestone or simply to provide a way for a certain group of people to enjoy themselves. As such, these goals must be incorporated into the early phase of event design and the well-known SMART acronym is a tool for ensuring that goals or objectives are Specific, Measurable, Achievable, Relevant and Timebound. This framework ensures that goals are well defined and can be tracked for progress, that they are realistic and meaningful and that there is a clear timeline for achieving them. Setting SMART goals for an event is an essential element of event design. Sustainable and responsible events should also be designed to achieve sustainability goals in addition to other objectives. Fletcher (2023) suggests that in order to embed sustainability goals within event design, one must first understand the context within which event planning is taking place. For example, if you are planning an event for a corporate client, this assessment would involve looking at how the corporation currently operates and what that organization is trying to achieve in terms of sustainability goals. This might be assessed through the questions illustrated in Figure 6.2 which will help to gather relevant information that can be used to inform the setting of event sustainability goals.

By assessing the start point, or context within which the client operates, the event planner can begin to identify ways in which the event can contribute towards the company's goals and where the event may have the most positive, and measurable, impact. This may require the event planner to follow a sustainability mandate and related policies such as only providing plant-based catering at company functions or ensuring events are held within a certain radius of the company's offices. In addition to following such instructions, event planners may wish to design events that will drive the company's ambitions to meet certain measurable key performance indicators (KPIs) or goals such as to reduce the use of paper or single-use plastics in all company endeavours.

Figure 6.2 Contextual questions for setting event sustainability goals list

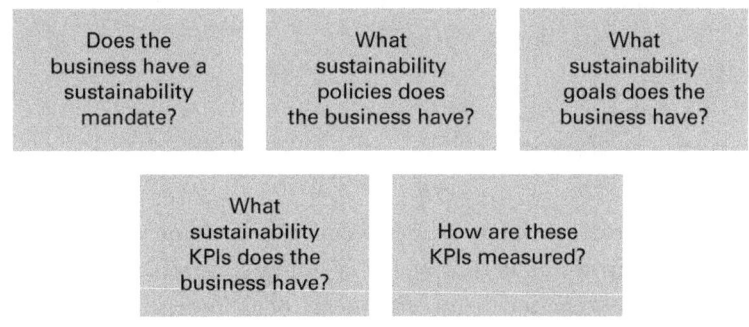

Figure 6.3 Event sustainability goals list (adapted from Jain, 2024)

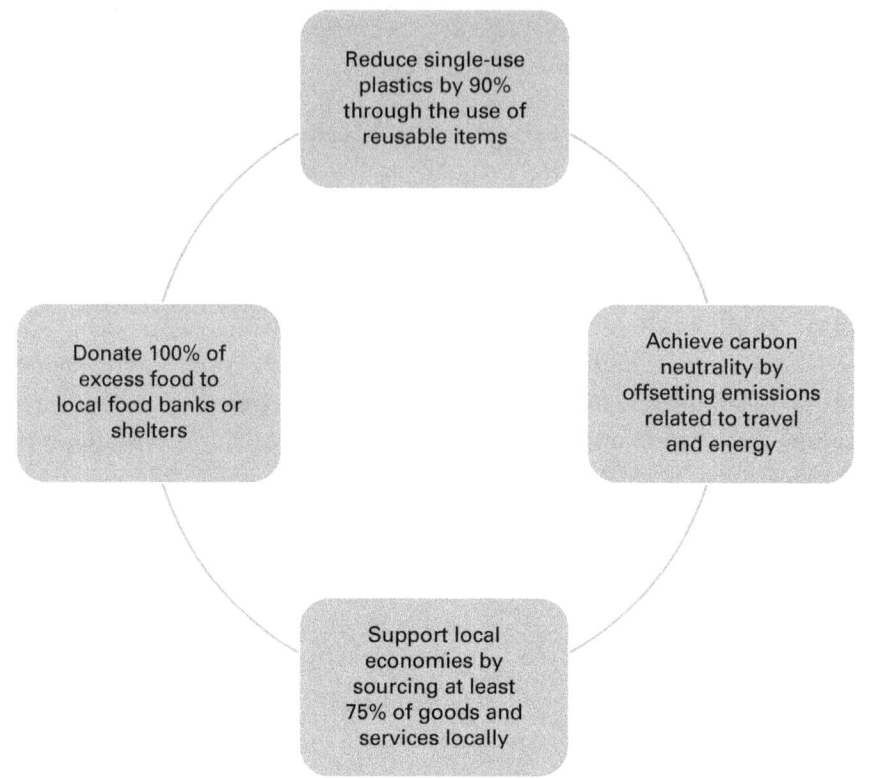

Jain (2024) gives further examples of how an event planner may set specific sustainability goals for an event which can also determine its vision and tone and these are illustrated in Figure 6.3.

Ultimately, setting SMART sustainability goals for the event will help to focus the design process on achieving these targets. Furthermore, publishing and sharing these goals with event stakeholders, particularly members of the planning team and event suppliers, will ensure that they are prioritized.

Event psychology

As part of the event design process it is worth taking some time to consider the role of psychology in shaping an event that will have specific outcomes and will create a memorable experience for attendees. Behaviourism is the theory that how we act is influenced by conditioning and therefore how we behave can depend on how our senses are stimulated. For example, at an event if we start to smell delicious food being cooked, we are likely to feel hungry and start to anticipate being fed. Seeing beautifully dressed tables and food being served by well-dressed waiters onto china plates will create an expectation that the food will be of high quality and we are likely to adapt our behaviour to reflect what we believe is normal behaviour in this situation (in other words we will put on manners as if we were at a top-class restaurant). Furthermore, operant conditioning suggests that we are aware that our behaviour has consequences and how we behave will result in us being punished or being rewarded, as illustrated in Figure 6.4. So if at this event we smell the food, see it being served, sit down, put a napkin on our lap and politely wait for our food, we know we will be rewarded with a delicious meal. If we are rude to the waiter and smash the crockery we know that we may be asked to leave as punishment.

What this means to the event planner is that when we design an event which stimulates the senses in a particular way, we will be encouraging attendees to behave in a certain way, as illustrated in Figure 6.5. Both positive and negative stimuli can be used to do this as they will affect behaviour in different ways. Examples of positive stimulation are altering the lighting at an event to control the mood (dimming lights to get people to pay attention to a film or speaker or concentrate), playing lively music to get people feeling energized or positive.

Figure 6.4 Behaviourism

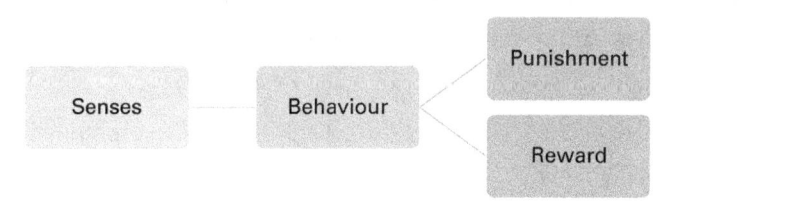

Figure 6.5 Positive and negative stimuli

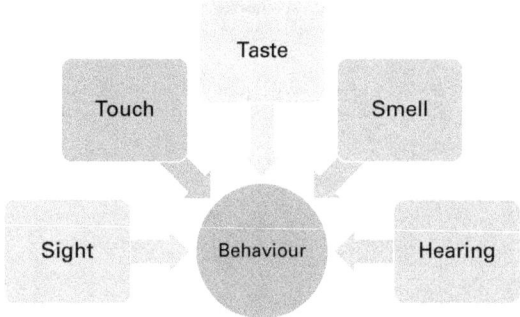

Negative stimuli can also be used to control behaviour, for example, at most events attendees will have to do certain things that they don't particularly want to – queue to get in, fill in paperwork, etc. To ensure that attendees comply and accept these as necessary parts of the event, stimuli can be used, such as putting up signage, making announcements and having formally dressed security staff at entrances to reinforce the importance of these processes. Therefore, event design means considering how to make the event a sensory experience for the attendee (so that they will engage with the event and remember it) but also looking at how the attendee's senses can be stimulated in order to get them to behave in a certain way.

Symbolic interaction theory suggests that how human beings act is also affected by what meaning we give to everything around us. In other words, what we think about people, objects and less tangible things such as ideas influences our behaviour. What things mean to us and what we think about them will be shaped by the lives we have lived up to now. Where people have had a common upbringing or common life experiences they may have similar opinions about other people, objects or ideas. This means that event planners can influence the way people behave at events by using symbols to encourage attendees into thinking, and therefore behaving, in a certain way about other people, objects or ideas. Symbols might include words, logos, icons or pictures and as part of the event design process, they may become important elements of a central theme, all designed to create a sensory experience to influence how attendees behave at an event and ultimately how they connect with and experience the event. Figure 6.6 shows how event design should be based on the event's objectives and be designed to incorporate a theme, sensory stimulation and symbols.

Figure 6.6 Event design

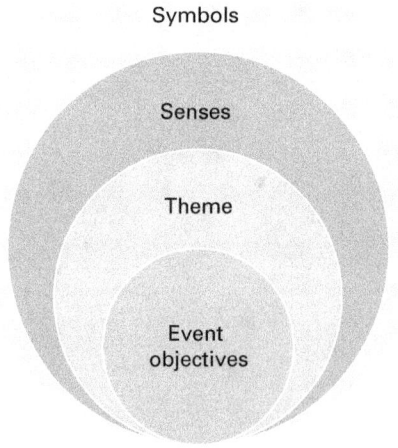

Figure 6.7 Event elements list

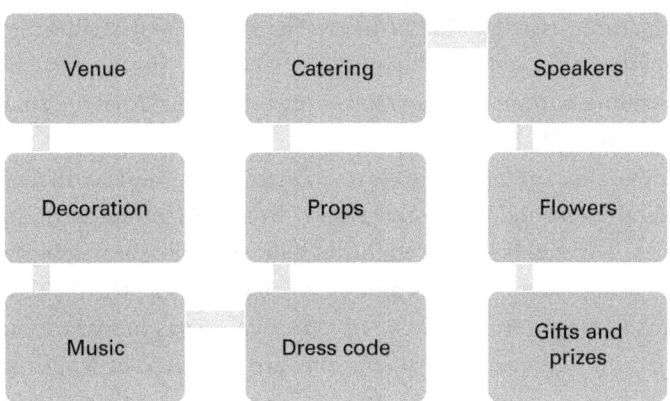

Event theming

Having a distinct theme for an event can help to create an experience that attendees will recognize, understand and engage with. Themes can be tangible or intangible, visual and sensory, elaborate or simple. A theme might be very obvious and repeated throughout design elements. As Getz and Page (2024) explain, the use of a particular colour, for example, can be reflected in the décor of the venue as well as the type of nature of entertainment provided. Colours can influence the atmosphere within a venue and the mood generated at an event, for example a blue colour palette will imbue a sense of calm whereas yellow is more energetic. The most recognizable theme is when it is overlaid as a story, in other words, when a fantasy world is created for attendees to inhabit for a short time (Dowson et al, 2023). This could be a fantasy theme such as a fairytale or space, a historical theme such as the roaring twenties, a TV or film-based theme. This theme would then be evident in the décor, catering and entertainment. Alternatively, a theme could be connected with an emotion or it could be intellectual in nature and relate to an event that is focused on education or problem solving.

Once a theme has been chosen, the design elements of the event should incorporate the theme as much as possible. Figure 6.7 illustrates the elements of an event that can be themed.

Biophilic event design

Biophilia is the human tendency to interact with nature, or to have an affinity for other forms of life. As many people spend much of their time indoors, biophilic design is an architectural concept that attempts to blend built environments with natural ones to improve the human experience (Resonics, 2025). This concept is underscored by the notion that people have a strong biological need to interact with and observe nature and that this promotes happiness and wellbeing. In terms of bringing biophilia into events, Ashwin (2024) describes this as designing events by seamlessly blending natural elements into events to boost attendee emotions and to further sustainability goals.

Biophilic design means finding ways to connect event guests with nature by incorporating natural elements into the designed event environment or by mimicking natural settings. This can be achieved through the use of natural lighting and natural materials and using water features and green space. Evidently, the choice of venue will have a great impact on the extent to which an event planner can achieve a biophilic event design and venue considerations are discussed at length in Chapter 4. Choosing an outdoor space for an event, rather than a building, will naturally lend itself to a more biophilic event. However, even structures can be maximized to achieve this, particularly when there is limited need to add in décor to create a visual impact. Furthermore, as McKanna (2025) suggests, planners may choose a venue with a rooftop with skyline views or beautiful gardens or source venues decorated with earth tones, natural textures and soft lighting as the basis for an enriching event experience. The following steps provide detailed examples of how to incorporate biophilic design elements into an event.

INCORPORATING BIOPHILIC DESIGN ELEMENTS

Step one: choosing a venue or site

The first stage of biophilic event design is to choose a location, venue or site that lends itself to this concept. This may include a space with:

- gardens and/or outdoor green spaces
- outdoor terraces or balconies
- views of water (e.g. sea, lakes)
- plenty of natural daylight (e.g. large windows, clear doors, skylights)
- natural décor (e.g. wood or stone).

Also look for venues that have a green wall, indoor plants or a rooftop garden. A green wall is a living wall or a vertical garden and it is a structure covered with vegetation. Such structures can be installed indoors or outdoors and are designed to support plant growth vertically. Event planners may wish to partner with a venue and a specialist to design and install green walls in key areas of a venue, where they will bring long-term benefits to multiple users of the space. This might be an area such as a reception, foyer or lobby, meeting rooms, or breakout spaces.

Rooftop gardens are green spaces created on the tops of buildings. They provide a natural setting and can help regulate building temperatures. Where possible, planners should choose venues with an existing rooftop garden or collaborate with venues to develop temporary rooftop gardens for the event. These spaces may work well for networking sessions, break areas or informal gatherings that form part of an event.

Step two: décor and furniture

The second stage of biophilic event design is to use natural materials like sand, water, wood, stone and bamboo throughout the event as much as is possible. These materials create a warm and inviting environment and they are often more sustainable than synthetic materials, thus contributing to eco-friendly event planning. Additionally, these textures stimulate biophilic responses, attracting us to explore and touch them so they may work in areas such as breakout spaces or lounges.

Venues and sites can be adorned with low-maintenance plants as these will add to the aesthetics and improve air quality by filtering pollutants and releasing oxygen. Planners can strategically place plants throughout the event space, focusing on high-traffic areas and places where attendees spend significant time. Using a variety of plants will add visual interest and texture.

Step three: Water features and patterns

The next stage of biophilic event design is to incorporate water features into the plans for the event, as much as is possible, as the sound of running water can reduce stress and promote relaxation. Planners may be able to incorporate small fountains in lounge areas or reception spaces. If the venue has an existing water feature, design event layouts to highlight this natural element and for indoor events, consider using aquariums as focal points.

McKinley (2015) suggests that patterns should be incorporated into biophilic event design where possible, which could include using natural materials (e.g. seashells) to create backdrops or exhibits or draping fabric that will billow and move to contrast with light and shadow to create an airy feel to a space.

The benefits of biophilic event design include creating a healthy environment for attendees, reducing the risk of respiratory issues and allergies and creating better air quality. This then allows attendees to focus and engage more effectively during the event. Creating a sense of calm at events will reduce stress levels and enhances the overall experience for attendees; this can also stimulate productivity and can boost creativity (Ashwin, 2024).

Ultimately, a carefully thought through and planned biophilic event may create a strong visual impact with attendees and generate a memorable experience that will leave them with a lasting, positive impression of the event.

Ambience and sustainable décor

The ambience or the mood of an event is important as it will influence the success of the event. When planners get it right, the event will be remembered by attendees, but the opposite is also true, and an event lacking in ambience is likely to be forgotten, or remembered for the wrong reasons. Although creating ambience relies on having attendees and guests behaving in a way that is appropriate to the event, it can be influenced through design. As a planner, if you are trying to create a particular mood for your event, you must consider how the venue or location for the event will contribute to this. If the venue does not naturally imbue the right ambience, then to create this you will need to invest in additional decoration, lighting and sound effects, as well as props, entertainment and food. The contribution of the venue to the overall mood will be significant, and to a certain extent this can be shaped and controlled by the event designer. The venue may already compliment the theme of the event but if not it can usually be transformed in order to match the theme and imbue the right ambience, although this may come at a significant design cost. However, many event designers take a different approach and will visit the venue during the design phase to absorb the pre-existing venue atmosphere and aim to incorporate the personality of the venue into the design of the event for greater effectiveness (Nolan, 2018). For example, a historical venue may have creaking doors, dark corridors with nooks and crannies that enhance ghostly-themed events, while a famous sporting venue may be filled with competition memorabilia that instils a sense of glorious determination that will complement a celebratory or competitive event.

There are a number of ways in which sustainability can be embedded into the design of event décor and creating an engaging and inviting environment does not mean spending a lot of money on items that will generate excessive waste. It is possible to rent equipment, props and scenery for events, thus minimizing waste and contributing to the repurposing of event decorations. In terms of furniture, if the venue is not able to supply items, then it may be possible to source vintage or second-hand items. Upcycled or repurposed décor not only supports sustainability but also adds depth, character, and storytelling to an event (McKanna, 2025). When designing props, table decorations and other decorative elements, planners should use repurposed items and reclaimed materials such as glass jars, wooden crates and wine bottles. Any gifts or prizes to be given out at the event should be eco-friendly and reinforce the event's sustainability goals. Incorporating biophilic ideas into event design, such as the use of potted plants or flowers instead of plastic or cut options, means that these items can be replanted or reused after the event. Single-use items should be avoided, so rather than balloons or confetti, digital displays or reusable banners can be used to enhance the attendee experience while reinforcing a commitment to sustainability (Jain, 2024). Items that cannot be reused could be repurposed or donated after the event, perhaps to the venue or to a local charity. As McKanna (2025) suggests, 'The key to sustainable event design is balance and by combining eco-friendly practices with smart planning and local sourcing, planners can craft meaningful, high-impact events that reflect a commitment to the planet but without compromising elegance or innovation.'

The checklist presented in Table 6.2 provides a summary of tips and suggestions for designing sustainable events.

Table 6.2 Tips for designing sustainable events

Area	Sustainable options
Sustainable materials	Pick reusable or compostable tableware
	Purchase locally grown flowers
	Use reclaimed wood or repurposed metal for signate or displays
Lighting	Use solar lights or candlelight to create an relaxed atmosphere
	Use dimmers and motion sensors where possible
	Use or mimic natural daylight
Décor	Use reclaimed materials and share the background of these materials as part of the event narrative
	Source vintage or repurposed furniture and props
	Repurpose items such as wooden crates, wine bottles or glass jars

Taking such steps ensures that the event demonstrates a commitment to sustainability, but it does not mean compromising on the quality of the event, as illustrated in the example below.

REAL-WORLD EXAMPLE   Impactful and sustainable event design

Planners that make a conscious shift towards using eco-friendly materials, embracing natural landscapes and being mindful of the environmental footprint of an event, may be able to design events that are impactful and sustainable (McKanna, 2025)

For example, Zentive, an events agency based in London, UK, organized a sustainable breakfast briefing at the famous Gherkin building in London. The event brought together more than 70 senior stakeholders, government representatives and industry media, which advocated for global Net-Zero goals (Zentive, 2025). The event was designed to reduce food waste and carbon emissions. It used onsite registration to avoid paper waste, digital screens were used instead of signage and branded marketing materials, and guests were served a vegetarian breakfast using reusable serve-ware (Zentive, 2025). Thus, the event achieved its goals by calculating and offsetting its carbon emissions and waste.

Green Sense Events are an events management company that focus on supporting, educating and inspiring event organizers and clients to delivery environmentally and socially sustainable events (Green Sense Events, 2025). In 2022, they designed and delivered the Partnerships for Forest Forum, an event attracting 400 delegates and 60 exhibitors to celebrate sustainable agriculture and forestry (Sweeting, 2022). The event needed to be carbon neutral and the University of Chicago Booth School of Business was chosen as the venue due to its proximity to public transport, airy and modern feel and energy efficiency (Sweeting, 2022). The event was designed to feature a menu that was 35 per cent plant based and 85 per cent vegetarian and all exhibitors were provided with pre-printed displays on recyclable material (Sweeting, 2022).

Digital solutions

Advances in event technology means that planners now have a number of ways in which technology can be incorporated into events. In terms of designing sustainable events, planners can choose digital options to embed into their event plans to help to reduce waste and enhance the event experience for all involved. As Jain (2024) explains, the digital landscape offers a wealth of opportunities to streamline event planning and reduce resource consumption and integrating digital solutions into the design of an event can enhance attendee engagement. Reducing paper usage when hosting an event is crucial because paper consumption contributes to deforestation, water consumption and energy usage, all of which have significant environmental impacts. By minimizing paper usage through digital alternatives, double-sided printing, and encouraging electronic communication and documentation, event organizers can significantly reduce their event's carbon footprint (ICC Belfast, 2024).

Figure 6.8 illustrates these and additional ways in which technology can be embedded into event design.

Event apps can now replace paper schedules or programmes and be used to provide guests with all the information that they need about an event. Using an app rather than printed alternatives also allows planners to keep the information up to date with any last-minute changes. Creating an event app instead of printing paper programmes not only reduces paper waste but also enhances attendee experience by providing interactive features, push-notifications, real-time updates and the ability to

Figure 6.8 Embedding technology into event design list

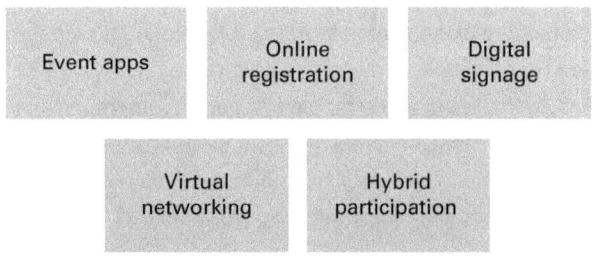

access information conveniently on their mobile devices. Apps can also feature exhibitor lists and maps so that attendees can navigate their way around a site or venue and surveys, so that guest feedback can be captured during an event.

Using an online registration or ticketing platform for events is another way to reduce paper usage but it can also be a much more time efficient way for guests to be admitted to an event. Similarly, using digital signage throughout the venue provides a sustainable alternative to printed posters and banners, allowing event organizers to display schedules and announcements in an environmentally friendly manner. It also allows planners to change signage throughout the event and update it with relevant messages or directions as the event progresses. As with apps, virtual networking platforms also give event guests the freedom to engage with each other as and when it is convenient to them, and remove the need to swap business cards. Virtual networking can also feature in events that are delivered in a hybrid format, thus allowing guests to attend virtually and to connect with each other digitally and without the need for travel. Ultimately, all of these steps can contribute towards streamlining event logistics, enhancing attendee engagement and reducing waste. As McKanna (2025) asserts, 'going digital isn't now just about being modern, using technology can be meaningful.'

Incorporating co-creation in event design

The concept of co-creation has emerged as a transformative paradigm within the field of event design, reshaping the traditional relationship between the event manager and event attendee. Co-creation emphasizes the collaborative value generated by actively involved stakeholders, particularly those attending, in the design and delivery of events. This participatory model challenges the notion of passive consumption, instead positioning audiences as co-designers and co-producers of the event experience. Rudi (2023) suggests that co-creation is important for three specific reasons:

1 Co-creation represents an experience itself, based on active participant engagement for the common good.
2 Event co-creation defines the new era of a conscious attendee who has control over his or her environment.
3 Collaboration relies on authenticity and crowd expertise, indicating a broader notion of value creation.

In other words, events designed through co-creative methods tend to be more engaging for audiences, as co-creation means democratizing the event with those who will experience them (Morgan, 2016). Figure 6.9 illustrates Morgan's (2016) six steps to co-creation.

Figure 6.9 Six Steps to co-creation (adapted from Morgan, 2016)

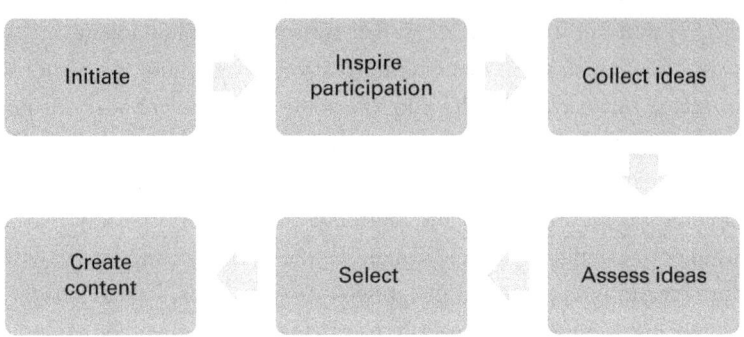

Initiating the process of co-creation requires identifying the objectives of the event and building a framework for participation in achieving those goals. The framework may invite contributions on the event's entertainment, catering, speakers, workshops and other elements of the proposed programme. The framework should also consider how people will contribute their ideas, and this might be via social media, an online survey or a forum. It is then important to encourage participation in idea generation so that ideas can be collected. The third step is to assess the ideas that have been generated, which can also be done by attendees such as through a vote or through social media metrics such as likes or shares. Selecting an idea needs to balance attendee views with event objectives but announcing the winning ideas can form part of the event promotion strategy as the ideas then form part of the content creation of the event programme (Morgan, 2016).

Co-creation is not without challenges as democratizing the event may create power imbalances and logistical constraints. In other words, attendees may want something that cannot be incorporated into the design of the event, for example, if logistically it does not work, if it is too expensive or if the suggestions do not fit with the sustainability criteria of the event. Additionally, divergent stakeholder interests can complicate the co-creative process. Therefore, the plan to develop co-created content must be carefully planned in advance.

ACTIVITY 6.2

Using Figure 6.9, devise a range of ways for different types of event attendees to be active participants in the book festival.

Intersectionality, equality, diversity and inclusion in event design

Another concept that is redefining event design is intersectionality, which refers to the interconnected nature of social categories such as race, gender, class, sexuality and disability. Intersectionality explores how various social identities overlap and collectively shape an individual's experience of oppression and privilege within systems of power. The term was coined by Crenshaw (1989) to highlight how black women's experiences were overlooked in both feminist and anti-racist discourses, because these frameworks treated race and gender as separate, rather than interconnected, factors.

Traditionally, many events have been designed through a 'one-size-fits-all' approach, often privileging dominant identities while marginalizing others. However, to achieve genuine sustainability and inclusion event planners must understand how systems of power operate within events. Intersectional event design considers how overlapping identities affect people's ability to access an event. This may be in terms of physical access, for example, a queer woman with a disability may face multiple barriers if a venue lacks gender-inclusive toilets, accessible rooms or sensory-friendly spaces. Economic access must also be considered, as for example, low-income attendees, especially those from racialized backgrounds, may be excluded by high ticket prices. Additionally, the digital accessibility of an event must be considered so that captions, sign language or interpretation are available to ensure equal access and participation at an event.

As many marginalized groups often experience harassment at events, event design can ensure that safe spaces are available for participants, and these might also help to meet some of the needs of attendees who are neurodiverse or who have hidden disabilities. Additionally, it is particularly important to consider meaningful representation, in other words performers, artists and speakers, as well as discussions and planned activities, should consider multiplied marginalized groups (e.g. a careers event might have a session on navigating career barriers for Asian homosexual professionals).

Intersectionality will therefore challenge event designers to move from token inclusion, for example, simply ensuring an inclusive conference speaker panel (e.g. in terms of gender or race) to addressing the structural inequalities embedded in how events are conceived, organized and experienced. This requires a shift in perspective from designing *for* people to designing *with* a diverse range of people, particularly those from historically marginalized communities. It goes beyond surface-level diversity to address systemic barriers and create equitable, inclusive spaces. An intersectional approach demands diversity in terms of how events are designed as well as delivered, as illustrated in the examples below.

An intersectional approach to events management challenges event designers to consider whose voices are amplified and whose are marginalized in the design and delivery of an event. This may be particularly relevant in cultural, political and corporate events where programming, speaker selection and sponsorship often reflect systemic inequities. Incorporating carefully planned co-creation activities into event design may ensure more representative and responsive programming so that events can affirm, rather than erase, the multiplicity of human experience.

REAL-WORLD EXAMPLE   Diversity in events

There is a renewed focus in events management on hiring from underrepresented backgrounds, as having a broader range of people within a business leads to a more diverse way of looking at things. Evidence confirms that there are black technologists moving into the tech sector, but this is happening at a very slow rate and the lack of representation in the tech sector is very apparent despite diverse organizations outperforming others (Daley, 2023). This is in spite of the work being done by organizations such as WeAreTechWomen, Code First Girls and Tech Global Advocates, all of whom are committed to driving real change around equality, diversity and inclusion.

Julia Streets, executive producer of DiverCity podcast, suggests that all organizations are on a journey in terms of equality, diversity and inclusion and there are five areas that will have the greatest, positive impact on the tech sector:

1 Corporate culture and leadership: organizations should establish a diverse and inclusive culture. CEOs set the tone – how they lead, others will follow.

2 Enlightened middle management leadership: making changes to the metrics for annual appraisals and rewards can mean enlightened leaders are supported.

3 Hiring and retention: ensuring adverts and recruitment partners deliver diverse candidate lists and ensuring the organization has talent retention and career development plans that make employees feel valued and supported.

4 Role models and allies: encouraging the management team to be role models and encourage others to step forward.

5 Networks and intersectionality: if organizations are serious about change, they need to be aware of siloed networks; we all have multiple identity attributes, so intersectionality really matters (DiverCity, 2021).

While these steps are aimed towards tech, they apply equally to all kinds of events businesses as creating an environment that leads with equality, diversity and inclusion and is conscious of its representation (especially within a live setting) can provide tangible benefits. In addition, with more diverse talent comes better event experiences.

REAL-WORLD EXAMPLE   WeAreTechWomen

WeAreTechWomen was founded in 2015 to help women working in technology to maximize their potential. Since then it has helped thousands of women in tech enhance their careers through events, conferences and awards. WeAreTechWomen has worked with over 100 multi-sector corporate organizations, helping them to attract, retain and develop their female tech talent. They have provided over 30,000 women with the opportunities to upskill through their events and conferences, as well as highlighting the achievements of 850 future tech leaders through their TechWomen100 awards. WeAreTechWomen currently has a membership of over 40,000 diverse women and 26,000 active social media followers, working across a multitude of industries and tech disciplines. WeAreTechWomen aims to:

- contribute to an increase in women working in technology industry (currently 20 per cent)
- support clients, helping them to attract, retain and develop their female tech talent
- raise the profile of women working in the industry through their awards
- upskill women working in tech through events and conferences
- provide access to resources that will enhance the careers of women working in tech (e.g. job opportunities/networks/learning/volunteering)
- support initiatives that encourage young girls to pursue STEM careers
- support women who wish to return to the tech industry
- encourage members to give back and act as role models for the industry
- collaborate with other women in tech organizations and programmes, sharing initiatives through their website and across their social media channels
- support women in tech not-for-profit organizations and charities.

SOURCE Printed with permission from WeAreTechWomen

Designing events for engagement

One of the key ways in which event planners can ensure audience engagement at events is by carefully designing ways for them to be active or included in the event. Not only does this contribute to the programme and content of an event but it will influence the ambience and create lasting memories for attendees. Figure 6.10 illustrates some of the ways in which attendees can become active participants at events.

Attendee participation can be achieved by asking guests to vote, rate or make a choice on a topic and this can be orchestrated through event technology, such as an event app or through the use of smartphones. Question-and-answer sessions, round tables, panel discussions and debates are another way to give attendees the opportunity to get involved and direct a discussion. Workshops or taster sessions at events can be very popular as these give guests a short trial of or attempt at an activity or skill. Individual or team quizzes, games and competitions work well in a variety of event types, as do an assortment of individual or group activities, particularly when they are linked to the event's objectives or theme.

Participation and engagement is not just about ensuring that guests have a good time. Events can be powerful tools for change, and they can be an effective platform for educating and empowering a group of people. Carefully designed events can therefore further sustainability goals by raising awareness and inspiring participants to adopt sustainable practices in their own lives (Jain, 2024). An event programme could be developed so that it includes the communication of messages that clearly explain sustainability objectives and provides attendees with tips and advice on how to adopt more sustainable practices. There could be incentives or rewards for attendees who participate in sustainable activities, such as bringing their own reusable bottle to the event or travelling to it by public transport. Fletcher (2023) gives further examples of how event planners can capture information about guests that can be used to encourage responsible behaviour, limit waste and promote sustainability by gathering data on predicted arrival and departure times and food preferences. For example, capturing guest arrival and departure dates and times can allow for organized group transportation. Asking attendees to register for their meals can help to get an accurate food and beverage estimate to avoid excess waste. It is also a way to influence choice and encourage good behaviour, for example by promoting vegan options. The careful design of the different elements of an event programme can be tailored to ensure attendee engagement and satisfaction and the attainment of key event sustainability goals.

Figure 6.10 Participation ideas for event guests

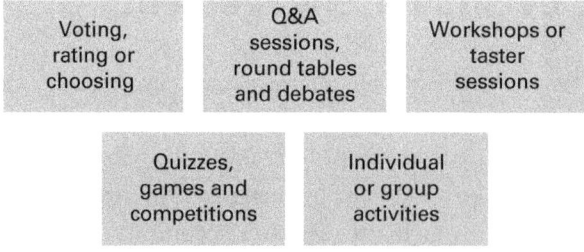

Summary

This chapter has explored the concept of sustainable event design as a process that places environmental and social responsibility at the heart of the event concept. Given the temporary nature of events, and the significant emissions that even a well-designed event will generate, sustainable event design has become essential. Sustainability may be seen as a limitation or a restriction on the creative process but this chapter has illustrated how sustainably designed events can benefit the environment, enhance a brand's reputation and inspire people to adopt sustainable practices. Sustainable event design includes considering the fundamentals of events such as guest behaviour, activities and décor, but it goes further to include elements such as biophilia and sensory stimuli. This chapter has also discussed how co-creation of an event programme can be a way to encourage participation in events and educate attendees about sustainability. Finally, this chapter has introduced the concept of intersectionality and through case studies, it has demonstrated how different organizations are furthering equality, diversity and inclusion in the events industry. This chapter has shown that sustainable event design is no longer a trend but a movement that is transforming the way we approach the creation of unforgettable experiences and demonstrates the integrity of all those involved.

Further reading and viewing

Ashwin, A (2024) Embracing biophilic design: How to plan sustainable and eco-friendly events, The Event Production Company, www.theeventcompany.com/news/embracing-biophilic-design-how-to-plan-sustainable-and-eco-friendly-events

Thant, A C M, Bibliophilic Design: Connecting people with nature, www.youtube.com/watch?v=iHGVpU_3yY0

References

Ashwin, A (2024) Embracing biophilic design: How to plan sustainable and eco-friendly events, The Event Production Company, www.theeventcompany.com/news/embracing-biophilic-design-how-to-plan-sustainable-and-eco-friendly-events

Crenshaw, K (1989) Demarginalizing the intersection of race and sex, *University of Chicago Legal Forum*, 1989 (1), 139–67

Daley, L (2023) Visibility matters, Conference News, 9 January, www.conference-news.co.uk/features/visibility-matters/

DiverCity (2021) About DiverCity Podcast, divercitypodcast.com

Dowson, R, Albert, B and Lomax, D (2023) *Event Planning and Management: Principles, planning and practice*, Kogan Page, London

Fletcher, M. (2023) Creating sustainable events: 5 steps for success, Cvent blog, 31 August, www.cvent.com/en/blog/events/creating-sustainable-events

Getz, D and Page, S J (2024) *Event Studies: Theory and management for planned events*, Routledge, Abingdon

Green Sense Events (2025) News, www.greensenseevents.co.uk/news

ICC Belfast (2024) 10 Sustainable event ideas that matter in 2024, iccbelfast.com/blogs/sustainable-event-ideas#hat-is-a-sustainable-event

Jain, K (2024) 11 Steps to planning sustainable events and meetings, Skift blog, 7 November, meetings.skift.com/2024/11/07/steps-to-plan-sustainable-events-and-meetings/

Matthews, D (2016) *Special Event Production: The Process*, Routledge, Abingdon

McKanna, M (2025) Discover sustainable event design without compromising luxury, Hosts Global blog, hosts-global.com/eco-friendly-luxury-corporate-events/

McKinley, S (2015) The benefits of nature based event design, Skift Meetings, 13 August, meetings.skift.com/2015/08/13/benefits-basics-biophilic-event-design

Morgan, J (2016) Co-creation and collaboration: Tricks and tools for event planners, 29 June, meetings.skift.com/2016/06/29/co-creation-collaboration-tricks-tools-event-planners

Nolan, E (2018) *Working with Venues on Events*, Routledge, Abingdon

Powell, C (2015) How to shortlist your 'brainstormed' event ideas, The Event Expert blog, 11 August, www.theeventexpert.co.uk/shortlist-your-brainstormed-event-ideas/

Resonics (2025) Biophilic design – The new way to reduce office noise? resonics.co.uk/our-blog/biophilic-design-office-noise-acoustics/

Rudi, V (2023) The real value of event co-creation and how it works, Eventtia, 20 August, www.eventtia.com/en/real-value-event-co-creation-works/

Sweeting, L (2022) Partnerships for Forests Forum 2022, 23 September, www.greensenseevents.co.uk/post/partnerships-for-forests-forum-2022

WeAreTechWomen (2025) What's our purpose, wearetechwomen.com/about/

Zentive (2025) Sustainability, www.zentiveagency.com/sustainability

07 | Delivering and evaluating the sustainable event

> **LEARNING OUTCOMES**
>
> By the end of Chapter 7, you should be able to:
> - appreciate the importance of reviewing sustainable events
> - recognize impacts of decision making
> - understand the significance of event measurements in future event planning.

Introduction

Reviewing events could potentially be the most important aspect of event planning. Bowdin (2024) outlines three phases of evaluation: pre-event, implementation and post-event. This chapter focuses on debriefing as part of the post-event phase. It has long been a part of the post-event process and provides a way to collect varied views and thoughts from stakeholders and suppliers. Feedback is vital to making improvements that matter, especially for those events that are infrequent, such as conferences or festivals. The clear definitions here cover event audiences, improvements, reputation and operations, as outlined by Bowdin (2024), while Berridge (2007) uses Rossman's (2003) six elements of symbolic interaction, applying them to event settings in an analysis of events. These consider how interaction shapes the meaning and outcome of event experiences (Berridge, 2007).

Reviewing events is not an easy process. Asking for opinions opens doors to more questions. Constructive criticism is not always received, but all feedback should be considered as good feedback to an event planner. Not only does it create a picture of your event, but it allows you to make constructive decisions about what others (including yourself as the event organizer) conclude about the event. However, the review of sustainable practices and effectiveness in this post-event analysis can only be as good as the data and information collected. Areas such as carbon reduction, community involvement and social health all require indicators to allow data to be collected and reviewed and some are not as easy to capture as others.

This is why post-event reviewing starts well before the event has finished. It must be factored into planning pre-event as part of feasibility studies to allow realistic and effective data collection for future event planning.

Making positive change only comes from working with other stakeholders to understand what positive change should look like. In sustainable planning, this must be mindful change that creates positive impacts for more sustainable future events.

Delivery

During the pre-event stage, communication is highlighted as a core factor of sustainable event planning. This creates a positive approach to achieving your sustainable event goals. There should be clear checks and subsequent indicators that create a smooth and transparent way for you and your stakeholders to deliver and measure these goals. Getz (2024) suggests that event operations and logistics apply to three subsystems:

- **Customer-oriented**: traffic, queuing, ticketing, information, essential services, comfort and safety, crowd management/
- **Supplier-oriented**: utilities, infrastructure, technical services and security systems.
- **Communications**: equipment, procedures, accreditation, hosting the media and scheduling.

These sections cover core areas of the event planning process; however, they can be adapted to consider sustainable approaches too. Elkington's (1994) sustainable practices – the triple bottom line (TBL) – can also help with understanding why this is important in the approach to sustainable planning. Adapted examples are shown below:

- **Customer-oriented**: transport options to the event, ticketing (including incentives and the customer journey), welfare and comfort of attendees, safety, crowd management (TBL: people, planet).
- **Supplier-oriented**: choice of supplier, venue choice, supplier's sustainable goals, SME business support (TBL: people, profit).
- **Communications**: community, messaging, media (TBL: people, planet).

Ultimately, the outcome of measuring goals should form a post-event sustainability report. This report should always stem from the sustainable policy and procedures determined as part of the pre-planning phase of the event.

The event venue(s) carry significant weight in terms of measuring your sustainable event goals, for example, venue emissions (TBL: planet), venue staff (TBL: people, profit) and venue suppliers (TBL: people, planet, profit) can be large contributors. In this textbook, communication is highlighted in the early phase of event planning, identifying relationship building. Understanding what can and cannot be measured and reviewed by you or the event's stakeholders is important in the pre-event phase, as this will have a significant impact on your post-event reporting.

Allegiant Stadium, Las Vegas, USA is a 65,000-seated capacity venue that opened in 2020. In 2023, it started working with nZero, a near real-time carbon accounting and management platform that helps track its carbon emissions and water consumption data (Allegiant Stadium, 2023). The platform allows venue management to assess and address in real time, allowing for quicker reduction as part of event planning.

Every venue is different; every event may use a different level of emissions that contribute towards its carbon footprint. For some venues, the setup/load-in phase will create higher levels of emissions than the event itself. Consider for example what a large-scale music tour may produce when transportation is factored in, compared to a stadium which may calculate a high percentage of attendees travelling by train.

Eventforce (n.d.) provides a list of the most sustainable venues in the UK, some of which are shown in Table 7.1. Table 7.2 lists some venues in Paris. The criteria to evaluate the sustainability of venues are similar to the 12 criteria used by The Production People (TPP, n d), a UK event production company.

Table 7.1 UK venues

	The Crystal (London)	Eden Project (Cornwall)	Manchester Central Convention Complex	Brighton Dome	Barbican Centre (London)	ICC Belfast
Rainwater harvesting	X		X			
Technology to reduce footprint	X					X
Recycling systems	X		X		X	
Renewable energy source		X	X			X
Water conservation		X	X			
Organic/local sources products		X			X	
Green roof				X		
Energy efficient lighting system				X		X

Table 7.2 Paris venues

	Palais des Congrès de Paris (France)	Parc des Princes, Paris (France)	Opera National de Paris (France)
Rainwater harvesting			
Technology to reduce footprint			X
Recycling systems and waste management	X	X	X
Renewable energy source	X		X
Water conservation	X		X
Organic/local sources products		X	
Green roof	X		X
Energy efficient lighting system	X		
Breeam in-use Certifications	X		
Accessibility for all	X		
Biodiversity strategy	X		X
Suppliers share sustainability values		X	
Food given to charities		X	

To implement these procedures and subsequently report on them, long-standing organizations such as Julie's Bicycle (n.d.) or those that are heavily impactful such as A Greener Future (n.d.) can help you to plan, record and report on your event goals. Industry support and advice is available in terms of carbon impact of your event, taking into consideration eco-consciousness. Julie's Bicycle, for example, offers a carbon calculator, while A Greener Future has a range of benchmarks and support to provide advice and record an event's footprint. The industry has made real steps forward here in the past decade. Some social, economic and cultural impact accounting is available, but is more complicated in its approach and of less note. Benchmarking and industry support can help this process but agreeing key performance indicators (KPIs) based on your own understanding and research into your event is an important tool. Much of this starts with those sustainable goals for your event, outlining some practical ways in which they can be achieved. If those goals are SMART, then measuring should have already been a consideration.

Social impacts can be challenging, given the unique approach taken, as this depend on the event's demographics, the local community and the type of event taking place. Most studies focus on the economic impacts, leaving the social impacts of event portfolios largely underexplored (Getz, 2012). However, some impacts can be simplified, considering the approach to community involvement discussed in other chapters of this textbook. One of the most common approaches is contingent valuation methods (CVM), which can offer a solution through non-use value – a measure of value that residents place on an event, even if they do not directly attend it. CVM is used in events to help understand a variety of data. Asking how much attendees would pay for a ticket is a good hypothetical approach to understanding audience views. Better still, if you can find out information on what attendees would pay for similar events, you can start to collect valuable data on economic status and social choices. These surveys are often seen as market research, using incentives to gather information through mailing lists and social platforms. The term 'non-use value' comes into the discussion when measuring views, because this is slightly less tangible than a question on ticket pricing. Social impacts encompass a range of outcomes, including community pride, social cohesion and cultural exchange, but there is little consensus on how these impacts should be defined and measured (Fredline et al, 2003; Wood, 2006). One of the core challenges in assessing and communicating social impacts lies in their subjective nature (Wallstam et al, 2025). It is therefore perhaps notable that the inclusion of stakeholders in event planning helps determine the impact that they have on the event, allowing a greater level of data collection post-event to understand how valuable the event actually was.

Not all event attendees will be positive about an event. That in essence could deter organizers from choosing to highlight this point. After all, less support means it is less likely an event may take place. One obvious KPI most outdoor event organizers or venue owners will be aware of is 'community quality of life' – the impact on the perceived living conditions of community residents. In many cases this is defined as local noise pollution, waste management, local transport links and more recently the debate of public park use.

REAL-WORLD EXAMPLE   Brockwell Park

Brockwell Park is a publicly-owned (council-owned) park in South London, UK. It has been used for large-scale events and festivals over the summer months since 2018. Festivals range from music to family inspired and the Lambeth country show.

A residents' group, Protect Brockwell Park (PBP), opposed the events, which require closing off sections of the park to the public for several weeks. They started a legal campaign which reached the high court, with the group arguing events were causing damage to the park's ecology, heritage and the broader community. A judge found in favour of PBP, noting the planned use of the land may be unlawful, given that the 37-day duration of the festivals exceeded the 28 days allowed for a temporary change of use.

Events continue to go ahead while the event organizers correct the administrative error; however, the subject of the campaign remains a live debate around use of public spaces, how councils generate income, and the impact that events of this size have on local residents. None of this is new to the industry, however it does pose a significant question to outdoor events organizers in terms of the land used, and to what extent community quality of life is impacted by it.

As important as these views are, given that legal battles can stop an event taking place, the event organizers must take a broader approach. Wider KPIs should include community pride, social capital (as discussed in Chapter 5), as well as community capacity enhancements, where the event finds ways for community members to build on civic projects. These indicators can provide real-life data to show positive social impacts. The latter of course is seen significantly in any mega-event plan, notably the Summer Olympic Games, which almost hails this as a given right. Mega-events do this, and they do it well – they have the budget after all, as well as the long-term vision to make positive change. The London 2012 Olympic Games established an independent body to monitor sustainable development of the Games, which might be considered a challenge, given that benefits are not seen immediately.

Pride, building social capital and creating a sense of community can often be seen as positive goals for event organizers. This is due to the need for them to ensure the event takes place, and perhaps because this is a constructive approach to turning what could be a negative view of an event into a much wider positive one. Such an approach is not wrong, but it is important to remember that building social capital is a process. Event organizers will have the event in mind first and foremost – the need to make it work and the hard graft that this will take. Community pride is not always instant and similarly, social capital is a marathon and not a sprint. While some people will feel instant gratification from attending an event, others do not share that need or passion. And, just like sporting mega-events which can be both positive and negative, the need to build an event from the inside out is often a course for leveraging a positive event legacy. The same should be applied to how events approach community inclusion.

REAL-WORLD EXAMPLE Cirkulär Festival

Cirkulär Festival is a newly formed small (below 1,000 capacity) festival in Dorset, UK.

It is a community event that provides entertainment, a speakers' forum, food and drink and kids' activities. The event model is based upon the circular economy and this approach is taken with regard to sustainability.

The festival's three sustainable aims are as follows:

1 Social health: including communities, groups and projects as part of the event, asking them to help shape and build the event for the future.

2 Economic growth: working towards a circular model by building an event that allows local businesses to grow with it.

3 Eco-consciousness: the festival captures the carbon footprint pre-, during and post-event operations, working towards reduction, but also intending for the event to be used as a blueprint for small to medium events of this size locally (Cirkulär Festival, 2025).

The event is interesting in terms of using data collection to create sustainable planning going forward. Alongside data from attendees in terms of their carbon impact, social connections and social economics are also addressed. The event asks questions of attendees, traders and residents about the impact of the event, and impact of attending or not attending, what main challenges traders face and what community pride means to local residents. The festival says that this data collection helps them determine how the event can become a sustainable model going forward.

Table 7.3 can help deliver and measure some important KPIs. Surveys, focus groups and meetings with community leaders, including local MPs, are all ways in which information can be gathered. The main objective is not to approach the subject by stating how the community will help your event, but instead how your event will help the community.

Framework

ISO20121 Event Sustainability Management system was developed in 2012 to help organizations deliver events that follow the principles of sustainable development. This framework should guide you in your initial event goals and help form the sustainable policy for your event. It should also be seen as a core guide to your event/company/charity's social responsibilities, a long-standing term within business. The framework continues to evolve and a 2024 update includes a stronger emphasis on social legacies and inclusivity.

Table 7.3 Assistance for event organizers in considering social aspects of an event

Quality of life	
What are the most significant local (and in some cases, national) impacts on people's quality of life?	Can your event address any of these? What tangible outcomes for the community could be created from the event?
Community pride	
What makes people proud of where they live?	Can your event address or impact any of these, even if there is no direct link to the event? What tangible outcomes could there be from your event that help the community be proud of where they live?
Social capital	
What currently creates happiness among local people? What does health and wellbeing look like to local people? Is there a strong connection between local people?	Can your event address or impact any of these, even if there is no direct link to the event? What tangible outcomes could there be from your event that help the community have a shared responsibility?

Linking with the discussion on post-event analysis, it highlights when evaluation and reviews should take place. This signifies the importance of continuous monitoring to gather the best possible information for future planning. ISO 20121 also contributes and interlinks with the United Nations' 17 Sustainable Development Goals (SDGs) – global goals aimed at ending poverty, protecting the planet and ensuring prosperity for everyone by 2030. These goals together with the ISO framework remain ongoing benchmarks for any event organizer, especially in the post-event/next-event phase, where aligning with these will allow for a clearer route towards developing the event.

The Birmingham 2022 Commonwealth Games concluded with a sustainability report, addressing operations, actions, challenges and successes of the event (Commonwealth Games, 2022). ISO2021 framework was used for the event and there were four core KPI targets as part of the event's plan to create a circular approach to the games. There are also a further three wider objectives linked to the broader approach. The report includes a greater level of detail of how these KPIs are determined and measured. KPI outcomes in the report's appendices suggested that each one had been achieved in some form, although there a greater level of detail was needed to determine some of the data.

Pre-event staffing for sustainable events

Staffing is one of the most vital components of pre-event planning for delivering sustainable events. No matter how robust a sustainability plan appears on paper, its successful implementation hinges entirely on people – individuals and teams who not only understand and believe in the event's sustainable goals but are also equipped to deliver them. The human element can make or break not only the attendee experience but also the operational and sustainability ambitions embedded in the event's core vision. As Bowdin et al (2024) emphasize in their framework of pre-event, implementation and post-event phases, each stage is intrinsically linked. Consequently, staffing must be meticulously planned with all three phases in mind. The pre-event phase in particular is where the foundational groundwork is laid, encompassing hiring suitable personnel, assignment of clear roles and responsibilities, establishment of expectations and the crucial alignment of every team member with the event's sustainability policy and targets.

A well-planned staffing strategy for sustainable events should commence by addressing a few key questions, integrating them into early feasibility studies and operational planning:

- What are the specific sustainability objectives of the event, and how do these translate into actionable tasks for staff? This requires a detailed breakdown of environmental, social and economic sustainability targets into measurable responsibilities for various roles.

- Who will be responsible for monitoring and reporting sustainability metrics before, during and after the event? Clear lines of accountability are essential for tracking progress and ensuring data integrity.
- How will staff be trained to handle the unique demands of sustainable practices, such as waste management, resource efficiency, responsible procurement, crowd control for eco-friendly transport or community engagement initiatives? Training must extend beyond general events management to cover the specific nuances of sustainable operations.

These questions highlight that staffing decisions must be integrated into feasibility studies and early operational planning. For example, if the event aims to minimize waste and ensure effective recycling, staff must be trained to guide attendees in waste separation and to liaise with suppliers and venues to enforce sustainable waste contracts. Without this, even the best sustainability intentions can fall apart during execution.

EXAMPLE

Green Team Coordinators

Consider a large music festival aiming to significantly reduce its carbon footprint and promote circular economy principles. During the pre-event phase, the organizing committee identified a need for 'Green Team Coordinators.' These individuals were hired specifically for their passion for sustainability and their organizational skills. Their pre-event responsibilities included:

- developing detailed waste management plans, including signage and bin placement strategies
- identifying and vetting sustainable suppliers for everything from food vendors to merchandising
- designing and delivering specific sustainability training modules for all event staff (e.g. security, ushers, cleaning crew) on topics like composting, recycling guidelines and energy conservation
- establishing communication protocols for reporting sustainability issues or successes during the event.

Community engagement liaisons

For a sporting event seeking to maximize its social impact and ensure ethical community engagement, pre-event staffing would include community engagement liaisons. These staff members would:

- research and identify local community groups, charities and social enterprises for potential partnerships
- develop clear communication strategies to involve local residents in the event planning process and address any concerns
- design and implement volunteer recruitment programmes from the local community, ensuring diverse representation
- establish frameworks for measuring the social benefits of the event, such as local economic impact or community participation rates (Brown and Davis, 2022).

ACTIVITY 7.1

Role-playing sustainable scenarios

Objective

To understand the practical implications of sustainable staffing in real-world event scenarios.

Instructions

1 Divide the class into small groups (3–4 students per group).
2 Assign each group one of the following hypothetical event scenarios:
   a. A large corporate conference aiming for ISO 20121 certification (Sustainable Events Management System).
   b. A community food festival focused on local, organic produce and zero-waste practices.
   c. An outdoor adventure race committed to minimizing environmental impact and promoting responsible tourism.
3 Each group must identify three key pre-event staffing roles crucial for delivering the sustainable objectives of their assigned event.
4 For each identified role, the group should outline:
   a. the specific sustainability-focused responsibilities for that role during the pre-event phase

> b. the skills or knowledge a candidate for this role would need to possess
>
> c. one potential challenge that role might face in implementing sustainability, and a pre-event strategy to mitigate it.
>
> 5 Each group will then present their findings to the class, briefly role-playing a short interaction between one of their identified staff members and a hypothetical stakeholder (e.g. a sustainable supplier, a venue manager or a community representative).

Building the right team

Building the right team for a sustainable event extends far beyond the traditional functional roles. While the core team will undoubtedly include seasoned event managers, dedicated sustainability officers, meticulous operations coordinators, strategic supplier liaisons and empathetic community engagement officers, the true strength of a sustainable event often lies in the comprehensive integration of all personnel. This includes a robust cohort of temporary staff and volunteers, all of whom are crucial in delivering the event's sustainability promise on the ground.

The recruitment process for sustainable events should therefore be redefined to prioritize not just technical skills but also a profound understanding of sustainability principles, cultural sensitivity and an unwavering commitment to community engagement. This is particularly salient for events with significant community interfaces, such as large-scale festivals, sporting events or conferences held in shared public spaces. As argued by socio-economic theories of community wellbeing (e.g. Putnam's (2000) social capital theory), the success and long-term viability of public events are intrinsically linked to their ability to foster positive relationships and avoid negative externalities within host communities. If staff lack awareness of local sensitivities, customs or environmental concerns, even a meticulously planned event can inadvertently cause unintended negative consequences for the community and damage the event's reputation for sustainability.

Drawing on resource-based view (RBV) theory, an organization's sustained competitive advantage comes from its unique and valuable resources (Barney, 1991). In the context of sustainable events, the 'resources' are not just financial or technological, but crucially, human capital imbued with sustainability knowledge and values. Hiring individuals who intrinsically understand and champion sustainability transforms human resources into a distinctive capability, enabling more effective implementation of eco-friendly practices and fostering genuine community connections. Furthermore, stakeholder theory underscores the importance of managing relationships with all groups who can affect or are affected by the event (Freeman, 1984). Competent and well-aligned staff act as critical conduits for engaging with diverse stakeholders – from attendees and suppliers to local residents and environmental groups – ensuring their concerns are addressed and their contributions are leveraged for a more sustainable outcome.

> **EXAMPLE**
>
> Recruiting for a sustainable marathon
>
> Consider a major city marathon aiming to be carbon neutral and minimize its impact on public parks while maximizing local community benefits. When recruiting event staff and volunteers, the organizing committee would need to go beyond standard event experience:
>
> - **Volunteer coordinators**: The organizing committee would seek individuals who not only have good organizational skills, but also experience in environmental education or community outreach, who are capable of training volunteers on proper waste segregation at aid stations, guiding participants to public transport options and engaging local residents about road closures and alternative routes in a culturally sensitive manner.
> - **Medical staff**: Beyond their clinical expertise, they might be briefed on sustainable procurement of medical supplies (e.g. minimizing single-use plastics where possible) and encouraged to promote responsible disposal of waste from medical tents.
> - **Route marshals**: In addition to directing runners, they would receive specific training on protecting park flora and fauna, reporting any environmental disturbances, and ensuring effective crowd flow that respects local residents and businesses along the route. Their cultural sensitivity would be paramount when interacting with residents whose daily routines might be temporarily impacted.
>
> This approach ensures that every individual, from the top-tier manager to the frontline volunteer, becomes a conscious and active participant in delivering the event's sustainability agenda, transforming intentions into tangible, positive impacts.

The most unusual and unique festivals in the world: a question on sustainability

Unique and unusual events of the world are interesting, but they also challenge sustainability principles and sustainable practices before, during and after the events. There are several examples that show how festivals and events can be both sustainable from a cultural perspective and unsustainable from other perspectives. These are elaborated below.

Health and safety

Las Bolas de Fuego (El Salvador), despite being a very dangerous festival, has been running for over 100 years. This longevity prompts us to consider: is the health and safety of participants necessarily a sine qua non condition for the sustainability of an event? How do event organizers weigh cultural preservation against participant wellbeing in the long term?

Each year on the evening of 31 August, residents of Nejapa gather to throw fireballs in commemoration of the 1658 El Playon volcanic eruption. History has it that the natural disaster forced the villagers of the old town to flee and settle in their current location. Today, residents split themselves into two teams to paint their faces like skulls and begin the festival by hurling palm-sized fireballs of kerosene at the opposing team.

Another event that can be considered dangerous is the Baby Jumping Festival, one of the most unusual festivals in the world. It takes place annually to celebrate the Catholic feast of Corpus Christi. During the El Salto del Colacho (Devil's Jump), men dressed as the devil wear red and yellow suits holding whips and oversized castanets to jump over babies who lie on mattresses in the street. This raises questions about the ethical implications for participants and the impact on the event's social sustainability.

Pamplona's famous Running of the Bulls, which takes place during the San Fermin festival, is one of the most extreme adrenaline-pumping events held in Spain. Taking place in July each year, this experience welcomes hundreds of thrill-seekers from all over the world to run in front of six wild, powerful bulls (plus six steers) through the city's old and narrow streets. In the mornings, the bull runs and, in the evening, visitors get to witness bullfights. However, the Running of the Bulls is an event that can be both considered dangerous for the participants and built on animal cruelty. How can such an event claim to be sustainable when it potentially compromises both human safety and animal welfare? What are the long-term societal and ethical considerations for events management?

Waste management

The Bun Festival (Hong Kong) is based on the use of food. The festival is the biggest and busiest event in Cheung Chau. What originally started as a celebration for the end of the plague on the island has transformed into one of the most popular cultural events today. The festival runs for almost a week, housing a vibrant yet traditional parade along with the famous Bun Scrambling Competition, where the participants conquer a massive 60 ft bamboo tower covered with buns, trying to grab as many buns as possible. One of the principles of sustainability is the reduction of food waste but this event is doing the opposite. How do event organizers reconcile cultural traditions involving large-scale food use with modern sustainability goals of waste reduction? What strategies, if any, are in place to mitigate the environmental impact of such practices?

Another event is the Lopburi Monkey Banquet, also known as Monkey Buffet Festival, which is based on the same model. With the aim of bringing good luck to the area and its people, the Lopburi Province north of Bangkok prepares a grand feast comprising 4000 kilograms of fruits, vegetables, cakes and candies that feed around 2000–3000 macaque monkeys every year. The festival first occurred in 1989, run by a local businessman. This raises similar questions about the sheer volume of resources consumed; how are these events balancing cultural significance with resource efficiency and waste generation?

The Battle of the Orange also challenges waste management as central to the sustainability of events. Imagine the UNESCO-listed Italian town of Ivrea witnessing a citrus battlefield where participants shoot 600,000 kg of oranges at one another, in celebration of Shrove Tuesday. Part of the city's popular historic carnival, the battle aims to recreate the 12th-century combat between the locals and the Royal Napoleonic troops. The teams of aranceri (orange handlers) on foot hurl oranges (representing old weapons and stones) against aranceri riding in carts (representing the tyrant's ranks). This symbolic festival marks one of the biggest food fights in Italy. Given the immense quantity of oranges used, what are the broader environmental implications, and how can events management address such significant organic waste streams responsibly?

Use of natural resources

The Florida Keys Underwater Music Festival (UMF) is aiming to raise awareness of the dangers faced by coral reefs, and for all divers and music enthusiasts, the festival is the place to be. Bill Becker, founder, coordinator and music director of UMF took music festivals to a whole new level with the aim of raising awareness of coral preservation. The quirky celebration held in July at Looe Key Reef has been running for more than 25 years, welcoming hundreds of snorkelers. However, this event attracts so many visitors that they might unwillingly harm the corals. This presents a paradox: how can an event designed to promote environmental awareness simultaneously pose a potential threat to the very natural resources it seeks to protect? What measures are in place to ensure that increased tourism does not negate conservation efforts?

Central criteria for the sustainability of events

Support and interests of participants

As long as people are interested in the event, it will continue to run. Indeed, the common point between all the most unusual events in the world is the large number of people involved. For instance, up to 10,000 men take part in the festival of Saidai-ji Eyo

Hadaka Matsuri. The event has been going on for over 500 years. The World Body Painting Festival attracts participants from over 40 countries. This consistent engagement suggests social sustainability, but how do event organizers maintain this interest while potentially adapting to modern sustainability demands?

Las Bolas de Fuego in El Salvador is about the commemoration of the 1658 El Playon volcanic eruption. The Bun Festival is the celebration for the end of the plague in Hong Kong. The Baby Jumping Festival aims to ward off evil spirits, for a safe passage through life. The Day of the Dead is an opportunity for family and friends to gather to pray and remember their loved ones who have died. These deep cultural roots clearly contribute to these events' longevity, but how can events management leverage this cultural significance to promote sustainable practices without compromising tradition?

How long the event has been going is also an indication of its sustainability: Las Bolas de Fuego dates back to 1658, while the Baby Jumping Festival also started in the 1600s. The Battle of the Orange dates back to the 12th century, while Saidai-ji Eyo Hadaka Matsuri started 500 years ago. Finally, the Underwater Music Festival has been running since 2000. While longevity suggests resilience, does a long history automatically equate to sustainable practices, or is there a growing need for these established events to re-evaluate their environmental and social footprint?

Cost

Some of the most unusual festivals in the world are low cost or no cost events as they are run by the local community or based on natural resources. This minimal financial burden suggests a model of economic sustainability, but does it inherently lead to environmental sustainability as well, or are there hidden costs related to resource extraction or waste disposal that are not immediately apparent? Under cost could also be included whether the event is free entry or ticketed.

Free entry festivals make up 75 per cent of global events and include:

- Las Bolas de Fuego, El Salvador
- Cheung Chau Bun Festival, Hong Kong
- Lopburi Monkey Banquet, Thailand
- World El Colacho, Spain
- Kanamara Matsuri, Japan
- Running of the Bulls, Pamplona
- Battle of the Oranges, Ivrea
- Air Guitar World Championship, Oulu
- Cheese-Rolling Festival, England

- Día de los Muertos, Mexico
- Busójárás, Mohács, Hungary
- Naki Sumo, Japan
- Saidai-ji Eyo Hadaka Matsuri, Japan
- World Toe Wrestling Championship, Ashbourne

Ticketed festivals make up the remaining 25 per cent of global events, for example:

- Underwater Music Festival, Florida
- Boryeong Mud Festival, South Korea
- Up-Helly Aa, Scotland
- World Bodypainting Festival, Austria
- Water Gun Festival, South Korea

The prevalence of free entry festivals points to strong community involvement and accessibility, which are aspects of social sustainability. However, how do these events manage their environmental impact without a direct revenue stream for green initiatives? Are there implicit environmental costs associated with mass participation that are not being accounted for?

Training for sustainability

Hiring individuals with a predisposition towards sustainability is undoubtedly a crucial first step, but it is through effective and comprehensive training that sustainability policies truly come to life. Training sessions are not merely informational briefings; they are immersive educational experiences designed to embed the event's sustainability ethos into every operational layer. These sessions should clearly communicate the event's overarching sustainability goals, introduce the foundational concept of the triple bottom line (TBL) – people, planet, profit (Elkington, 1994) – and meticulously detail specific tasks aligned with these interlinked objectives.

By grounding training in the TBL framework, staff gain a holistic understanding of how their individual actions contribute to the event's broader environmental stewardship, social equity and economic viability. This directly aligns with Getz's (2024) conceptualization of events as comprising three interconnected subsystems: customer-oriented, supplier-oriented, and communications. Each subsystem requires tailored training to ensure sustainable practices are not just understood but actively implemented:

- Customer-oriented staff: These frontline personnel are the direct interface with attendees. Their training must extend beyond traditional customer service to

07 | Delivering and evaluating the sustainable event 171

empower them as advocates for sustainable choices. This includes educating them on promoting and facilitating eco-friendly transport options (e.g. directing attendees to shuttle buses, public transport links, designated bicycle parking areas or ride-sharing hubs), explaining waste segregation protocols at recycling stations and encouraging responsible consumption behaviour. As O'Brien and Dowling (2021) highlight, customer engagement is critical for the success of green initiatives, and well-informed staff are key enablers of this engagement.

- Supplier-oriented staff: Individuals in roles interacting with suppliers (e.g. procurement, logistics, food and beverage management) must be thoroughly versed in the event's sustainable supplier standards. This involves understanding criteria for ethical sourcing, waste reduction commitments from vendors, energy efficiency requirements, and fair labour practices within the supply chain. Training should equip them to monitor compliance, negotiate for sustainable alternatives and foster collaborative relationships with suppliers who share the event's sustainability vision (Jones and Smith, 2022).

- Communications staff: This team is responsible for crafting and disseminating messages to various stakeholders. Their training needs to focus on consistent and accurate communication of the event's sustainability journey, including community messaging, media interactions and public relations. This involves understanding how to transparently report on sustainability metrics, address potential environmental or social concerns, and highlight positive impacts without engaging in 'greenwashing.' Effective communication builds trust and reinforces the event's commitment to responsible practices (Chen and Wang, 2023).

This integrated approach ensures that every staff member, regardless of their primary function, understands their role in weaving sustainability into the very fabric of the event, thereby maximizing the chances of achieving ambitious TBL targets.

REAL-WORLD EXAMPLE The 'Green Guardians' programme
at the Paris 2024 Olympic and
Paralympic Games

The Paris 2024 Organizing Committee implemented a comprehensive 'Green Guardians' training programme for its vast workforce, encompassing both paid staff and thousands of volunteers. Beyond general operational training, specific modules were dedicated to sustainability. For customer-facing roles, this involved detailed briefings on encouraging spectators to use public transport, guiding them to water refill stations to reduce plastic bottle use, and educating them on waste sorting at designated bins. Supplier-facing teams received in-depth training on the ethical sourcing guidelines, circular economy principles for venue fit-outs and criteria for low-carbon catering. Communications teams were trained on transparently sharing sustainability progress and challenges with the public, focusing on the event's reduced carbon footprint targets and social inclusion initiatives.

This holistic training ensured that sustainability was not an add-on but an intrinsic part of every role, transforming personnel into active proponents of the Games' ambitious environmental and social goals.

Monitoring and feedback

Staffing should also include mechanisms for collecting feedback during and after the event. Post-event debriefings benefit greatly when frontline staff contribute observations about what worked and what didn't. For example, did recycling stations work effectively? Did attendees follow guidance? Such insights are often overlooked by senior planners but can drive future improvements.

A sustainable staffing legacy

A thoughtful approach to staffing can have a legacy effect too. Many events now offer sustainability roles as part of graduate internships or community volunteer programmes. This builds capacity in the local workforce, contributing to the social pillar of sustainability by equipping people with new skills and employment opportunities.

ACTIVITY 7.2

Build your sustainable staffing plan

Objective

Students will apply principles of sustainable event staffing by designing a staffing plan for a hypothetical festival.

Instructions

1. Divide the class into small groups (4–6 students per group).
2. Give each group a brief for a fictional two-day music festival in a public park with an audience of 5000 attendees. The festival has strong sustainability goals: zero waste to landfill, reduced carbon footprint and positive community engagement.
3. Each group must:
    a. Identify at least five key staffing roles required to meet these goals.

b. Describe how they will recruit, train and deploy these staff.

c. Create a plan for how staff will monitor and report on sustainability targets during the event.

d. Develop two creative staff-led initiatives to engage the community (e.g. green ambassadors, recycling competitions).

4 Each group should present their plan to the class in a 5-minute pitch.

5 After all presentations, hold a short class discussion: What staffing ideas were most innovative? How realistic were the plans? What challenges might they face in practice?

Activity outcome

This activity reinforces the real-world challenges and creative solutions involved in aligning staffing with sustainability. It helps students see how people, when supported by thoughtful planning and training, become the backbone of sustainable event delivery.

The BCOPS framework: a holistic approach to sustainable events

In the evolving field of events management, achieving genuine sustainability demands more than isolated actions or well-intentioned but ad-hoc efforts. A comprehensive framework like BCOPS (Behaviour, Communication, Operations, Policy and Strategy) brings much-needed clarity to the complex, interconnected elements that determine how events fulfil their sustainability promises and evaluate their true impacts. BCOPS is not simply a checklist; it is a systems-thinking approach. To effectively deliver and evaluate sustainable events, planners must understand how behaviour, communication, operations, policy and strategy intersect to produce tangible, positive change.

In practice, the BCOPS framework ensures that sustainability is not relegated to a single officer or department. Instead, it becomes a shared responsibility embraced by every volunteer, supplier, manager and attendee. This collective ownership provides the foundation for rigorous post-event debriefing and honest self-assessment that Bowdin (2024) describes as vital for continuous improvement. In this way, BCOPS transforms sustainability from a mere aspiration into an achievable standard, making every event a catalyst for progress toward a more resilient, responsible and regenerative industry.

The BCOPS approach aligns seamlessly with Bowdin et al's (2024) three phases of evaluation – pre-event, implementation and post-event – by embedding sustainability not only in planning but also in delivery, measurement and legacy. Each element of BCOPS acts as a crucial pillar supporting the entire sustainability cycle.

Behaviour

At its core, delivering a truly sustainable event hinges on shaping human behaviour among staff, suppliers, attendees and the wider community (Getz, 2024). This resonates deeply with Berridge's (2007) application of Rossman's (2003) symbolic interactionism, which posits that meaning and outcomes are produced through dynamic social interaction. Sustainable event managers must proactively create environments that encourage and facilitate desirable behaviours: conscious recycling, responsible transport choices, active waste reduction and respectful community engagement. For instance, the Glastonbury Festival's 'Love the Farm, Leave No Trace' campaign stands as a prime example of actively shaping attendee behaviour. Through a combination of subtle 'nudges' (e.g. clear signage, designated waste zones), highly visible volunteer engagement and even explicit deterrents like fines for littering, the festival embeds behavioural science into its operations. This makes sustainability tangible and actionable for thousands of attendees, demonstrating how large-scale events can foster a culture of environmental responsibility. Moreover, ISO 20121 (ISO, 2024), the international standard for event sustainability management systems, stresses that sustainability must be driven by a culture of responsibility.

Effective staff training and robust stakeholder onboarding processes directly influence how individuals behave on-site and, crucially, during debriefs, ensuring the collection of accurate data for evaluation (Wallstam et al, 2025). This aligns with social cognitive theory, which emphasizes that learning occurs in a social context and that self-efficacy (belief in one's ability to succeed) and observational learning are key to adopting desired behaviours (Bandura, 1986). By providing clear guidance, positive reinforcement and visible examples, events can foster pro-environmental and socially responsible actions among all participants.

Communication

Communication is the essential glue that connects and energizes all elements of the BCOPS framework. Sustainable goals, expectations and results must be communicated clearly, consistently, and transparently to all stakeholders (Bowdin et al, 2024). Poor or inconsistent communication can undermine even the most meticulously crafted sustainability plans, while effective and compelling messaging empowers attendees, staff and partners to make informed, better choices. Elkington's (1994) TBL framework strongly reinforces the need for communication that seamlessly integrates and aligns environmental, social and economic goals. For instance, Allegiant Stadium's pioneering partnership with nZero for real-time carbon tracking would be largely meaningless without effectively communicating these dynamic impacts to staff and stakeholders. This real-time data allows for immediate adjustments to behaviour and operations, maximizing efficiency and minimizing environmental footprint (Allegiant Stadium, 2023).

Communication also extends critically to post-event reporting. Publishing comprehensive sustainability reports not only demonstrates accountability but also allows the wider public to scrutinize and hold organizers to their stated commitments. Furthermore, methods like contingent valuation, which involve asking audiences how much they would hypothetically pay for greener events, can both inform future planning and actively engage audiences in a shared sustainability mission (Fredline et al, 2003). This participatory approach, rooted in engagement theory, fosters a sense of collective responsibility and investment.

Operations

Operations represent the practical actions on the ground that bring sustainable behaviour and communication strategies to life. As (Getz 2024) outlines, operations span three critical subsystems: customer-oriented, supplier-oriented and communications. Each of these must be meticulously optimized for sustainability. For example, customer-oriented logistics such as transport planning directly affect an event's carbon emissions. Operational teams should proactively promote and facilitate eco-friendly options, such as dedicated shuttle buses, ample bike parking and clear public transport information. Supplier-oriented logistics demand stringent oversight to ensure that all contractors meet established sustainability standards, for instance, by prioritizing local caterers, utilizing sustainably-sourced materials and verifying ethical labour practices. The operations team also bears the crucial responsibility of coordinating accurate data collection during the event, which then feeds into robust post-event reporting (Bowdin et al, 2024).

Allegiant Stadium further exemplifies operational innovation by leveraging real-time carbon data to dynamically tweak heating, ventilation and air conditioning systems, lighting and water usage during an event – a best practice other venues can and should emulate (Allegiant Stadium, 2023). This level of granular control showcases how operational excellence can directly translate into measurable environmental benefits.

Policy

Policies are the formal, overarching frameworks that embed sustainability into the DNA of an event. These foundational documents set clear expectations and minimum standards that guide individual behaviour, shape organizational communication and directly influence operational procedures. They transform good intentions into mandatory practices.

ISO 20121 (ISO, 2024) provides a robust and internationally recognized template for event sustainability management systems. Its cyclical 'Plan-Do-Check-Act' approach directly aligns with the BCOPS framework, mandating clear policies that are continuously refined through rigorous monitoring and evaluation. Glastonbury's sustainability policy, for instance, includes strict guidelines for waste management, renewable energy use and community partnerships. This ensures that everyone involved, from performing artists to individual attendees, is aligned with the festival's ambitious environmental and social vision. These policies are not mere suggestions; they are legally binding, feeding directly into contracts with suppliers, volunteers and local authorities, thereby reinforcing a unified and non-negotiable standard for sustainability across all facets of the event. This systematic approach, deeply rooted in institutional theory, suggests that organizations adopt certain practices, like sustainability policies, not just for efficiency but also to gain legitimacy and conform to societal expectations.

Strategy

Finally, strategy is the overarching element that ties together behaviour, communication, operations and policy to deliver a coherent and long-term vision for sustainability that extends far beyond the confines of a single event. A well-articulated strategy ensures that each event builds upon lessons learned, systematically contributing to broader, long-term goals such as the UN Sustainable Development Goals (SDGs). Fredline et al (2003) and Wood (2006) emphatically argue that social impacts must be an integral part of this strategy, for instance, by consciously strengthening community pride and building local capacity through targeted local employment programmes or sustainable partnerships with community groups. A strong sustainability strategy also defines clear, measurable KPIs. Organizations like Julie's Bicycle and A Greener Future provide invaluable carbon calculators and benchmarking tools, helping event organizers translate their strategic sustainability ambitions into trackable, actionable data (Julie's Bicycle, n d; A Greener Future, n d).

Mega-events like the London 2012 Olympic and Paralympic Games stand as powerful demonstrations of how a well-conceived, long-term sustainability strategy can profoundly shape urban development and transport infrastructure and leave a positive community legacy that endures for decades. This strategic vision must logically trickle down to all levels, including smaller festivals, corporate events and conferences that may only run once a year. Even these seemingly smaller events can set crucial benchmarks and contribute significantly to progress toward a more resilient and responsible future for the entire industry. This echoes strategic management theory, where long-term vision, resource allocation and adaptive planning are key to achieving sustained competitive advantage and fulfilling an organization's mission, in this case, its sustainability mission.

ACTIVITY 7.3

1. In small groups discuss the potential outcomes if an event is not reviewed throughout its life cycle
2. Discuss and write down the people who may be responsible for recording and reviewing the sustainable objectives of an event.
3. In pairs, choose an event of your choice.
   - Note the venue where the event took place. Research and discuss how the venue could record and evaluate sustainable objectives.
   - Note the attendees for the event. Research and discuss how the event organizer could record and evaluate attendee data from the event.
   - Consider and discuss how an event organizer could measure any potential changes from the event regarding:
     o quality of life
     o community pride
     o social capital.

CHECKLIST

Sustainable events succeed when sustainability is embedded throughout behaviour, communication, operations, policy and strategy and is planned in advance, delivered with care, reviewed with honesty and improved for the future.

Here is a checklist that may help in sustainable event planning and evaluation.

Pre-event planning

- Define clear sustainability goals aligned with ISO 20121 and the UN SDGs.
- Integrate sustainability targets into feasibility studies and operational planning (Bowdin et al, 2024).
- Select venues and suppliers that align with sustainability criteria such as the TBL (Elkington, 1994).
- Develop SMART indicators for carbon reduction, community involvement and social impacts.
- Build sustainability into staff recruitment, onboarding and training plans.

Staffing

- Recruit staff and volunteers who understand and support sustainability goals.
- Provide training on waste management, carbon monitoring and community engagement.
- Assign clear roles for sustainability monitoring and data collection.
- Include staff in pre-event, on-site and post-event debriefing.
- Use examples like Glastonbury Festival's 'Leave No Trace' to inspire practical training.

Operations and delivery

- Apply (Getz's 2024) three subsystems:
  - Customer-oriented: Sustainable transport; waste facilities; crowd safety.
  - Supplier-oriented: Local, ethical suppliers; green contracts.
  - Communications: Clear signage; public messaging; media relations.
- Collaborate with industry tools (e.g. Julie's Bicycle, A Greener Future) for measurement and reporting.
- Monitor venue sustainability, such as real-time tracking (e.g. Allegiant Stadium and nZero).
- Include community input and local impact measures.
- Have contingency plans for unexpected sustainability challenges.

Communication

- Communicate sustainability goals clearly to attendees, staff, suppliers and local communities.
- Use nudges and signage to influence positive attendee behaviour (Berridge, 2007).
- Provide incentives for sustainable choices (e.g. discounts for public transport).
- Be transparent in communicating post-event results and improvements.

Reviewing and evaluating

- Use Bowdin et al's (2024) three-phase model: pre-event, implementation and post-event evaluation.
- Plan for data collection in advance – don't leave it until after the event.
- Gather feedback from all stakeholders, suppliers, staff and attendees.
- Debrief honestly – use both positive and negative feedback to make improvements.

- Apply Rossman's symbolic interaction framework to understand how interactions shaped the event experience (Berridge, 2007).
- Report on all sustainability KPIs: carbon footprint, community quality of life, waste reduction.

Policy

- Develop a clear sustainability policy that all stakeholders agree to follow.
- Include sustainability clauses in contracts and agreements.
- Refer to ISO 20121 for an integrated management system.
- Connect policy to wider corporate social responsibility (CSR) frameworks.

Strategy

- Align event strategy with long-term sustainability commitments.
- Ensure behaviour, communication, operations and policy all support the strategy (BCOPS).
- Benchmark against industry best practices and case studies (e.g. London 2012 Olympics, Allegiant Stadium).
- Evaluate and refine strategy after each event to continuously improve.

Community and social impact

- Measure not just economic impact but also community pride, social cohesion and non-use value (Fredline et al, 2003).
- Use methods like contingent valuation to capture intangible benefits.
- Plan initiatives that build social capital (e.g. local training, capacity building).
- Monitor local concerns regarding noise, waste and transport effects.
- Celebrate community benefits in post-event reporting to strengthen legacy.

Final reporting

- Produce a clear, honest post-event sustainability report.
- Share results with stakeholders and the public.
- Highlight lessons learned and planned improvements for future events.

Summary

Delivering and evaluating a sustainable event is an evolving, multi-layered process that does not end when the last attendee departs or the final piece of equipment is dismantled. As this chapter has explored, the true measure of an event's success – particularly from a sustainability perspective – depends greatly on how diligently, honestly and creatively organizers review and learn from each phase: pre-event, implementation and post-event, as outlined by Bowdin (2024).

Debriefing represents a crucial component of the post-event evaluation phase and its importance cannot be overstated. It is not merely a formality or a polite exercise in gathering stakeholder sentiments but a deliberate, strategic opportunity to collect diverse insights, perspectives and constructive criticisms that can shape the future sustainability and effectiveness of events. As Berridge (2007) highlights, applying Rossman's (2003) symbolic interactionism framework, the way stakeholders interact with the event influences its meaning and legacy. Hence, a robust debriefing process that welcomes interaction and candid feedback enables event planners to capture this complex interplay and turn it into actionable improvement.

Yet, reviewing an event is never straightforward. Constructive criticism can be uncomfortable, and sometimes stakeholders are reluctant to share negative feedback. Nevertheless, every piece of feedback, whether glowing or critical, is a valuable asset. It reveals truths that planners might otherwise overlook and provides the evidence needed to make informed, impactful changes that resonate with both people and the planet.

Crucially, the effectiveness of post-event sustainability analysis is limited by the quality of the data collected. This underlines why review and evaluation cannot be an afterthought. Planning for meaningful, measurable data must begin at the pre-event stage. Feasibility studies, stakeholder agreements and the integration of clear, realistic sustainability indicators – whether measuring carbon reduction, community impact or social health – are essential. This proactive approach ensures that data is relevant and reliable, empowering organizers to demonstrate tangible outcomes and track progress against meaningful benchmarks.

Delivery relies on the seamless coordination of operations and logistics across customer-oriented, supplier-oriented and communications subsystems (Getz, 2024). When these elements are adapted through a sustainability lens, aligned with Elkington's (1994) TBL framework, they become tools for embedding sustainability into every touchpoint of the event. Transport choices, local supplier partnerships, community engagement strategies and effective stakeholder communication each offer opportunities to minimize negative impacts and maximize positive legacies.

An event's venue is often a linchpin for achieving and evaluating sustainable goals. The Allegiant Stadium case illustrates how embracing real-time carbon management technologies can set new standards for venue accountability and impact reduction. Each venue, with its unique characteristics and community context, must be assessed individually. It is only through honest, transparent partnerships with venues and suppliers that realistic, actionable sustainability reporting can be achieved.

Beyond environmental metrics, this chapter has emphasized the equally important social dimension of sustainability. Social impacts like community pride, social cohesion and local capacity building are harder to quantify but no less vital. They speak directly to an event's legacy and its social licence to operate. Contingent valuation methods (CVM) and non-use value surveys, although imperfect, offer practical ways to gauge these intangible impacts. Mega-events like the Olympics demonstrate how investing in social legacies can become a cornerstone of responsible events management, although smaller events must find their own scalable pathways to deliver similar community benefits.

Frameworks like ISO 20121 provide valuable guidance for integrating sustainable development principles into events management. Their cyclical model of planning, doing, checking and acting underscores the need for continuous monitoring and improvement. Moreover, alignment with global frameworks such as the UN SDGs ensures that local actions contribute to wider societal and planetary wellbeing.

In essence, delivering and evaluating a sustainable event is not a linear or isolated exercise but an integrated, cyclical process that depends on mindful planning, collaborative delivery and transparent evaluation. Each phase feeds the next: insights gathered during debriefing inform future planning; lessons learned shape operational choices; and stakeholder engagement ensures that sustainability goals remain relevant and inclusive.

Sustainable events management requires courage and humility. Courage to ask difficult questions, to confront inconvenient truths about an event's real impacts, and to challenge the status quo of 'business as usual.' Humility to accept that sustainability is an ongoing journey of improvement rather than a fixed endpoint. It is about progress, not perfection.

Ultimately, the ability to deliver and evaluate a sustainable event rests on a planner's commitment to listen deeply, plan proactively, act responsibly and report transparently. It demands that sustainability is not treated as an add-on but as an integral thread running through every decision, every stakeholder relationship, and every measure of success.

In closing, as this chapter has highlighted, the most resilient, relevant and responsible events are those that see sustainability not as a checkbox but as a continuous promise – to their audiences, communities, suppliers and the wider world. When debriefing and evaluation are embraced wholeheartedly, that promise becomes more than words: it becomes an evolving standard that shapes not just individual events but the future of the entire events industry.

Further reading

Masterman, G (2022) *Strategic Sports Events management*, Routledge, Abingdon

Wallstam, M, Ioannides, D and Pettersson, R (2020) Evaluating the social impacts of events: in search of unified indicators for effective policymaking, *Journal of Policy Research in Tourism, Leisure and Events*, 12, 2

References

A Greener Future (n.d.) Event Sustainability Support and Benchmarks, www.agreenerfuture.com

Allegiant Stadium (2023) Allegiant Stadium and nZero: Real-Time Carbon Tracking. www.allegiantstadium.com/sustainability

Bandura, A (1986) *Social Foundations of Thought and Action: A social cognitive theory*, Prentice-Hall, Upper Saddle River, NJ

Barney, J (1991). Firm resources and sustained competitive advantage, *Journal of Management*, 17 (1), 99–120

Berridge, G (2007) *Events Design and Experience*, Butterworth Heinemann, London

Bowdin, G A J, Allen, J, Harris, R, McDonnell, I and O'Toole, W (2024) *Events Management*, Routledge, Abingdon

Brown, K and Davis, L (2022) Measuring social impact in events management, *Journal of Sustainable Events*, 15 (2), 87–101

Chen, L and Wang, H (2023) Communicating corporate social responsibility: Strategies for credibility and engagement, *Business Ethics Quarterly*, 33 (1), 45–67

Cirkulär Festival (2025) www.facebook.com/events/the-quomps-christchurch-dorset/cirkul%C3%A4r-festival/593880930186234/

Commonwealth Games (2022) Birmingham 2022 Sustainability Report, sustainabilityreport.birmingham2022.com/64-1

Elkington, J (1994) Towards the sustainable corporation: Win-win-win business strategies for sustainable development, *California Management Review*, 36 (2), 90–100 http://dx.doi.org/10.2307/41165746

Eventforce (n d) Embracing Sustainability: Unveiling the UK's Top Ten Most Sustainable Event Venues, www.eventsforce.com/blog/post/embracing-sustainability-unveiling-the-uks-top-ten-most-sustainable-event-venues/

Fredline, L, Jago, L and Deery, M (2003) The development of a generic scale to measure the social impacts of events, *Event Management*, 8 (1), 23–37 doi.org/10.3727/152599503108751676

Freeman, R E. (1984) *Strategic Management: A stakeholder approach*, Pitman, London

Getz, D (2012) *Event Studies: Theory, Research and Policy for Planned Events*, Routledge, Abingdon

Getz, D (2024) *Event Management and Event Tourism*, CABI, Wallingford

ISO (2024) ISO 20121: Event Sustainability Management System – Requirements with guidance for use, International Organization for Standardization, Geneva, www.iso.org/standard/50030.html

Julie's Bicycle (n d) Carbon Calculator and Resources, juliesbicycle.com/resources

Jones, R and Smith, L (2022) Sustainable supply chain management in the events industry, *Journal of Cleaner Production*, 350, 131345

O'Brien, M and Dowling, M (2021) The role of customer engagement in driving green behaviour, *Journal of Marketing Management*, 37 (13–14), 1321–45

Production People, The (n d) The most sustainable venues in the world: The corporate buyer's guide, The Production People, theproductionpeople.com/the-most-sustainable-venues-in-the-world/

Putnam, R D (2000) *Bowling Alone: The collapse and revival of American community*, Simon & Schuster, New York

Rossman, J R (2003) *Recreation Programming: Designing leisure experiences*, Sagamore Publishing, Champaign, IL

Wallstam, M, Kronenberg, K and Pettersson, R (2025) Assessing the social impacts of event portfolios through non-use value, *Journal of Policy Research in Tourism, Leisure and Events*, miun.diva-portal.org/smash/get/diva2:1950128/FULLTEXT01.pdf

Wood, E (2006) Measuring the social impacts of local authority events: A pilot study for a civic pride scale, *International Journal of Nonprofit and Voluntary Sector Marketing*, 11 (3), 165–79, doi.org/10.1002/nvsm.21

08 | Making the event safe as an important aspect of sustainability

LEARNING OUTCOMES

By the end of Chapter 8, students should be able to:
- understand the link between risk and sustainable event planning
- recognize the challenges in event planning for core groups of people
- include sustainable thinking in the safety planning of an event.

Risk management: an overview

Risks and uncertainties are closely related and are inherent to the organization of events (Quinn, 2013). Conducting a risk assessment is an ongoing procedure which consists in identifying, controlling risks (Becker, 2006; Edger and Oddy, 2018), and to minimize them (Quinn, 2013). 'A key area of risk that events must plan for is crowd management' (Quinn, 2013: 113). Traffic management, the use of temporary structures, electrical devices, adverse weather and the demographic of the attendees are all examples of factors to consider when conducting an event (Dowson and Bassett, 2018). Whatever the factors considered, the principles of risk management are the same, and are summarized below:

1 Identify potential hazards that could cause harm or damage. Ensuring that attendees are safe is part of the duty of care of the event organizer. There are a range of regulations that relate to the organization of events. In the UK, these

include the Health and Safety at Work Act (1974), Working at Height Regulations (2005) and Equality Act (2010). Conducting risk assessments is therefore important beyond the fact it is a legal requirement for the organization of events (Becker, 2006). Other reasons include ensuring a smooth run of the event, which is central for the experience of attendees, and to avoid negative publicity that may harm the image of the event should something happen.

2 Identify what the harm or damage might be, who (audience, contractors, performers, volunteers) it would affect and how seriously. The risks related to hazards can be either low, medium or high. Indeed, low-risk events are generally indoor events that involve no unusual or specialist activities. Medium-risk events are usually large indoor events designed for a large number of attendees. High-risk events are often unusual or specialist events for a large number of people. The risk assessment procedure also implies the development of contingency plans. The safety officer is the main person in charge of risk assessments and related procedures. However, anyone who has identified a risk must flag it to the safety officer, hence the importance of having a procedure in place (Shone and Parry, 2004).

3 Identify the likelihood (high, medium or low) of the risks involved in putting on the event.

4 Take action to reduce or mitigate risks through a clear procedure.

5 Monitor and re-evaluate the action plan put in place to deal with incidents and, equally important, update the action plan and risk assessment (Dowson and Bassett, 2018; Jeynes, 2002). This is particularly important for the next run of the event.

Completing a risk assessment form is part of the risk management procedure (see Figure 8.1 for a summary of the risk assessment procedure). A risk assessment form may be presented in different ways. Table 8.1 is a template of the risk assessment form.

Once the risk has been identified, a risk control plan needs to be developed. Table 8.2 is a template of a risk control plan.

Core groups in safety planning

There must be a clear understanding between the role of social sustainable practice in event planning and the need to ensure the safety of people throughout an event, whether attendees, staff and volunteers, or other stakeholder groups. Outlining key groups and their potential risks is a good way to ensure that safety is not compromised during the event planning process. A risk assessment should be a fundamental part of identifying this, but through the prism of sustainable event planning, there should be a greater level of consideration to what this means in terms of the event life cycle and the long-term planning of the event. One core example includes discussion around equality, diversity

Figure 8.1 Risk assessment procedure (adapted from Dowson and Bassett, 2018; Edger and Oddy, 2018; Jeynes, 2002)

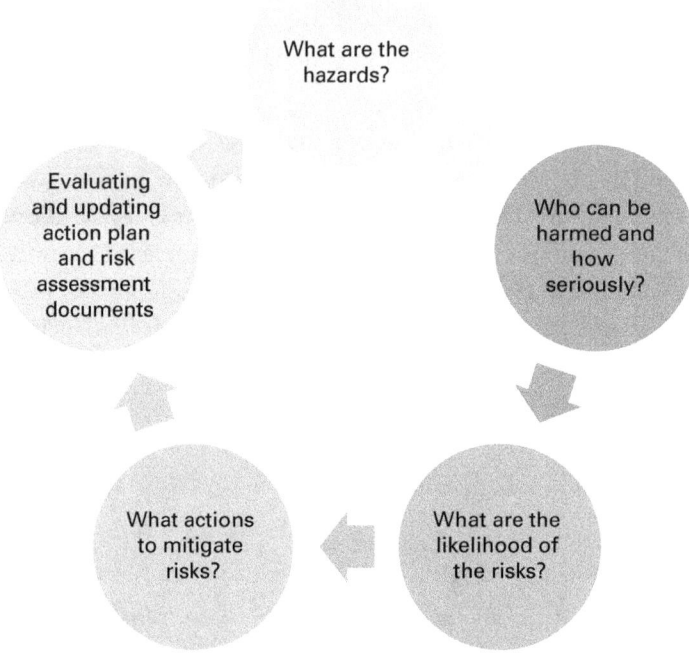

Table 8.1 Risk assessment form template (adapted from Shone and Parry, 2004: 171)

Event name: Location: Date of first assessment Date of review:				Date of event: Reviewed by:	
Risk ratings					
Hazard	People at risk **Staff** **Contractors** **Attendees**	A: Worst case outcome **Slight** **Serious** **Major**		B: Likelihood **Rare** **Possible** **Likely**	Rating **A x B**

Table 8.2 Risk control plan form template (adapted from Shone and Parry, 2004: 172)

Event name: Location: Date of first assessment Date of review						Date of event: Reviewed by:		
Risk Control Plan								
Hazard	Existing control measures	Additional control measures required	Priority	Person responsible for measure	Complete by	Action taken	Review date
1								
2								
3								
4								
5								
6								

and inclusion (EDI) in the events industry and is a core piece of the overall sustainability jigsaw of an event. Fletcher and Hylton (2018) state that the events industry is beset by a lack of diversity in terms of race and ethnicity, remaining a predominantly white space in terms of senior management and leadership positions. There has been some progression in terms of gender in the industry. Some events companies are acting locally to try and support women in the sector and overcome some of the barriers to progression they face in their individual careers (Page, 2020). As discussed partly in other chapters, the inclusion of groups in the event planning process, whether that be pre-, during or post-phases, can add positive value to the longevity of an event. In other words, to make an event sustainable over time, key groups considered as part of EDI awareness must not just be addressed by organizers within risk planning; but be included as part of the event's core values. As discussed in Chapter 5, key stakeholders should be part of objective setting. The same applies to groups of people considered within risk management of an event.

REAL-WORLD EXAMPLE Access to live events

UK consumer champion 'Which?' surveyed 705 members of the Research Institute for Disabled Consumers panel between October and November 2023, asking them about access to live events (Downes, 2024). Half of those surveyed outlined problems with experiencing live events. Event organizers, under the umbrella of venues, promoters and ticketing outlets, must all follow the Equality Act 2010 to ensure people with disabilities can access their events. However, the survey revealed various problems, from little information available regarding accessible ticket options, to a lack of information on car parking or even just accessing the venue safely. Half of those surveyed outlined problems while being at the event itself, with viewing and lack of staffing support at the venue being noted.

Every event is different, and the venue type, location and existing infrastructure will dictate so much of the customer experience. There is, however, a very important need to factor this type of customer journey into event planning. Not only are there laws to protect groups such as people with disabilities but there is a moral and sustainable obligation to ensure all groups are part of events in the future, helping to grow an event and ensuring it remains safe and inclusive. This is, of course, part of a wider conversation regarding continuing high levels of inequality in society generally, and in turn an imbalance when it comes to event attendance.

A key area of consideration for event organizers in risk planning is accessibility and how the event fits the needs of those attending. Finkel et al (2018) suggest that 'Accessibility can be understood in terms of the measures put in place to address participation by those with impairments, both permanent and temporary, as well as both physical and mental, including perceived class and cultural barriers.' There are perhaps two schools of thought here, especially with outdoor event planning, which can be a greater challenge. First:

- What space is being used, and does it usually serve a purpose (separate to that of the event)?
- By removing this space could it compromise safety (physical and mental) for some people?

Second:

- When discussing the needs of attendees to an event, the narrative can often be how the individual struggles to fit into the environment created. As with the wider view of disability, this should be the other way around. If the environment does not fit the needs of the individual, it is the role of the event organizers to accommodate this where practical to do so.

Page (2020) suggests that while there is great potential for festivals to encourage greater intercultural engagement and facilitate social cohesion, the way they are conceived, planned and delivered can impact on their accessibility for persons with a disability. Cited in Lytras and Visvizi (2020), Rahman and Zhang (2018) carried out research into the accessibility of public urban green spaces to different socially vulnerable groups of people. Their research investigated areas such as urban open parks, which are core aspects to urban green environments and key to sustainable urban development and sustainable social health in urban populations. 'They are focal components to advance living quality in urban areas, attributable to their commitment to a decent urban condition, the experience of nature and to expanding the interest for nature-based recreation facilities' (Rahman and Zhang, 2018 p. 2).

Event organizers should be sensitive to spaces such as these when used by the public, and whilst the event's sustainable objectives may feel they are met by utilizing green spaces proactively, consideration should be given to what adjustment or removal of spaces will mean for groups who may use, value and need open air spaces and access to these kinds of facilities (see also the real-world example of Brockwell Park in Chapter 7).

Consideration must also be given to the event itself and those who choose to attend but require a greater level of support. As outlined in Chapter 5, the inclusion of stakeholder groups is paramount to sustainable objectives. Vulnerable groups such as those with a greater level of accessible needs due to a physical or mental health disability, or groups defined by age, must be clearly understood in terms of their challenges and needs before they can be encouraged to attend the event. Both indoor and outdoor venues can be challenging environments for those that require a greater level of accessible support. While organizers of events have a duty of care to all attendees and staff members, and to give support where it is practical and appropriate, further focus on who is attending and what the event may look like to them can be an effective exercise to plan more sustainably. Event organizers could therefore address five key areas when considering this, by asking themselves the following questions and detailing some of the answers to use when objective setting:

1 Who is being invited to the event? (Demographic, customer profile, etc.)
2 What does the event environment give to non-vulnerable groups of people, that it cannot give to vulnerable groups of people?
3 As event organizer, do I need a greater level of guidance or support regarding understanding a group's needs?
4 As event organizer, what am I required to do by law, what is my duty of care, and where can I go further in implementing plans?
5 As an event organizer, how do I communicate information to customers?

Making an event safe for children, young people and their carers

This section discusses safety at events from the perspective of children, young people and their carers. More specifically, it addresses the following question: What needs to be considered to make events targeting children and young people, and their carers, safe?

From a safety perspective planning, designing and delivering events for children and young people is no different from events organized for adults as in both cases the safety of attendees is paramount. This means that all the information provided earlier in this section is applicable to events for children. Obviously, planning events for children have some additional requirements, which includes for instance having some licences, having a lost/found child policy, etc. (Delaney, 2023; Knapton, 2023; Powell, 2023). These will be discussed later. It should also be noted that children and young people at events can be split into two groups: those attending and those performing at events. In the case of children performing at events, a licence is needed. If many children are scheduled to perform at the event, a Body of Persons Approval (BOPA) needs to be obtained by the event organizer.

Risk management at events for children, young people and their carers

When it comes to the health and safety of children, there are specific bodies concerned with their welfare, such as the National Society for the Prevention of Cruelty to Children (NSPCC) and local authority child protection services. There is also specific legislation in the UK, including the Children and Young Persons Act (2008) and Working to Safeguard Children (2023) statutory guidance. These highlight the responsibilities of adults involved with children (in any capacity) to keep them safe and to act accordingly if they are not. Such legislation naturally impacts on the planning, design and delivery of events for children. An example of a direct impact could be the need to have a lost/found child policy, which would lead to the following needing to be considered.

- What to do in case of a missing/found child.
- How to record cases of missing/found children.
- Where to keep paperwork to record cases of missing/found children.
- Who is responsible for found children while waiting for carers – a background check (Disclosure and Barring Service (DBS)) of staff will be needed prior to the event, as this is required for all those who work with children.
- What to check when returning a child to an adult.

Every event may take a different approach to lost children, depending on the event's own risk assessment outcomes and the size and nature of the event. Essentially, the following should be done in the event of a lost child at an event (Knapton, 2023:158):

1 Inform event control immediately in coded language (referring to a lost child using an internal radio call sign, for example Moses, Disney).
2 A description of the child and other relevant information (name, gender, age, build, height, hair colour, hair style, eye colour, distinguishing features, clothing, medical concerns, contact number, name of the person reporting, time of the report). This should be reported to event control together with completed documentation.

3 Take the carer to the lost children point (which must be staffed by DBS checked members of the events team).

4 Explain to the carer what is being done to help but do not promise anything that is beyond your control.

Once the child has been located (Knapton, 2023:159):

1 Inform event control.

2 Confirm identity of child.

3 Inform carer that child has been found.

4 Escort child to the carer.

5 Confirm ID of carer. Note that if the child is unwilling to go with the carer, the police should be contacted (Knapton, 2023).

6 Complete relevant reunited confirmation documentation (to be kept for six months), which includes (reunited with, relation to child, contact number, ID check, signed off document).

If the events management team cannot locate the lost child, the procedure is as follows (Knapton, 2023: 160):

1 If after 10 minutes, the child is not located the event manager should contact the police. (The length of time before this is done should be assessed on an individual basis, for example, a competent 15 year old can be searched for after a longer period than a vulnerable 2-year-old child.)

2 Inform carer of actions being taken.

3 Staff and volunteers should continue to search while they wait for the police.

4 One staff member to remain with the carer until the child is located or police take control of situation.

In summary, the longevity of an event should be considered and addressed as part of an event risk assessment and the sustainable planning of an event is directly linked to its safety. The consideration of 'groups at risk' and how they are included in an event is a core part of planning a sustainable and safe event.

Operational management

As part of the risk assessment process for a large-scale event, core areas often considered are crowd management and contingency planning. These are fundamental areas to consider in terms of safety planning for any event and can be the main reasons some events are unsafe to continue. There are many aspects of event planning that require back-up plans; however there are some elements of events that may lead to worst-case scenarios such as postponement or cancellation. This is because safety (including both physical and mental welfare) will always come first. This is correct of course given that the health of people may be at risk, but the decisions made to keep attendees and staff safe can affect the long-term strategy of an event, as discussed further in this section.

Financial considerations

Some events operate on very small profit margins, and/or have large initial costs. As significant expenditure is often required in the initial phase of event planning (for example, website development, venue deposits, promotional activities) prior to any income being received, the task of cash flow management can be challenging (Bowdin et al, 2024). The effects of changing or in the worst case cancelling an event can have a substantial impact on whether the event continues to operate again, whether staff are employed again and whether the many social and economic benefits are received. The global Covid-19 pandemic affected the event industry significantly. Post-pandemic, the rising cost of living continues to affect a proportion of events. Many events were forced to close in March 2020, some with little to no financial support. Multiple challenges for the industry coming out of the global pandemic period has meant that many events have either altered/adjusted their provision or removed their event entirely from the events calendar. Often viewed as a 'perfect storm' by some, the challenges of a post-pandemic environment have changed consumer behaviour, created a heavy reduction in resources and all against a backdrop of economic instability. Greenbelt Festival cited in Bowdin et al (2024) states,

> Plenty of us are experiencing the cost-of-living crisis, as rising prices start to bite. We know that money is tighter than ever before. For our festival that pressure is combined with the post-pandemic impact on the events industry. There's an accompanying cost-of-festivaling crisis too, as the sums involved in producing a festival have – and we hope you don't mind the technical language here –absolutely gone through the roof.

It is also clear that budgets play a core role in other major sectors of the industry. Post-pandemic, the wedding industry worked through a significant backlog of bookings following postponement of larger weddings over an 18-month period. However, as costs increase per household as part of the economic squeeze, the emphasis for many customers has been on 'cost cutting' and 'value'. Lainston House, a 5-star,17th-century country house hotel in Hampshire, UK, offers weddings for up to 200 people. Their Weddings Manager commented, 'The luxury weddings market is seeing significant change … Our current challenge is offering the premium product for all, without compromising on the quality.'

There are also discussions around larger corporations swallowing smaller events and venues, the topic of ticket pricing (and public access to tickets) as well as event demand (for ticketed events) increasing significantly. All of this has an effect down the pyramid and has resulted in not all events having survived the turmoil of the last five to six years. This is not to suggest that some areas of the industry have not started to thrive and have continued to do so, but the post-pandemic years thus far have shown that there is a significant demand for in person (as well as online) events, subject to the type of event and core values. Global conference spending in 2024 was estimated at $50 billion (MIA, 2024). However, as many historical national or international moments such as these have shown us, not all events escape unscathed or intact to continue to operate in new climates.

REAL-WORLD EXAMPLE   Secret Garden Festival, UK

The Association of Independent Festivals (AIF) announced that 60 UK festivals had been postponed, cancelled or closed for good in 2024. It also reported that 96 events were lost to the Covid pandemic and 36 in 2023. So, some 192 UK festivals have disappeared since 2019 (AIF, 2025). A notable example of this was the UK's Secret Garden Party Festival, which started in 2004 and grew to a capacity of 30,000 people – a significant number given the independent operation of the event. Like all festivals, it stopped during the pandemic years before re-opening with a reduced capacity to combat what the festival called turbulent rising costs and a lack of support in the industry generally.

Organizers announced that the 2024 festival was to be their last in the current format, publicly stating that the outdoor festival sector is a 'broken model.' The festival carried out a symbolic end to its 20 years with a ceremony burning the main stage (safely!). A community of people spanning two decades celebrate the end of the festival.

In 2025, a partnership was created with other independent festivals alongside the Music Venue Trust to use the same festival site as a platform for growth, with Secret Garden Party festival organizer Freddie Fellowes giving the land free of charge to festivals with the aim to grow something new and sustainable.

It signals an interesting time for a business model that many see as unsustainable. During the pandemic, many conversations within the industry turned to how events such as these could combat contingency planning should lockdowns on such a scale take place again. With the economic uncertainty post-pandemic, and the changes in social decision making, comes a great question on the future of this sector. Outdoor music festivals have always carried risk; however, those pressures have become too much for some. A rebirth of a sustainable model is an interesting and notable moment for the sector, especially given that the music industry is having a conversation about grassroots support more widely.

The pandemic also had a significant effect on the industry in terms of personnel resources. When events stopped in 2020, so did the chain of those people in work because of them. Pre pandemic, 70 per cent of the entire industry workforce were made up of freelance workers (Parry, 2020). The abrupt stop to events taking place ultimately forced many freelancers working in events into other industries; those that were simply able at that time to survive financially were also seen to be more stable over time. As many events returned slowly during 2022, the recruitment drive found that previous freelance workers were carrying out delivery work for supermarkets or had started their own local trade and/or perhaps found the slower and less varied hours of guaranteed work more appealing. 'From the offset [sic] of the pandemic, the absence of live events forced audio visual (AV) technicians to seek employment in other industries' (Live Recruitment, 2024).

When the uncertainty of the pandemic led many event professionals to explore alternative careers, some temporarily but many permanently, it damaged the industry's emergence. Staff shortages have also been exacerbated by the UK's staggered EU exit (Great Potential Consultancy, 2024). It has exposed an industry that could become paralysed, but also an industry that could remain resilient to external change and be able to re-ignite. There have been strong signs of financial recovery in these post-pandemic years. It is estimated that the UK's event industry generated £62 billion in 2023, noting corporate events such as conferences, trade shows, exhibitions and product launches generated £33.6 billion, while leisure and outdoor events including music festivals, sporting events, and cultural festivals, contributed £28.053 billion (Great Potential Consultancy, 2024).

A 2024 survey that reflects the response of 117 professionals representing organizations within the business meetings and events sector suggested that almost half (49 per cent) of organizations state their workforce was bigger on 1 January 2024 than it was on 1 January 2023, while 40 per cent of organizations state it has stayed the same (MIA, 2024; Great Potential Consultancy, 2024). There is also a noted shift in employment with more freelance roles available. After years of unpredictable restarts followed by a cost-of-living crisis for many, self-employment is growing once more. While not the same level as pre-pandemic of over 5 million freelancers, as of October 2024 the UK had approximately 4.38 million self-employed workers (Statista, 2025). In 2024, approximately 1200 freelancers in the live event sector were surveyed by the UK LIVE Event Freelancers Forum on aspects such as available work, job confidence and financial arrangements. More than 60 per cent said they felt 'optimistic' about the next 12 months (Clift, 2024). Further afield, in a US workforce study of business event freelancers, 36 per cent of the US workforce across all industries were engaging in freelance work in 2023, an increase of 4 million total professionals from 2022 (Upwork Study, 2023).

The UK LIVE Event Freelancers Forum report also highlighted areas where changes are required to improve the experience of freelancers, which include financial security, better pay, flexibility and work–life balance, all factors that are becoming increasingly important (Clift, 2024). Workers have always remained a core part of event planning. Casual staff, freelance workers and shift workers – the nature of the industry requires and relies on it. It is widely recognized that people are one of the most valuable resources for an event (Rutherford Silvers and O'Toole, 2020). Post-pandemic, the flexibility and approach to home working in many industries has created a wider conversation on the work–life balance. Anderson (2021) discusses a workplace enabling employees to achieve work–life balance is particularly motivating and gratifying to employees. Happy employees, whose needs for a good work–life balance are achieved, tend to stay with their employer and are more productive.

Nobody working in the events industry expects the conditions of an event to change, given the nature of the environment or the passion that comes in being a part of delivering an event. However, they do quite rightly expect to have an employer who can see past the often fast-paced, extensively complex environment, and address the importance of employee support. Event organizers should consider this, giving a much greater level of recognition, care and contingency during event planning in the important area of human resources.

The more obvious risk of course is that without workers there will undoubtedly be no event; however as part of an event's sustainable goals and Elkington's triple bottom line, the impact of event workers socially, economically and ecologically driving positive change should all be at the heart of sustainable event planning.

Cancellation

As discussed throughout this textbook, sustainability is often about collaborating in order to succeed. Chapter 4 outlines the importance of venue finding and venue relationships. It is, however, an important part of financial management to consider the chain of impact of cancellation of an event. This is useful in terms of the conversation around financial planning, as just like within mega-event planning, we must consider the wider implications of events and the location in which they take place. When industry statistics on generated income are compiled, they include a wide range of beneficiaries including the catering supplier, the events agency, the merchandise and the charity. It is one of the reasons why the events industry can be so fragile especially in the shadows of a global pandemic and the cost-of-living crisis.

The stakeholder and supplier chain in event planning can be vast and is often an overwhelming consideration when talking about the sustainability of the industry. It therefore requires breaking down. As event organizers, we cannot be solely responsible for each aspect that the chain feeds. However, if we are the source of income that helps feed it, which the event often is, then there must be moral and ethical considerations. Earlier in this chapter, it was identified that event cancellation must be factored into the event planning risk assessment. Each supplier at an event will have their own cancellation terms including insurance and this to some extent offers a level of financial security. It cannot be the responsibility of an event organizer to manage this, but where cancellation affects groups of suppliers and stakeholders who are less protected, then a greater level of accountability is required. As part of risk assessment, cancellation should not be ignored simply because it is too complicated to consider or seen as something which must only be dealt with at the time. When putting together a risk assessment pre-event, consider the following points:

- What insurance policies do direct suppliers have in place to reflect loss of earnings and staff recruitment from event changes?
- Discuss with the event insurers whether there is support for suppliers directly affected by changes to an event. (Direct suppliers could be those considered needed in order for the event to take place.)
- What other events are taking place locally at the time of the event? Could suppliers utilise their staff resources or stock for these, in the event of a cancellation?
- To what extent is a charity intending to benefit from the event? Can they plan for a contingency?

Changing risks

Social change, technology advances, as well as the expected generational shift in event attendees have all suggested that expectation of event experience, shared moments and the need to document it all are paramount to attending an event. This era also seems to suggest that there is a greater desire to speak up, to 'shout about' an experience and make it clear what is acceptable and what isn't. It is a welcomed change in society but also comes with high-level expectations, especially when attendees are paying for an event that they expect to enjoy.

The event industry could also perhaps be in a place of its own making. For example, improved technology in society being implemented into event design only delivers a greater level of attendee convenience. There are many attendee positives to event tech, however the more that it is included, the more that it is expected. At the same time, the improved level of attendee experience at an event, whether that's the implementation of technology into venues such as the Las Vegas Sphere, or the immersive show Abba Voyage, all contribute to raising the bar in terms of customer satisfaction. ABBA Voyage grossed £100m in 2023 with a profit of £6m. Tickets in 2024 start at a widely accepted £55 per person (see Chapter 9 on tickets). The show/venue cost £141 million to create (Hanley, 2024). Yet to some extent, there is a level of customer understanding when it comes to the type of event – nobody would expect a high level of immersive activity at a small local community festival, for example.

Crowd management

When looking at the fundamentals of operational risk and the subject of crowd management we may discover that attendee expectations go deeper than that of digital improvements and immersive experiences. The core aspects of event planning do not disappear. One of the most frequently cited theories in crowd psychology is social identity theory (Drury, 2018). Crowds can be seen as a social group, and social identity theory suggests that people identify with groups to increase their self-esteem and sense of belonging (Drury et al, 2019).

Crowd dynamics are a well-researched area of academia, but post-pandemic crowd decisions by potential attendees are less so. There is little research into the effect on mental health issues relating to the global pandemic linked to people's decisions to attend an event. Many people are physically and mentally unable to carry out the same functions they once did. For instance, there has been an estimated additional 76.2 million cases of anxiety disorders globally, an increase of 25.6 per cent (Kindred and Bates, 2023). While health concerns such as these are hard for us to influence as event organizers, it does highlight the importance of crowd safety when people arrive at an event. Rutherford Silvers and O'Toole (2008) suggest that the event risk manager must analyse the physical and behavioural factors that could influence a crowd and incorporate the appropriate crowd controls necessary to mitigate negative outcomes. Crowd management has become a leading area of the industry, but as we so devastatingly see globally, there are still risks resulting from poor crowd planning. Recent disastrous examples include Astroworld in 2021, where 10 people between the ages of 9 and 27 tragically died; lawsuits continue against the event organizers and individual performer Travis Scott (Savage, 2023). The event was not stopped to manage casualties in the crowd safely, resulting in a widespread conversation about the culture of this: 'The language around stopping shows has become more prominent but also more debated. The industry has always had the ability to stop shows but the culture around when and how to use that power is shifting, for the better.' (Hancox, 2025)

Aside from this, crowd control problems can also arise when event organizers do not consider the level of expectation that customers may have. Crowd management and crowd control are synergistic rather than synonymous (Fruin, 1984, 1993). This can be a hard balance to find, yet every year there are examples of crowds during events becoming confused, leading to problems. There is no disputing that the most important aspect of crowd management for event organizers will always be to reduce the risk and protect lives. While the increased use of mobile phones at live music events divides opinion in terms of social interaction, organizers can use them to share important messages. Glastonbury Festival in Somerset, UK becomes the most densely populated event in Europe for four days each year. With crew, around 240,000 are on site. Organizer Emily Eavis says her event uses push notifications on the official festival app as a way to communicate any updates to the masses and signalling in real-time higher capacity areas in the approximately 1500 acres of farmland festival site. This approach is a positive crowd movement technique as well as addressing individual concerns of some customers.

However, for some events, it is necessary to go deeper into customer behaviour and whether this becomes a factor in risk. Notting Hill Carnival in London, UK attracts up to 2 million attendees annually to the streets of West London (London Assembly, 2025). The event, which is non-ticketed, means that crowd management is a carefully addressed but unpredictable process. Some attendees of the carnival may expect this; however, many attending are swept up in the event and do not realize the risk there is to the movement of people around the open streets. The event is a superb example of sustaining culture and celebration, and its impacts are far reaching in terms of social health, protecting cultural heritage and economic growth. It fosters intergenerational connection and cultural pride. Quinn (2005, 2013) suggests that festivals are vital mechanisms for the safeguarding and evolution of intangible cultural heritage, and their absence can disrupt this. The event is important in the culture calendar, and event organizers and local authorities must protect the values and traditions to ensure that the event is sustainable in the long term. Notting Hill Carnival is about freedom and expression in a street carnival format, but this comes with problematic risks such as crowd management. There are continued warnings of a potential mass casualty event due to increasing crowd crushing incidents (Grew, 2025). Ultimately, this risk will outweigh everything else if it leads to injury or death. As we have seen in other global event examples, this can lead to significant change or event cancellation should it be deemed an unsafe environment. It is therefore important that an event organizer of any event considers that the risk of 'no change' is sometimes a risk to the overall sustainability of a cultural event.

REAL-WORLD EXAMPLE   Boardmasters Festival

Boardmasters festival takes place on the coastline in Cornwall, UK, welcoming over 50,000 people to the event on an annual basis. It started in 1981 as a surfing competition and then grew in the early 2000s into a music festival.

The event's location is problematic for a few reasons. The natural coastline is part of the event's USP. Its history is based upon the connection of sea and beach. However, ensuring 50,000 people are in a safe environment when the site is so open to the elements of the British weather can be problematic.

In 2018, the weather was a significant challenge for festival organizers. The weather pattern altered more significantly than expected and the decision was taken to cancel the festival hours before gates were due to open. That decision was made between the festival, the safety company hired to manage risk at the event, and the local emergency services and council. The cancellation of any festival poses risk, however the timescale meant that the event faced a greater level of issues to overcome. The decision to cancel was based on attendee safety. Although much discussion would have taken place to carry out a dynamic risk assessment of the situation, the severe weather warnings would have started to make the decision easier.

Event organizers had a significant number of the 50,000 + attendees on their way to the event or in the vicinity of the festival site. The communication with ticket holders, and the safe removal of existing people on site such as traders, vendors and artists, along with the need to derig infrastructure as quickly but as safely as possible given the extreme weather impacts, all resulted in a greater level of crowd management planning.

The events management plan included crowd management as a core aspect of risk and planning and would have also included plans around cancellation.

The Boardmasters example shows that cancellation was ultimately out of their control. However, given the expected risks, their events management plan sought to cover many potential risks and details of planned outcomes. There was initial significant upset at the festival's cancellation because many attendees expected better weather forecasting plans given the decision to cancel seemed so late. For some of them the impact would go on to be greater personally, as the event would then not take place for another three years due to the global pandemic.

This example is also perhaps one that can be viewed as having less long-term impacts in terms of event sustainability. After some understandable disappointment, most attendees would understand that the weather itself cancelled the event, not the organizers. Yet it highlights how an incident such as this can be considered, and equally as to how well attendees respond post-cancellation. The cancellation in 2019 was pushed aside somewhat by three years of further disruption due to the global pandemic. By the time the event came back in 2022, the welcomed return of events, the festival's USP as well as high profile artists attracted an audience, all of which helped to market the event. The same can be said for many music festivals, for example, if one year there is problematic queuing to get in or out of carparks but the next year they have a popular headline act, this will wipe most of those memories away. In some way, music festivals can perhaps remain sustainable in terms of sales, based upon who is performing at them.

In summary:

- Financial considerations are a significant risk for an event's longevity.
- The events industry employs a wide range of people in it, with freelance workers making up a considerable number.
- Communication is vital to help attendees understand the process of risk.
- An event risk assessment should take into consideration and address how to reduce the impacts on returning customers, post-cancellation of an event.
- Cultural importance of an event must be balanced by an assessment of risk, and how these two are integrated should be considered in the pre-event risk assessment.

Political challenges

The industry is no stranger to the direct and indirect impacts of the political landscape. The discussion is wide, and this section of the chapter only aims to discuss some of the core risks seen in event planning (see *further reading* at the *end of this chapter for more*).

Funding

A 2024 report from the University of Warwick with the Campaign for the Arts, suggested that the UK's arts and culture sector was in crisis, with the government cutting culture budgets by 6 per cent since 2010 (Warner and Kassim, 2025). In comparison over this period, there was an increase in spending of up to 70 per cent in Germany and France. It has been widely portrayed that the UK's art sector has seen, like many other sectors, cut after cut. As part of a wider cultural review by the UK government, funding is on the agenda.

Resources

Recognition is a vital aspect of the relationship between the industry and central government. The 2024 Events Report 2024 outlined a need for a campaign from government and business to recognize the people who work in the events industry and to encourage more people to enter it because of its value to the overall economy. It suggests that events should be recognized as part of the creative industry. UK government figures estimate there were 2,419,000 filled jobs in the UK creative industries during 2023 (MIA, 2024).

For most political figures, events can be seen as positives, and when they hold national or international status then they become symbols. Events that support local businesses and are deemed part of a destination's identity are praised. However, many people would suggest that events are much lower down the political plan. After all, by definition, they are not a public service.

Social policy

As discussed in Chapter 5, fostering social integration and protecting community is a significant part of sustainable event planning. Social health can be improved by events but as can the cost of public services. Social prescribing is something that the National Health Service (NHS) in the UK has increased. Some of this prescription includes social interaction within community groups and events. A 2024 report entitled 'The impact of social prescribing on health service use and costs: Examples of local evaluations in practice', concluded a study of various NHS schemes around England and suggested that connecting people to groups, services and activities in their communities can reduce pressure on NHS services (O'Connell Francischetto, 2024).

Social policy must be at the heart of political minds if society is to thrive, but it is also about making better financial decisions for public services. As event organizers, we cannot influence this alone, but we can collectively demonstrate positive change.

Property and licensing

There has been discussion for many years about UK music venue closures and the lack of government support. This ranges from little recognition of culture to problematic licensing requirements. Notably, institutional locations in the live event industry such as small to medium music venues are affected most by this. Again, where not seen as a public service, local residents are often (and sometimes quite rightly) prioritised over commercial property. This, however, comes at the detriment of licensed premises and the vital chain that these provide.

REAL-WORLD EXAMPLE Small venues

In 2023, Music Venue Properties (MVP), a charitable community benefit society created by the Music Venue Trust launched the 'Own Our Venues' project – an initiative to secure the future of iconically recognized grassroots music venues across the UK through community ownership. The initiative's main objective is to remove grassroots music venues from what they call 'vulnerable commercial leases,' The initiative places the venue into community ownership in the hope that this will provide long-term stability to the venue.

The Music Venue Trust's sole purpose is to protect the cultural value that venues of this nature bring to the community as well as a focus on continuing to produce local artistic talent to keep this sector of the industry (and this part of the live music pyramid) sustainable in the future. The venue lease gives the venue a greater level of security such as fairer sustainable rents as well as a greater package of support from the MVP, including ongoing maintenance and sharing good practice – aspects a commercial lease would be unlikely to do.

Tourism

Tourism is a well-researched yet ever-changing area. Getz (2024) suggests that many governments at all levels develop policies and strategies regarding the events sector – often with tourism as the main priority, but increasingly adding social, cultural and environmental goals as well. Destination branding and regional development by local and national governments is required to provide long-lasting economic, social and cultural change to a destination. Event tourism can lead to longer lasting support, but comes with variables and challenges.

The European Union

The UK left the European Union in 2019, and post-Brexit; the industry sees a number of hurdles that have arisen from it. The subject matter is vast, complicated and this chapter does not aim to tackle it. However, it is important to touch upon this subject as part of the core discussion on risks to event organizers and considerations as part of risk assessing when it comes to the political climate. Planning post-Brexit has been painful for some organizers. Generally, it has been agreed that Brexit has made travel for artist and performers more difficult, and often more costly. Warner and Kassim (2025) reported that 87 per cent of musicians report financial losses, with average EU tour earnings down 45 per cent. Slowly, political decisions seem to be easing some of these problems, but there is still little sign of any return to an easier pre-Brexit process on this matter.

Climate change

As seen in a real-world example in Chapter 5, Conference of the Parties (COP) brings together world leaders and industry figures to discuss, showcase and work towards global climate change targets. The important targets to reduce global temperatures are missed regularly, something that is considered by many as a failure to combat human-made global climate change and the fight to reverse the impact that fossil fuels have had. Chapter 5 also discusses the role that local councils play on sustainable climate goals for an event. Specific targets are yet to be imposed on event organizers, but undoubtedly will be in the future. This decision is perhaps positive if real change is to take place, however there is still work to be done on supporting event organizers in public and private sectors to ensure events reduce carbon emissions. Infrastructure is a core consideration here and much of this textbook outlines the importance of planning to accommodate this. However, a government-led target is a risk to the event nonetheless and should be treated as one. Just as an event may not generate enough income from ticket sales to proceed or be awarded a licence due to safety risks in its EMP, a local carbon reduction target is perhaps also not off the table.

In summary:

- Gaps in government support or funding can create uncertainty and easily dilute the significance of the industry.
- Politically focused risks should be considered in an event's risk assessment.

Long-term planning and returning customers

Of course, much that has been discussed in this chapter is concerned with the long-term planning of an event. These are all valid aspects to consider as event organizers must ensure that an event is sustainable. Event organizers should consider the best way that they can plan the long-term benefits of an event, as it will increase the likelihood that the event's life cycle is positive and it remains in place in the future. This can bring several benefits, often referred to within discussion of sporting mega-events such as the Olympics, where event leveraging and wider impacts are measured more broadly. Tourism Area Life Cycle (TALC) framework (Butler, 1980) is applied to events and festivals by Holmes and Ali-Knight (2017) where seven event trajectories are outlined to describe an event beyond the TALC framework:

1. Accelerated development: the event goes beyond the continued growth phase and develops very quickly.
2. Continued growth: the event continues to grow steadily, building further support, resources and consistently innovating to maintain and build its audience.
3. Survival: the event neither increases nor declines.
4. Redevelopment: the event is substantially changed but still operating successfully (e.g. change of location).
5. Hiatus: the event experiences a temporary major problem that halts further development (e.g. it misses a year).
6. Decline: the event reduces in attendance, income or support services.
7. Cancellation: the event is cancelled for various reasons.

Event growth, rather than decline and cancellation as discussed earlier in this chapter, should of course be the core aim. These seven event trajectories may help event organizers achieve this and consider their event in terms of 'future planning'. Not all future planning will be positive though, and so allowing time to carry out this work can help manage those negative aspects. There is also a clear need to address the impacts of risk on returning customers. The Notting Hill Carnival discussed earlier in this chapter is a good example of this. Those who feel that the carnival is a significant part of their lives may ignore any risk to safety. Those who visit the event and suffer the negative impacts of large crowds may not return.

It could be suggested that the hiatus, decline and cancellation stages of those seven trajectories outlined by Holmes and Ali-Knight (2017) are the elements in which attendees are turned off to the idea of returning to an event. The circumstances in which this happens may define the outcome, as in the case of The Secret Garden Party festival which received solidarity in decline followed by its cancellation. However, when an event is cancelled due to other reasons, then we can still see a negative response. Whether this remains a long-term problem for the event can depend on varying factors relating to marketing, communication and of course branding.

Marketing

The Co-Op Live Arena in Manchester, UK became the newest and largest arena to be built in the UK, opening in 2024. It was built as part of the wider Manchester City FC group's site development and now has the largest arena capacity in the UK, built with live entertainment in mind compared to its predecessors (which were mostly built in the late 20th century when basketball was becoming a popular spectator sport). However, the Co-Op Live Arena went through a series of bad public relations ahead of opening, resulting in failed opening dates due to safety concerns. Some were errors in planning, and some just installation delays which would be expected in a venue of this size. However, despite its size and significance as a venue, the cancelled events were communicated late, not only affecting customers' views but also impacting the marketing of this new venue. To some extent, this is comparable to the Boardmasters Festival discussed earlier in this chapter; these impacts are forgotten by most people after a few years of high-profile shows and successful experiences. However, given the pyramid of live music venues and the impact on grassroots venues as discussed earlier in this chapter, it offers constructive questions on how event organizers can manage the longer-term impacts on attendees due to event cancellations.

The following should be considered when it comes to managing the impact of cancellation on customers:

1 Be personable as possible in your communication.
2 Whether you created the incident or not, apply empathy rather than simply expressing sympathy with attendees.
3 Remember that building back up locally is an important sustainable goal.
4 Do not promise what you cannot achieve.
5 Build into your EMP what you have learnt.

In summary:

- Holmes and Ali-Knight's (2017) seven trajectories can be considered when addressing the longevity of an event.
- When communicating with attendees, empathize and look to find ways to reduce the impact of risks becoming greater problems.

ACTIVITY 8.1

1. What does having an accessible event mean to you? List five considerations for event organizers when planning for accessibility at an event.
2. Consider and discuss in small groups:
   a. Three risks that could lead to a cancelled event decision.
   b. How the cancellation could then impact the long-term sustainability of the event.
3. What reasons could there be for an event cancellation, and how can these be met by the event organizers in the pre-planning phase?
4. Write down three areas which you as an event organizer could focus on for protecting an event's longevity (i.e. ensuring the event will be repeated).
5. Some venues in the UK have been recognized as providing outstanding experiences to families with children, including Tapton Hall in Sheffield, the Royal Welsh College of Music and Drama and Bournemouth International Centre (Delaney, 2023). Research three other venues hosting events for families with children that you consider to be outstanding. Justify your choice.

CHECKLIST

A list of questions and considerations that support this chapter's discussion of risk in relation to an event's sustainable goals.

- Does your event risk assessment consider groups of people who may be identified as a higher risk?
- Does your event risk assessment include longevity measures (e.g. measures that reduce the risk that the event may not take place again in the future)?
- Have you held conversations regarding the financial stability of the event taking place with your internal stakeholders in the pre-event phase? Do you understand concerns or risks from stakeholders (such as freelance staff)?
- Does your event risk assessment consider and address how to reduce the impact of customers not returning, following an event cancellation?
- Have you considered the cultural importance of your event in the pre-phase event planning?

Summary

This chapter considered the important link between risk and sustainable event planning. Undoubtedly there are challenges in any event plan, which is why the subject of risk is justifiably the most important part. However, understanding attendees and visitors, as well as considerations of how to accommodate these groups should be at the heart of sustainable planning. As discussed throughout this textbook, sustainable goals for an event can only be achieved by working with people. Staff resources (from any type of contract) are a considerable part of this as they undoubtedly help reduce the risks of an event, while also building relationships to ensure future collaboration.

The chapter also highlighted the often-fragile process of event planning, especially for large-scale events that take a considerable amount of time and money to prepare with no guarantee of generating enough income. The chapter identified rising costs for UK event organizers, post-pandemic changes and Brexit as all contributing to challenges which become risks for event organizers.

This chapter has identified making the event safe an important aspect of sustainability. Many risks in event planning are seen as tangible, but it is often the non-tangible risks which should be addressed and reduced to make an event more sustainable. Some risks are out of our control as event organizers; where the source is difficult to influence or change, we have seen how some events use collaboration and circular approaches to reduce such risks.

While demand generally has increased for many public events, the challenges for attendees have also increased. Cost of living and post-pandemic health all are concerns for attendees. It is therefore fundamental to the process of sustainable event planning that we consider this as part of the pre-event phase as a long-lasting approach to an event and factor this into risk assessments.

Further reading

Rutherford Silvers, J and O'Toole, W (2020) *Risk Management for Events*, Routledge, Abingdon

Séraphin, H (ed) (2022) *Children in Sustainable and Responsible Tourism*, Emerald Publishing Limited, Leeds

References

Anderson, D (2021) *The New Normal Work Life Balance*, eBookit.com.

Becker, D (2006) *The Essential Legal Guide to Events. A practical handbook for event professionals and their advisors*, Dynamic Publishing, Tasmania

Bowdin, G A J, Allen, J, Harris, R, McDonnell, I and O'Toole, W (2024) *Events Management*, Routledge, Abingdon

Butler R W (1980) The concept of a tourist area cycle of evolution and implications for management of resources, *The Canadian Geographer*, onlinelibrary.wiley.com/doi/10.1111/j.1541-0064.1980.tb00970.x

Clift, C (2024) LIVE survey reveals event freelancer concerns, Standout Magazine, 22 May, www.standoutmagazine.co.uk/live-survey-reveals-event-freelancer-concerns/

Delaney, E (2023) Venue considerations when planning child centric events. In: Séraphin, H (ed) *Events Management for the Infant and Youth Market*, Emerald Publishing Limited, Leeds

Downes, H (2024) Half of disabled consumers face access issues at live events. *Which?* Online report. www.which.co.uk/news/article/half-of-disabled-consumers-face-access-issues-at-live-events-aaXh24m218Eq

Dowson, R and Bassett, D (2018) *Event Planning and Management. Principles, planning and practice*, Kogan Page, London

Drury, J. (2018) The role of social identity processes in mass emergency behaviour: An integrative review, *European Review of Social Psychology*, 29 (1), 38–81

Drury, J, Carter, H, Cocking, C, Ntontis, E, Tekin Guven, S and Amlôt, R (2019) Facilitating collective psychosocial resilience in the public in emergencies: Twelve recommendations based on the social identity approach, *Frontiers in Public Health*, 7, 1–21

Edger, C and Oddy, R E (2018) *Events Management: 87 key models for event, venue and experience (EVE) managers*, Libri Publishing, Faringdon

Finkel, R, Sharp, B and Sweeney, M (eds) (2018) *Accessibility, Inclusion and Diversity in Critical Event Studies*, Routledge, Abingdon

Fletcher, T and Hylton, K (2018) Race, ethnicity and whiteness in the governance of the events industry, *Journal of Policy Research in Tourism, Leisure and Events*, 10 (2), 164–79

Fruin, J (1984) Crowd dynamics and auditorium management. In: *Auditorium News*, International Association of Auditorium Managers, www.gkstill.com/Support/crowd-flow/fruin/Fruin3.html

Fruin J (1993) The causes and prevention of crowd disasters. In: *Engineering for Crowd Safety*, R A Smith and J F Dickie(Eds), Elsevier Science Publishers, Amsterdam

Getz, D (2024) *Event Studies: Theory, research and policy for planned events*, Routledge, Abingdon

Great Potential Consultancy (2024) UK Events Report 2024, ukevents.org.uk/research-and-publications/research/bvep-research/uk-events-report-2024-full-version

Grew, T (2025) Met police fear 'mass casualty event' at carnival, BBC News, 22 April, www.bbc.co.uk/news/articles/clyqd79ljv9o

Hancox, D (2025) 'Poor management leads to fatal crushes': how Glastonbury and others are dealing with big crowds, *The Guardian*, 25 June, www.theguardian.com/music/2025/jun/25/glastonbury-festivals-crowd-management-disaster-astroworld-emily-eavis

Hanley, J (2024) ABBA Voyage hands huge boost to UK economy, *IQ Magazine*, 9 December, www.iqmagazine.com/2024/12/abba-voyage-generates-huge-boost-to-uk-economy/

Holmes, K and Ali-Knight, J (2017) The event and festival life cycle – developing a new model for a new context, *International Journal of Contemporary Hospitality Management*, 29 (3), 986–1004.

Jeynes, J (2002) *Risk Management: 10 principles*, Butterworth Heinemann, Oxford

Kindred R and Bates, G W (2023) The influence of the COVID-19 pandemic on social anxiety: A systematic review, *International Journal of Environmental Research and Public Health*, 20 (3), 2362, pmc.ncbi.nlm.nih.gov/articles/PMC9915904/

Knapton, A (2023) Sport Events and Children: Rees Leisure management approach. In: Séraphin, H (ed) *Events Management for the Infant and Youth Market*, Emerald Publishing Limited, Leeds

Lainston House (2025) www.exclusive.co.uk/lainston-house/

Live Recruitment Blog (2024) Covid-19 and the impact on AV candidates in the Events Industry. www.live-recruitment.co.uk/blog/2024/08/covid-19-and-the-impact-on-av-candidates-in-the-events-industry?source=bing.com

London Assembly (2025) Review Notting Hill Carnival crowd numbers before 'mass casualty event' occurs, 22 April, www.london.gov.uk/who-we-are/what-london-assembly-does/london-assembly-press-releases/review-notting-hill-carnival-crowd-numbers-mass-casualty-event-occurs#:~:text=Notting%20Hill%20Carnival%20is%20an,two%20million%20visitors%20each%20year.&text=This%20volume%20of%20people%20also,stewards%20required%20across%20the%20Carnival

Lytras, M and Visvizi, D (2020) *Sustainable Smart Cities and Smart Villages Research: Rethinking security, safety, well-being and happiness*, Multidisciplinary Digital Publishing Institute (MDPI), Basel

MIA (2024) UK events industry generates £61.653 billion annually, demonstrating post-pandemic resilience, UK Events Report 2024, www.mia-uk.org/news/uk-events-report-2024-published-uk-events-industry-generates-61653-billion-annuallydemonstrating-post-pandemic-resilience/278358

O'Connell Francischetto, E (2024) The impact of social prescribing on health service use and costs: Examples of local evaluations in practice. National Academy for Social Prescribing. https://socialprescribingacademy.org.uk/resources/new-report-shows-impact-of-social-prescribing-on-health-service-use-and-costs/

Page, S (2020) *The Routledge Handbook of Events*, Routledge, Abingdon

Parry, A (2020) The event staffing revolution is here!, Event Industry News, 17 September, www.eventindustrynews.com/news/the-event-staffing-revolution-is-here

Powell, C (2023) 7 Steps to the perfect children's event. In: H Séraphin (ed) *Events Management for the Infant and Youth Market*, London: Emerald Publishing

Quinn, B (2005) Arts festivals and the city, *Urban Studies*, 42 (5–6), 927–43

Quinn, B (2013) *Key Concepts in Event Management*, SAGE, London

Rahman, K M A and Zhang, D (2018) Analyzing the level of accessibility of public urban green spaces to different socially vulnerable groups of people, *Sustainability*, 10 (11) 3917

Rutherford Silvers, J and O'Toole, W (2008) *Risk Management for Events*, Routledge, Abingdon

Rutherford Silvers, J and O'Toole, W (2020) *Risk Management for Events*, Routledge, Abingdon

Shone, A and Parry, B (2004) *Successful Event Management. A practical handbook*, Cengage, Boston, MA

Savage, M (2023) Travis Scott breaks silence on Astroworld tragedy, BBC News, 16 November, www.bbc.co.uk/news/articles/cd1pd66y9k6o

Statista (2025) Number of self-employed workers in the United Kingdom from 1st quarter 2000 to 1st quarter 2025, www.statista.com/statistics/318234/united-kingdom-self-employed/#:~:text=As%20of%20April%202025%2C%20there%20were%20around%204.4,over%20five%20million%20at%20the%20start%20of%202020

Upwork Press release (2023) Upwork study finds 64 million Americans freelanced in 2023, adding $1.27 trillion to U.S. economy, www.upwork.com/press/releases/upwork-study-finds-64-million-americans-freelanced-in-2023-adding-1-27-trillion-to-u-s-economy

Warner, K. Kassim, H (2025) How UK creative industries are navigating Brexit alone. https://ukandeu.ac.uk/how-uk-creative-industries-are-navigating-brexit-alone/

09 | What is needed to run the sustainable event?

> **LEARNING OUTCOMES**
>
> By the end of Chapter 9, you should be able to:
>
> - understand the concept of sustainable procurement
> - apply a range of questions about sustainability to event suppliers
> - recognize the contribution of different event suppliers to an event's success
> - appreciate the role that event staff and suppliers have in achieving event sustainability.

Introduction

As the lifecycle of an event transitions from the design phase into event production and delivery, the event manager will need to procure various products and services to bring the event to life. This will involve securing suppliers and making many decisions about purchasing or hiring various items. This chapter will explore the management of a sustainable event inventory, or the list of all the resources, equipment, materials and services needed or used for planning, organizing and executing an event. An event inventory will typically include both physical assets (like decorations, furniture and AV equipment) and intangible resources (such as contracted services and permits). The inventory helps to ensure that everything required for a smooth event is identified, sourced and managed effectively.

Historically, the goal of procurement has been to get the best possible value in terms of cost and quality; however, it is now extremely important that sustainability is a key feature of the procurement process. There is an increasing requirement for event organizers to use resources that are eco-friendly, but there is also mounting pressure to make events cost effective (particularly when they are financed with public money). This chapter will focus on how sustainability can be at the core of the procurement of inventory items and services and how emerging technologies in events management are increasingly relevant in this process.

Given the temporary nature of events, it can be particularly challenging to deliver events that are sustainable. As such, this chapter provides an overview of key elements of typical events that may need the support of a supplier, including event registration or ticketing, technical production, catering, furniture, décor and props, speakers, artists and performers and event staff. The chapter includes a comprehensive set of questions that can be used and adapted into conversations with potential suppliers to determine their sustainability credentials and several case studies are presented to showcase examples of best practice from suppliers to the events industry.

Sustainable procurement

Procurement is the process of identifying, acquiring and managing the goods and services required by an organization to fulfil its objectives. This can include sourcing items from suppliers, negotiating the terms and conditions of purchase or hire and the administration of supplier relationships. Procurement is a critical business function that supports the operational, strategic and financial goals of an organization. It involves more than just purchasing; it includes the entire lifecycle of a product or service as illustrated in Figure 9.1.

- Procurement starts with needs identification or recognizing the necessity for a product or service to deliver an event.
- This is followed by sourcing a supplier, which can involve identifying potential suppliers and evaluating them based on criteria such as quality, cost and reliability. It may also involve a tender process, which is when suppliers are invited to submit bids for the provision of products or services. This process can ensure transparency, competition and fairness in the selection of suppliers or service providers.
- Negotiating the terms and conditions of either hiring or purchasing a product service then follows, and this may involve the issuing and signing of a contract outlining the agreement (particularly when hiring products or services).
- Careful discussion must be had with suppliers as to when products or services will become available or when the order can be fulfilled (and any delivery instructions) and this may involve the venue to ensure items can be delivered to site.
- Post event, it is important to evaluate each product or service in terms of value for money and quality of what was provided by a supplier.

Figure 9.1 Key stages in the procurement process

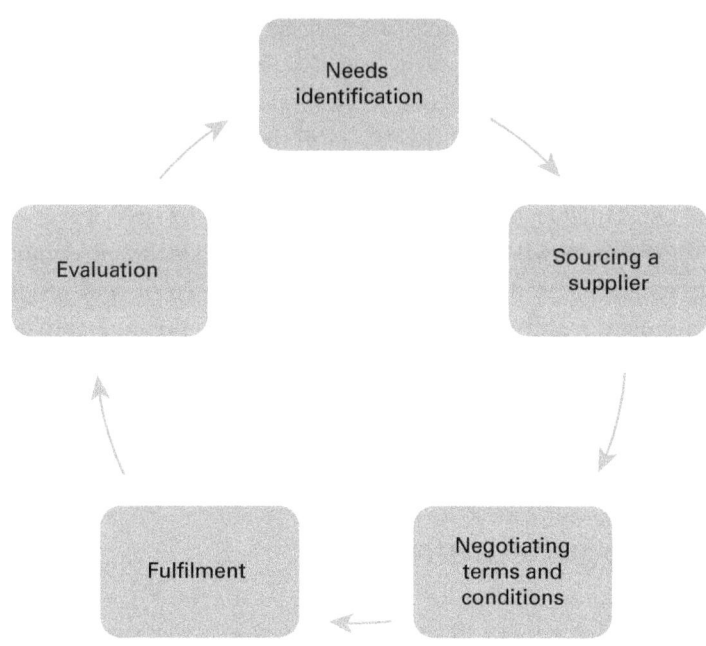

Typically, the goal of procurement is to secure the best possible value in terms of cost, quality and delivery while managing risks and fostering long-term, sustainable supplier relationships (Bowdin et al, 2024). However, given the temporary nature of events, it has become essential that sustainability is at the heart of the procurement process.

Sustainable procurement is the process of acquiring products and services in a way that ensures value for money while generating benefits for the client, guests and the wider community. Sustainable procurement considers the full lifecycle of products and services, from production and use to disposal or reuse, with the goal of minimizing negative impacts and maximizing positive outcomes. Sustainable procurement goes beyond traditional purchasing, which typically focuses on cost, quality and delivery. It integrates environmental, social and economic considerations into all stages of the procurement process (Tinakhat and Viriyachaikul, 2023). This approach involves selecting products and services that reduce pollution, greenhouse gas emissions and waste and that use resources efficiently across their life cycle. Where possible, procurement should ensure economic sustainability by promoting innovation, supporting local businesses and ensuring long-term value for money. It should also support broader goals such as reducing carbon emissions, conserving natural resources, promoting ethical labour practices and encouraging local economic development.

09 | What is needed to run the sustainable event?

It is often assumed that environmentally friendly or sustainable products and services will be more expensive or inferior in quality than alternatives. However, allowing time to research purchases can lead to finding products and companies that will meet the needs of an event through sustainable options. Table 9.1 provides a checklist of questions that can be put to suppliers of different types of event products and services.

Table 9.1 Checklist of sustainability questions for event suppliers

Materials and sourcing	
Renewable resources	Is the product made from renewable materials (e.g. bamboo, organic cotton, recycled metals)?
Sustainable sourcing	Are the raw materials sourced sustainably (e.g. certified by FSC, Fair Trade)?
Recycled content	Does the product contain recycled materials, and what percentage is recycled content?
Non-toxic materials	Are the materials free from harmful chemicals, such as heavy metals, PVC or phthalates?
Production process	
Energy efficiency	Was the product manufactured using energy-efficient processes or renewable energy sources?
Waste minimization	Does the production process minimize waste and by-products, or does the manufacturer have waste-reduction practices in place?
Factory conditions	Is the product made in factories that adhere to sustainable practices and responsible labour conditions (e.g. low carbon footprint, fair wages, ethical working conditions)?
Design and durability	
Longevity	Is the product designed for durability and longevity, reducing the need for frequent replacements?
Modular or repairable	Can the product be easily repaired, refurbished or upgraded to extend its lifespan?
Upgradable	Is the product designed in a way that allows for parts or features to be upgraded, thus reducing overall waste?
Packaging	
Minimal packaging	Does the product use minimal packaging, avoiding excess plastic, foam or other non-recyclable materials?
Recyclable or compostable packaging	Is the packaging recyclable, compostable, or biodegradable?
Sustainable materials	Are sustainable packaging materials, such as recycled paper, cardboard or plant-based plastics used?

(continued)

Table 9.1 (Continued)

Transport and distribution	
Local production or sourcing	Is the product produced locally or sourced close to where it will be sold, reducing transportation-related emissions?
Efficient transport	Was the product transported using fuel-efficient or low-emission methods (e.g. rail vs. road)?
Carbon offset	Does the company offset carbon emissions associated with the transport or production of the product?
End-of-life considerations	
Recyclability	Can the product be easily recycled at the end of its life?
Biodegradability	Is the product biodegradable, or will it decompose safely in the environment if disposed of improperly?
Take-back or reuse programs	Does the company offer a take-back programme or recycling options for its products at the end of life?
Certifications and labels	
Environmental certifications	Does the product have any environmental certifications (e.g. Fair Trade or Global Organic Textile Standard (GOTS))?
Eco labelling	Does the product carry an eco label that confirms its environmental friendliness, such as the EU Ecolabel, Green Seal, or the Forest Stewardship Council (FSC) certification?
Social impact	
Fair labour practices	Are fair labour practices adhered to during the production of the product (e.g. fair wages, safe working conditions)?
Community impact	Does the company support sustainable community development, such as investing in local economies or ethical sourcing practices?
Carbon footprint	
Carbon emissions	Has the product or its manufacturing process been assessed for carbon emissions, and does it minimize its carbon footprint?
Offset programmes	Does the company invest in carbon offset programmes to neutralize its environmental impact?

Many industries are now choosing, or being led by legislation, to reduce the chemical input to their manufacturing processes. Event managers should therefore look for these reassurances when making purchases, particularly when buying or hiring something that has no suitable eco-alternative. If an item is essential to the event, a reduction in its chemical input may be the only eco-saving to be made. The amount of recycled content in new items is another sign that a manufacturer is taking steps to lower the footprint of its goods and be more sustainable. The concept of lean manufacturing is becoming more evident and businesses may now state that they have a lean manufacturing policy or demonstrate awards that they have won for their approach to minimizing waste. These are also signs to look out for during the procurement process.

Ultimately, one of the main challenges in event procurement is that as events are temporary, may of the items purchased for it become surplus to requirements after the event and cannot easily be stored by the event owner. Thus, when purchasing items over hiring them, it is advisable to choose products that can be easily reused or recycled. The market for second-hand or refurbished pieces of equipment has grown in recent years and charities or local organizations (local to the event site) will often come and pick up used items that still have life left in them. The venue or site owner may be able to advise on this and connect the event manager with suitable local groups or you could work with a company such as Event Cycle (2025), as shown in the real-world example.

Ultimately, as the event organizer, you may have or may decide to create a procurement policy to outline your approach to making responsible purchasing decisions with the aim of reducing the footprint of events on both people and planet. This may include having a traceable supply chain and working with suppliers and contractors that meet sustainability criteria or responsible sourcing guidelines. By aligning procurement activities with sustainability goals, organizations can influence market behaviours, support ethical supply chains and contribute to achieving broader sustainable development objectives.

REAL-WORLD EXAMPLE   Event Cycle asset dissolution

Event Cycle (2025) is an organization set up to help project planners with sustainable solutions that create a lasting social legacy in the process. Ultimately, they want to change mindsets, reduce event waste and encourage a change to a more circular economy. One way that Event Cycle do this is by asset dissolution. Event planners can let Event Cycle know what they've got to donate, where it is and when it needs to be collected. It helps them to know the number of items, type of item, approximate height and weight. Event Cycle can take everything from graphics to giveaways, planks of wood to plants, from furniture to topsoil and nearly everything in between. They will then find homes for these items within their network of organizations and they aim to distribute items donated on a first-come-first-serve basis but with a local-first approach, which means they limit the distance items have to be transported. If the event manager or their client have a specific type of organization in mind for the donation, they will try to accommodate this. They will then send a certificate to show where the donations went and they can also issue a full report detailing how items have gone on a journey from the event to a charitable organization or recycling facility.

In 2023, the Gamescom Exhibition was staged by the agency Walbert Schmitz at the Messe Koln in Cologne, Germany. This event brings the gaming world together and demonstrates new and established games on different mediums. For 2023, it was decided that the event should achieve change through determining repurposing routes for leftover material after the exhibition and to keep sustainability and social impact at the top of everyone's agenda. Event Cycle were appointed to conduct asset dissolution research to identify whether items could be repurposed within the local Cologne area. Event Cycle concluded that local charities would benefit from repurposed graphics, carpet and furniture after the event. In summary they achieved the following:

- 100 per cent of the donations were placed within North Rhine-Westphalia.
- 83 per cent of the donations were placed within approximately an hour's drive from the Messe Koeln.
- Social impact of equivalent to £24,116.00 was donated to charities as part of material donations. This is the approximate cost of a charity purchasing these items new and how that money can now be spent on further projects.

Graphics from the B2C (business to consumer) part of the exhibition:

- 400 m² of graphics saved from landfill
- Carbon saving due to a charity not having to buy an item new: 401.85 kg CO_2e
- Carbon saving due to waste diversion from landfill: 0.89 kg CO_2e
- Donation of approximately £15,116.00 in item value to charity. This is also the equivalent of the approximate cost of a charity purchasing these items new meaning that money can now be spent on other projects.

Carpet from the B2C part of the exhibition:

- 250m² of exhibition carpet saved from landfill.
- Carbon saving due to a charity not having to buy an item new: 502.31 kg CO_2e
- Carbon saving due to waste diversion from landfill: 1.11 kg CO_2e social impacts.
- Donation of approx. £2,500.00 in item value to charity. This is the equivalent of the approximate cost of a charity purchasing these items new and how that money can now be spent on further projects.

Furniture (including a wall plinth used for demonstrations, as well as gamer tables):

- 3 tables and 6 plinths were saved from landfill.
- Carbon saving due to a charity not having to buy an item new: 134.42 kg CO_2e
- Carbon saving due to waste diversion from landfill: 397.85 kg CO_2e social impacts.
- Donation of approximately £6,500.00 in item value to charity. This is also the equivalent of the approximate cost of a charity purchasing these items new and how that money can now be spent on further projects.

Figure 9.2   The Event Cycle team © Event Cycle

Registration and ticketing

Making decisions about sustainable procurement should extend to services and products that will be used in event registration and ticketing. Event registration is a core component of event planning and execution, acting as the gateway between organizers and participants and it often includes the collection of attendee information, preferences and payments. This process by which individuals formally sign up or are enrolled to attend an event may occur online, in person, or through hybrid systems. To avoid the unnecessary printing of tickets or documents, much of this can be done online and event guests can store this information on a smartphone. The real-world example below illustrates how this can be done even for low-budget, small-scale events. For events where in-person registration is essential or when it is important for guests to have visible ID (such as exhibitors and visitors at exhibitions), then sustainable options are now widely available including lanyards made from recycled or lower impact materials such as bamboo.

> **REAL-WORLD EXAMPLE**   Alternatives to paper tickets
>
> There are now many companies offering event planners online event ticketing services. Event registration and ticketing software allows planners to monitor attendance and can provide useful guest information in advance of the event. Ticket Tailor (2025) is one such platform that has been used by over 70,000 planners and offers round-the-clock support. They offer pay-as-you-sell packages or charge an upfront cost and offer 50 per cent discounts to charities.
>
> Another provider is Ticketpass, set up by Rodrigo Bautista, who felt he could create a fairer ticketing solution to one that often profits from high fees, lack of transparency and rip-off practices (Ticketpass, 2025). Ticketpass's mission is to provide an ethical alternative that is fair, friendly and social, that truly makes for great experiences, from planning through to participation (Ticketpass, 2025).
>
> Whova is another company that offer paperless events via their app, which can include event agendas and maps as well as a document-sharing facility to replace paper handouts (Whova, 2025). Using the app for events can save up to 60 per ent of printing costs and can increase attendee engagement tenfold (Whova, 2025).

Working with the venue and their preferred suppliers

As an event manager, it is prudent to work closely with the venue or site owner in the run up to any event. They can usually provide a lot of help, advice and suggestions throughout the project management of the event and are a useful resource. Typically, venues will have an excellent network of local contacts including fairly standard suppliers such as florists and photographers to specialised equipment or unique performers. They can usually recommend reliable suppliers that they have worked with before and who therefore know the venue well. Using local suppliers will contribute towards keeping transportation of items to a minimum; however if the preferred supplier list does not give any indication of the green credentials of the suppliers, this is something to discuss with the venue (see Chapter 4).

Many venue managers will be able to book suppliers and make arrangements on your behalf. This is sometimes provided in exchange for a small charge or commission but it can be worthwhile as the venue may be able to negotiate good rates with suppliers that they contract on a regular basis. Furthermore, if they are making arrangements for you this service will usually extend to fully liaising with the supplier in the run up to the event, including putting in place all of their venue requirements and arranging the invoice. Alternatively, the venue may be able to suggest suppliers that meet your sustainable procurement policy. However, as Chapter 4 has covered in detail, many venues will only allow event planners to work with preferred suppliers and will provide a list of options to choose from. This is often the case for event catering and event technology provision.

Technology

The technical elements of an event can range from basic items such as staging and microphones to an extensive list of requirements to include dressing rooms, power, lighting and other equipment. Furthermore, as event attendees are likely to own a smart phone event planners may incorporate technology into every aspect of the event to ensure attendees engage with it in a range of ways. The use of cloud technology and an ever-developing range of apps designed for such interaction are making this possible.

Typically, most events will require large screens for projections, changeable lighting, staging and a dedicated AV technician (Nolan, 2018) and as such, it is important to work with a venue or supplier that uses up-to-date equipment that will be the most energy efficient. Most venues will be able to provide the hirer with a detailed list of what is available at the venue, either for free, included in the hire package or at an additional cost. This is usually referred to as a technical specification, which is often abbreviated to tech spec. The most competent and experienced event manager may struggle to fully comprehend a tech spec and if an event is going to involve stage production generally it is advisable to hire the services of a technician to manage this element of the event. However, a basic understanding of sound, lighting, equipment and staging is essential in event planning.

Sound and lighting

The acoustics (i.e. the properties or qualities of a room or building that determine how sound is transmitted in it) may be different in each room of the event venue. They will vary according to the size of the room (including ceiling height), the material of the building and the type and amount of furniture and equipment in the room. The best way to assess the acoustics are in person during a site visit and this will influence what type of activity is best suited to the space and whether or not sound equipment will be required. However, for a large event, sound equipment is usually essential to ensure that all attendees can clearly hear what is going on and proper sound provision will ensure that the event is accessible to all, including attendees or staff with hearing impairments. A system of microphones connected to speakers will ensure that human voices as well as music can be suitably amplified. A distributed system of speakers will usually work in small venues, particularly buildings with poor acoustics (e.g. those with hard reflective surfaces such as glass walls) and this involves dotting the speakers around the edge of the event (Matthews, 2016a). The technical specification may give full details of speakers, microphones and rigging at the venue and many venues will keep a selection of microphones in stock, including lavalier microphones (ones which usually attach to clothing), handheld or roving microphones (which are wireless) and lead or stand microphones (which are wired). The specification may also make reference to the use of, or suggested position of, a sound desk which will be used to control the sound equipment during the event. If the event will feature a band or noise-producing entertainment, it is important to check with the venue if there are any restrictions on noise levels. For example, it is quite common to find that venues located in residential neighbourhoods have noise restrictions in place, particularly for night times.

Lighting is an essential part of the event experience as it contributes to the first and overall impression of the event. Once again, the site visit is the best way to assess the venue's natural daylight and artificial lighting options, including any blackout facilities. There are a number of ways of creating a visual impact including positioning LED uplighters in order to enhance the venue's internal features, colour washes to give impact to the walls, ceilings and stage and gobos, to enliven drab spaces by shining patterns or logos onto them. Using modern equipment will generally ensure that lighting is energy efficient, but this should be checked with the supplier. If the venue has limited equipment available, then you may find that hiring additional lighting equipment will be expensive. However, lighting has the potential to add an extraordinary element to the event and is one of the key ways to create an emotional impact on guests, providing it is managed by a professional lighting designer (Matthews, 2016b).

Equipment and staging

The technical specification will usually give details of the power (electricity) service and distribution set up at the venue, particularly in larger venues. Typically, the power at venues such as hotels and conference centres is distributed via either single-phase or three-phase alternating current (AC) and depending on what is available, the equipment provider will determine if this is sufficient (Matthews, 2016a). Details of available projectors and screens may be listed on the specification and the specification may also include details for rigging, which is usually reinforced and equipped parts of the venue's ceiling, from which items may be hung (or flown). The venue may provide two-way radios (walkie talkies) which enable the users to communicate across the site via a specific radio frequency. These can be particularly useful if your event is spread across a wide area as they facilitate the brief communication of important messages to specific users.

If the rooms in the venue have a purpose-built stage, then the technical specification will usually include details about its dimensions, details of the proscenium arch and apron, rigging points and fly bars. Most stages are flat, but a number of theatres have raked stages to enhance the visual effect of scenery or props on the audience. Information about the availability of backdrops and tabs (stage curtains) will be useful in helping to establish how the stage can be used. For example, some stages are very large and can seem unsuitable to certain events as there is such as lot of room to fill and then to use. But carefully positioned curtains, scenery or props will reduce this space to something that is more manageable and creates a more intimate space and personable ambience, which might suit a sole speaker or performer, for example.

Venues without a fixed stage might have portable staging that will be available to use at events. Portable staging comes in different shapes and sizes, but it can be moved from room to room fairly easily and enables a stage to be set up in a variety of different ways. If the venue has no staging at all, you may wish to consider whether it is appropriate to create one. A stage can be a barrier between performer and audience (which may be desirable) but it also becomes a focal point for the audience and elevates speakers, performers, screens, marketing messages, etc. It is fairly straightforward to hire equipment and staging but Table 9.2 later in this chapter can be used to identify suppliers that meet a sustainable procurement policy.

Catering

For indoor events that are going to be held in a venue, there are three principal ways in which the catering operations are provided. These are when the catering is in house or provided by an appointed caterer, when the venue does not have its own team but provides a list of preferred suppliers, and when the event manager can hire any company to cater the event or provide the catering themselves. For outdoor events, it is usual for the event manager to hire either one or several companies to cater the event or to provide refreshment options for attendees.

If the venue has a catering team based permanently at the building this will either be an in-house department or an appointed company. An in-house department refers to when the venue employs its own catering staff and has a fully equipped kitchen within the building. The catering team may include chefs and waiting staff and be led by a banqueting co-ordinator or a food and beverage manager (often abbreviated to F&B manager). Hotels and other venues whose primary function is to offer hospitality will naturally have an in-house catering team as providing regular food service will be central to their day-to-day operations.

If a venue does not have an in-house team, but needs a regular catering service, they may appoint a caterer. This refers to the process of forming a contractual agreement with an outside catering company. The contract will normally require the catering company to have a certain number of their staff working permanently at the venue to manage the kitchens and meet all of the venue's catering needs. Typically, the catering company will enter into a financial agreement with the venue in order to take sole control of the catering provision at the venue. The agreement may include an annual payment to the venue and an additional payment of a percentage of their annual takings at the venue. This payment is in exchange for exclusive rights to provide catering at the venue. As such, event managers and other users of the venue, will be obliged to work with the venue's appointed caterer or in house team.

There are certain benefits and drawbacks to working with in-house or appointed caterers. The benefits are that these teams or organizations will have the same or aligned values with the venue. Thus, a venue that places sustainability at the heart of its operations will ensure that this extends to the catering provision. Additionally, these catering staff will be very familiar with the venue and experienced in terms of what works particularly well. They are likely to have strong relationships with local suppliers. This commitment to corporate social responsibility and sustainability is evident through supporting local businesses to provide quality and authentic local produce and keeping food transport costs at a minimum. However, the obvious drawback of this type of catering provision is that it can lead to suppliers having high prices and an unwillingness to compromise on menus or prices. It is important to remember that if the caterer has the right to provide all of the food and drink at the event this will extend to alcohol, too.

Venues that do not have their own in-house or appointed caterer will normally provide event managers with a list of preferred catering suppliers that they are content to allow into their on-site kitchens or to bring in equipment in order to provide a catering service. Usually there will be several companies listed as preferred suppliers, giving the venue hirer some choice. Often, these will be fairly local to the venue and this will help to reduce food transportation costs. Occasionally the venue will allow the event manager free choice of caterer. This means that a planner can hire the caterer of their choice to provide all of the meals and refreshments at the event. Obviously this gives the greatest choice and scope to provide exactly what food and drink is required and at the best possible price. It also gives planners scope to ensure that the catering supplier has demonstrative sustainability protocols and uses appropriate goods, such as organic and fairtrade products and those that conform to high animal welfare standards. However, it can be high risk and prove to be more costly and less sustainable to bring caterers into a venue or onto a site. Venues that allow free choice often do so because they have limited kitchen space or equipment, which would mean that the caterer would be obliged to bring cooking and refrigeration equipment into the building as well as cutlery, crockery and everything else needed for a professional catering service. It is unsurprising that Bowdin et al (2024) confirm that the catering operation at the venue can frequently determine why you might choose one venue over another.

As catering is usually a significant element of an event, it is worth taking time to choose a venue and/or supplier to meet the specific requirements of each event. The discussions that take place with a caterer should include discussing the provision of food, drink (including alcohol) as well as items that may be required such as tablecloths and linen, table decorations, menu cards and a displayed seating plan. This may be provided by the venue or the caterer, or hired through them or through an additional supplier. Once again, the checklist in Figure 9.2 can help to steer conversations with these suppliers to determine their sustainability credentials. Of course, for certain events, such as outdoor festivals, it may be up to the event manager to provide catering or to ensure a range of refreshment concessions are available to guests. Having full control of the event catering will mean being able to source and contract the most suitable suppliers and therefore being able to choose those suppliers that place sustainability at the heart of their operations and values.

Food waste

Food wastage refers to food that is grown, processed and intended for human consumption but is not eaten. It can be the most significant negative impact of an event and represents a significant sustainability challenge, contributing to environmental degradation, economic inefficiency and ethical concerns. Large gatherings such as conferences, weddings and festivals often involve over-catering and poor waste management, leading to substantial quantities of edible food being discarded. According to WRAP (2021), food service and hospitality sectors in the UK produce over 1 million tonnes of food waste annually, with events playing a considerable role in this.

Reducing food waste at events requires a multifaceted approach, beginning with accurate guest forecasting and portion planning. Employing RSVP systems, real-time attendance tracking and historical data can help event planners to match food quantities to actual demand. Menu design also plays a crucial role; offering flexible serving options such as smaller portions or buffet-style services can minimize surplus. Many caterers will have a partnership with a food redistribution organization to ensure that surplus food is diverted from landfill to those in need and this may be another important question to ask suppliers during the procurement process. Additionally, some venues conduct composting on site (see Chapter 4), thus providing a more sustainable disposal option for unavoidable waste.

Additional furniture and props

Furniture and props play a crucial role in the design, functionality and atmosphere of events. They are functional assets that support the event's goals, influence guest interaction and can be used to convey brand or thematic messages. Furniture and props are integral to event logistics and can contribute significantly to event aesthetics. Their thoughtful selection and placement not only facilitate functionality but also enhance guest experience and event impact. Furniture and props will usually include items such as tables, chairs, signage and decoration as well as functional items such as storage space and coat racks. Props can also extend to items such as goody bags, merchandise, giveaways and prizes.

For indoor events, it is important to establish with the venue what they can provide in terms of furniture and equipment as ultimately it will be more sustainable and usually more cost effective to use these items than to hire them. It is also important to assess any rules the venue or landowner has about the use of decorations and wall or floor coverings. Some venues may have items of furniture that cannot be removed as well as architectural features, such as fireplaces, arches and columns, which must be worked around or incorporated into the design of the event. As Chapter 4 has highlighted, many historical or unique venues will provide quite a significant backdrop to an event through their existing features. Conversely, transforming an empty venue, such as an exhibition hall, into a meaningful and enticing event space could be more appropriate for some events but this will mean procuring a lot of items such as carpeting, lighting, screening and a significant number of props and decoration. Therefore, the selection of furniture and props can be a considerable element of event delivery and should align with the event type, venue constraints, audience profile and sustainability considerations. As such it may be prudent to work with a supplier of certain goods that places sustainability at the core of its operations.

REAL-WORLD EXAMPLE Event merchandise

It is possible to procure a range of items, or merchandise, for sale at events or to give away freely or as prizes to attendees or event VIPs. Merchandise can include clothing, stationery, drinkware, homeware, tech (e.g. power banks, charging cables), lanyards, bags, keyrings, etc. Merchandise can also be branded with either the name of the event or client. Branded merchandise can be used to increase brand awareness, drive customer loyalty and engagement and create a positive association between the brand and the user. As such, branded merchandise can be an effective part of an event's marketing strategy and procuring merchandise can constitute a major event purchase, particularly if items are going to be given away to all event guests. As a result, careful consideration should be given to what items should be purchased and how they will be used at the event. There are now many suppliers of branded merchandise that focus on creating bespoke but environmentally friendly products such as these three examples:

- Eco Branded is a supplier of ethically-sourced promotional products such as drinkware, bags and stationery. They suggest that branded products can enhance customer loyalty but they are also a way to show clients and attendees that the event organizers care about the planet. Their products include pens made from plastic bottles, pencils made from CD cases and fairtrade, organic cotton materials (Eco Branded, 2025).

- Totally Branded is a company that also offers a range of merchandise that can be branded, including reusable shopping bags, bamboo utensils and notebooks made from recycled materials. The company strives to produce merchandise made from recycled, biodegradable constituents so that clients can use products to raise awareness and demonstrate their leadership in eco-friendliness (Totally Branded, 2025).

- Fairware is a full-service promotional merchandise company that specializes in ethically sourced, sustainable promotional products. The company advocates for changing the way business is done and how supply chains are managed and they prioritize responsible sourcing, community impact, advocacy and environmental responsibility. Fairware believes that sustainability is more than having a few 'green products' in a merchandise assortment; it is about using merchandise to change behaviour, promote ethical manufacturing practices and amplify a cause or values as well as a specific brand (Fairware, 2025).

Speakers, artists and performers

Central to delivering memorable experiences for attendees is often the inclusion of speakers who deliver knowledge, insights or persuasive messages, and performers who entertain, evoke emotion and enhance the atmosphere of an event. Their roles are critical in achieving both the functional and emotional goals of an event. In conferences, seminars and educational events, keynote speakers and subject-matter experts serve as the primary vehicles for knowledge dissemination. Their credibility and authority can enhance audience trust and reinforce the legitimacy of the event. In corporate events, speakers often serve a motivational or inspirational function and influential speakers can boost morale, change perceptions or mobilize action, depending on an event's purpose. Speakers will often need to align with or reflect the values and objectives of the client or host organization and will contribute towards the event and organization's brand identity (Séraphin and Nolan, 2019).

Artists and performers, such as musicians, dancers, comedians or theatrical acts will contribute significantly to the atmosphere and enjoyment of events. Their role is often to emotionally engage the audience, creating lasting memories and positive associations (Nolan, 2018). Interactive performers can also increase audience participation, contributing to a more dynamic and inclusive event experience. Furthermore, at certain events, such as religious ceremonies or cultural festivals, performances often serve as ceremonial functions and are culturally significant or symbolically meaningful (Daniels and Wosicki, 2021). For some events it may be desirable or essential to secure high-profile speakers or well-known performers in order to draw in ticket sales and attract media interest, and in most events, speakers and performers can help structure the event timeline and theme. Much consideration should therefore be given to selecting speakers, artists and performers that are appropriate to each individual event. When selecting and liaising with potential speakers, artists and performers, sustainability should feature in associated discussions to ensure that, as with other suppliers, their practices and values align with the event. In particular this may be their use of recyclable or compostable materials and how they measure and offset their carbon footprint.

Supplier requirements

It is important to provide contracted suppliers with information about the event and certain instructions. This helps to ensure you receive a seamless and timely service from them and can meet their requirements of you and of the venue. Table 9.2 provides a checklist of some questions to ask suppliers and the instructions to give to them.

When contracting performers and entertainers, they will normally provide the person who has booked them with a rider. This is a type of contract or an addition to a contract which details all of the requirements of the artist. This can include their

Table 9.2 Checklist of questions and instructions for suppliers

Questions for suppliers	• What are your access requirements e.g. an unloading area • How long does it take you to set up? • How much space do you need to set up?
Instructions for suppliers	• The address and postcode of the venue and site map • Confirmation of their expected arrival time and what they should do on arrival (call, stay in car park) or who will greet them • Vehicle/event pass to access the site during set-up/break down • Confirmation of access times to get in/break down • Details of when they need to be set up by • Details of anything you have agreed to provide for them • Details of what you expect them to do when they are not performing, etc. • Details of break down requirements

staging and AV needs as well as what they expect in terms of facilities at the destination and the venue such as accommodation, dressing rooms and refreshments. Therefore, it is important to discuss the rider with the venue to ascertain whether or not the venue can provide the requisite items and services and if so at what cost. Many high-profile celebrities have been derided for their lavish and unreasonable rider demands and indeed a number of artists' green room requirements can be ridiculous (Matthews, 2016b) so it is important to check this document carefully against any sustainability claims.

Staffing

A final but important consideration in event planning and delivery is how the event will be staffed. Event stewards, marshals or staff will have operational responsibility for a range of areas from the logistical coordination of the event to guest services, technical operations and emergency response. Effective staffing contributes directly to audience satisfaction, safety and overall event quality and is therefore another element of event delivery that must be carefully planned. The venue may provide some event staff, but it may be up to the event manager to recruit, train and manage a number of temporary event staff to fulfil various roles including:

- front of house staff: to greet and register guests, provide directions and answer questions, manage guest flow and control access points, distribute event literature
- production staff: to set up and operate audiovisual equipment, stage management, rigging, artist liaison
- marshals: to monitor entrances and exits, conduct bag searches or screenings, manage crowd control, assist with emergencies.

Given the key role that each member of an event team will play in the successful delivery of an event, it is important to recruit suitable people into these roles and to invest time in training staff. As part of staff training, the sustainability values, goals and processes associated with the event should be discussed. This may include taking time to explain why event sustainability is important and to provide staff with clear, actionable guidance that connects their role and responsibilities to the broader environmental, social and economic goals of the event. Ultimately, event staff are likely to come into contact with guests much more than the event manager will, so it is important that staff understand the importance of event sustainability, act responsibly at the event and promote or encourage similar behaviour in event guests. Ultimately it is important to reinforce to event staff that sustainability is a team effort and staff are ambassadors of the event's values. By modelling sustainable behaviour themselves, staff will not only reduce environmental harm but also help inspire attendees to do the same. A checklist of suggestions for key messages to include in staff training is shown below.

CHECKLIST FOR STAFF TRAINING

Why sustainability matters at events and how everyone contributes

- Explain that events generate waste, consume energy and have a social and environmental footprint.
- Emphasize that reducing this impact is part of being a responsible, modern organization.
- Highlight that sustainability improves public perception, complies with regulations and can reduce costs.
- Every staff member, regardless of role, contributes to sustainability.
- Actions taken by staff, such as waste sorting, reducing energy use and communicating with attendees, can make a big difference.

Waste management

- Identify the types of bins (e.g. recycling, compost, landfill) on site.
- Guide guests on proper waste disposal.
- Report any overflowing bins or contamination.

Use of resources

- Turn off lights, AV equipment and taps when not in use and encourage guests to do the same.
- Limit the printing of materials.

Sustainable transportation

- Encourage guests to use public transport, carpooling, biking, or shuttle services (at least for their return journey).
- Know where bicycle parking or local transport stops are located.

Catering and food waste

- Monitor portions.
- Encourage guests to reuse (e.g. cups), recycle (e.g. packaging) and compost (leftovers) where possible.

ACTIVITY 9.1

Choose one of the world's most unusual and free festivals from the following list and undertake research to understand the concept of the festival before answering the questions below.

- Las Bolas de Fuego, El Salvador
- Busójárás, Mohács, Hungary
- Saidai-ji Eyo Hadaka Matsuri, Japan
- Naki Sumo, Japan
- World Toe Wrestling Championship, Ashbourne
- Día de los Muertos, Mexico
- Cheese-Rolling Festival, England
- Battle of the Oranges, Ivrea
- Air Guitar World Championship, Oulu
- International Hair Freezing Contest, Canada
- Lopburi Monkey Banquet, Thailand
- Cheung Chau Bun Festival, Hong Kong

Adapted from Headout (2023)

1. What types of suppliers will be required to support the delivery of the festival?
2. What are some of the challenges of delivering the festival in a responsible and sustainable way?
3. How could the festival be used to encourage guests to become more sustainable?
4. Based on your answers to questions 1–3, create ideas for new elements of the festival that could be delivered in a more sustainable way.
5. Identify suppliers local to the area where the festival is normally held and using some of the questions in Table 9.1, undertake an initial assessment of each supplier's commitment to sustainability.

Summary

Events will usually require the support of several suppliers that will be contracted to supply specific products or services at events. In order to deliver a truly responsible and sustainable event, these suppliers must be carefully assessed to determine their green credentials. Ideally, all event suppliers will have similar values and goals as the event owner or client and will ensure that their practices and policies are built around sustainable priorities. Investing time in choosing and working with aligned suppliers is an important part of events management and ultimately will contribute towards the success of an event. Suppliers and event staff have a crucial role to play in demonstrating sustainable practices and encouraging others to behave in a similarly responsible way. This can include elements of the event such as how it is ticketed, what technology is used at the event, how the event is catered and how food waste is kept to a minimum. Decisions around what props, furniture, décor and merchandise to use at an event can also have a significant impact on the events sustainability and ultimately event speakers, artists, performers and staff will help to convey the importance of event sustainability.

Further reading and viewing

For further information on sustainable procurement:

Welcome to the new self assessment tool at ISO20400.org with Shaun McCarthy, youtube/v0oQKg6dTKg

For further tips on working with sustainable event suppliers:

Sendino, M (2025) Key criteria for choosing eco-conscious event suppliers, Eventscase, 17 June, eventscase.com/blog/sustainability-at-events-main-criteria

References

Bowdin, G A J, Allen, J, Harris, R, McDonnell, I and O'Toole, W (2024) *Events Management*, Routledge, Abingdon
Daniels, M and Wosicki, C (2021) *Wedding Planning and Management: Consultancy for diverse clients*, Routledge, Abingdon
Eco Branded (2025) ecobranded.co.uk
Event Cycle (2025) www.eventcycle.org
Fairware (2025) Founding Canadian B Corp, https://fairware.com
Headout (2023) 20 Most Unusual and Unique Festivals in the World, www.headout.com/blog/unusual-festivals-in-the-world
Matthews, D (2016a) *Special Event Production: The process*, Routledge, Abingdon
Matthews, D (2016b) *Special Event Production: The resources*, Routledge, Abingdon
Nolan, E (2018) *Working with Venues on Events*, Routledge, Abingdon
Séraphin, H and Nolan, E (2019) (eds) *Green Events and Green Tourism: An international guide to good practice*, Routledge, Abingdon

Ticketpass (2025) Sell tickets the ethical way, ticketpass.org/
Ticket Tailor (2025) The world's most loved ticketing platform, www.tickettailor.com
Tinakhat, P and Viriyachaikul, V (2023) The role of collaboration and partnerships in achieving sustainability goals in event management, *Interdisciplinary Journal of Buriram Rajabhat University*, so02.tci-thaijo.org/index.php/journalfms-thaijo/article/view/263958
Totally Branded (2025) Eco Friendly Sustainable Merchandise, totallybranded.co.uk/collections/eco-friendly?srsltid=AfmBOoppeYrAAQRccxkulj726ur4BYvflrvwyYx9icDF-k5OOUka6iGO
Whova (2025) Award-winning mobile event app, whova.com/whova-event-app/
WRAP (2021) Food surplus and waste in the UK – Key facts, wrap.org.uk

10 | Digital marketing: the way forward for sustainable events

LEARNING OUTCOMES

By the end of this chapter, you will be able to:

- explain the evolving role of marketing in events management within the 21st century, particularly highlighting the impact of digital technologies and the increasing importance of sustainability
- analyse how digital marketing can be strategically leveraged to promote and enhance the sustainability initiatives of events
- identify and differentiate the expectations of various audience demographics, including Millennials, Generation Z, Generation X and Baby Boomers, regarding sustainability in events and their digital media consumption habits
- evaluate the application of the PESO (paid, earned, shared, owned) media model in developing integrated and sustainable digital marketing strategies for events
- discuss the significance of understanding target market characteristics, including demographics, psychographics, geography and behaviour, in creating inclusive and impactful digital marketing campaigns for sustainable events across diverse cultural contexts
- assess the future trends and ethical considerations at the intersection of digital marketing and sustainable events management, including the potential for digital tools to drive behavioural change and the importance of addressing the environmental and social impacts of digital technologies themselves.

Introduction

Marketing plays a pivotal role in shaping public perception, expanding audience engagement and amplifying the influence of events. The advent of the 21st century and the proliferation of digital technologies have significantly transformed the field of events management. This increasing digitalization is fundamentally altering the event sector, pushing organizations to re-evaluate and modify their operational processes to maintain their relevance and adaptability (Ophoff et al, 2020, pp. 161–88). Concurrently with this technological transformation, the event industry faces growing societal and regulatory demands to align with the United Nations Sustainable Development Goals (SDGs). This pressure arises from the inherent impact of events on environmental, social and economic systems through factors like resource utilization, waste production and carbon footprint. Annually, a vast array of events takes place globally (Jones 2014), ranging from local gatherings and school events to major international festivals, conferences and sporting and musical events. This continuous cycle of event production raises persistent questions about sustainability. Heightened worries concerning environmental decline, climate change and socio-economic disparities have focused public and institutional attention on the importance of sustainability. For example, in Mauritius, the Festival International Kreol actively incorporates digital narratives to emphasize Creole culture, sustainability and tourism centred around the local community. Through Facebook live sessions and collaborations with local influencers, the festival values cultural preservation. Its 'Zero Plastic' initiative gained traction via WhatsApp networks and podcasts adapted from community radio, contributing to notable reductions in waste during the event (UNWTO, 2021).

In an increasingly connected and ethically conscious world, digital marketing stands at the forefront of this transformation. It offers innovative pathways to reduce environmental impact such as minimizing printed materials through digital communications, encouraging eco-conscious behaviour via targeted messaging and leveraging data analytics to optimize audience engagement while reducing unnecessary resource expenditure. Additionally, digital platforms enable transparent communication about an event's sustainability efforts, thereby fostering trust and accountability among stakeholders. As audiences grow more attuned to issues of inclusivity, climate action and ethical governance, event marketing must reflect these values not just in content but also in delivery methods. As a result, the sustainability of an event is assessed not only by operational measures like carbon offsets or zero-waste initiatives but also by the ethics embedded in its branding, the inclusiveness of its outreach and the integrity of its messaging. Digital marketing allows event managers to adopt a lifecycle approach to sustainability – from pre-event awareness and behaviour change campaigns to real-time digital engagement and post-event impact reporting. Within this evolving landscape, digital marketing has emerged as a transformative tool not just for visibility and reach but also as a mechanism to support and amplify sustainability initiatives in events management (Getz and Page, 2016). Therefore, embracing sustainable digital marketing practices is not only essential for reducing the ecological footprint of events but also for fostering a culture of responsibility, innovation and stakeholder inclusivity. In light of these observations, digital marketing represents a powerful lever for integrating sustainability into the core strategy of events management, transforming events from transient gatherings into long-term drivers of positive change.

Against this backdrop, this chapter explores the intersection of digital marketing and sustainable event planning, focusing specifically on marketing practices that align with sustainability principles, as well as the expectations of increasingly conscious audiences. It aims to provide event marketers, planners and students with practical tools, theoretical insights and global case study examples that demonstrate how to build and implement effective digital marketing strategies for sustainable events. It delves into key models such as PESO (paid, earned, shared, owned), emphasizes the importance of understanding demographic and psychographic data and presents actionable recommendations for managing the dual challenge of reach and responsibility. In doing so, one of the most pressing questions in contemporary events management is addressed: How can we leverage the power of digital marketing to promote events that are not just profitable, but also ethical, inclusive and environmentally responsible?

Digital marketing and sustainable events

While marketing has traditionally been associated with persuasion and promotion, the 21st-century marketer is now tasked with balancing commercial objectives, social impact and ecological stewardship (Font and McCabe, 2017). This delicate balance becomes particularly pronounced in the context of events, which must attract large numbers of attendees – often from demographically diverse populations – while simultaneously minimizing their environmental footprint and ensuring inclusivity. Sustainable event is now the current buzzword for the event industry. The UN Environment Programme defines a sustainable event as one that is 'designed, organized and implemented in a way that minimizes potential negative impacts but also influences change and inspires those involved to live more sustainably' (Jones 2014).

Sustainability in event marketing involves aligning promotional activities with the triple bottom line of sustainability: economic viability, environmental responsibility and social inclusivity. It is about reducing the environmental impact of marketing operations (e.g. through paperless promotions), ensuring that messages and channels are accessible to diverse audience segments and doing all this within a financially sustainable model. Moreover, sustainability in marketing goes beyond the medium – it extends to the message. Promoting an event as sustainable demands authenticity and transparency as audiences today are increasingly savvy and demanding (Gowreesunkar and Dixit, 2017, pp. 55–68). They seek genuine commitments over greenwashed claims. Hence, digital marketing plays a vital role in advancing sustainability within the events sector. The content of digital marketing must reflect the actual practices of the event's operations, logistics and goals. Digital marketing offers alternatives such as email campaigns, social media engagement, content marketing and influencer partnerships, all of which can be more cost-efficient and less resource-intensive. An example is the African Network for Policy, Research and Advocacy for Sustainability (ANPRAS), a well-established not-for-profit organization in Mauritius which spearheads several sustainability initiatives directed towards the achievements of the UN SDGs and the African Union Agenda 2063 (Gowreesunkar and Séraphin, 2020; 2022, pp. 171–88). Several of those activities engage children as these segments of society play pivotal roles as agents of change in the society, a point highlighted in many children studies (Canosa et al, 2020; Norwood et al, 2019; Séraphin and Gowreesunkar, 2020; Maingi and Gowreesunkar, 2022). Students use their creations to popularize the SDGs and to educate and sensitize Mauritians on sustainable and responsible environmental practices. As such, ANPRAS organizes a series of sustainability activities such as sensitization campaigns in schools, painting and poems, road shows and exhibitions in collaboration with primary and secondary school students in Mauritius.

The TrashOut campaign targeted young people as ambassadors and utilized technology and digital platforms to target school children. TrashOut is a technological application, developed by secondary school students with the help of experts from the information technology sector and university students in Mauritius. The objective was to encourage young people to install the application and identify and report illegal waste dumping in their surroundings. In a nutshell, an individual simply needs to take a picture of the dump, indicate its nature and publish it with the attached location on TrashOut. The greatest cost for an individual to make use of TrashOut is a smartphone and internet connection. A server is required to receive and compile all pictures to generate a map marking the trash. By partnering with one of the largest digital network providers in Mauritius, Emtel, ANPRAS was successful in roping in young people in the attainment of this objective. Virtually, thousands of Emtel young users were targeted and every entry was made online on Facebook with the number of likes the determining factor. The winner was the one with most likes and they were rewarded with trophies during the award ceremony usually held in December.

Across Africa, digital innovation in support of sustainability is gaining momentum. Malawi's Lake of Stars Festival is a standout example, using mobile-first ticketing systems, SMS marketing and influencer-led content to minimize environmental impact and extend reach to rural communities with limited internet access. Sustainability messages are woven into the festival's social media presence through campaigns like #GreenStars and local clean-up events, amplifying both engagement and education (Moyo and Mhlanga, 2020). In South Africa, Rocking the Daisies festival has reshaped its brand to prioritize sustainability, employing dynamic digital strategies such as TikTok-based contests, 'travel green' campaigns and augmented reality filters on Instagram. These initiatives turn eco-conscious behaviour into engaging digital experiences, helping to build a loyal community of environmentally-minded participants who continue to advocate for the festival's green values after the event concludes (Gössling and Hall, 2019).

Rocking the Daisies reaffirmed its status as a premier music and lifestyle festival, seamlessly blending entertainment with a strong commitment to sustainability. Beyond its impressive lineup of international and local artists, the festival's digital branding and on-ground initiatives sent powerful signals about environmental responsibility and community engagement. The festival's digital platforms played a pivotal role in promoting sustainability. The Daisies app eliminated the need for printed festival guides, providing attendees with real-time information on schedules, water tap locations and waste stations. By going digital with their guides, the festival not only cut down on paper usage but also educated attendees on how to lessen their environmental footprint while at the event. Furthermore, the organizers established thorough sustainability guidelines, encompassing an eco-procurement policy, a waste management policy, a transportation policy and an overarching green strategy. These weren't merely internal rules; they applied to all vendors, suppliers, performers and sponsors, fostering a shared dedication to sustainability.

Audience expectations and digital media engagement

In an era characterized by increased awareness of environmental issues and widespread digital access, sustainability has become both an ethical necessity and a standard expectation in the market. For the events sector, which typically involves considerable resource use and intricate logistics, it is now crucial to incorporate sustainability into all phases, from initial planning to final promotion. A fundamental aspect of this shift is a deep understanding of the event audience: their identities, their values and their information consumption habits. Segmenting the audience based on demographics and recognizing their changing expectations are not just marketing considerations but vital strategies for integrating sustainability into the overall event experience.

The demographic composition of an audience – age, gender, geographic location, socio-economic status, education and cultural background – profoundly shapes both the content and delivery of marketing messages. Tailoring digital marketing strategies according to these characteristics allows event organizers to resonate more deeply with diverse audience segments and deliver messages in ways that foster engagement and promote sustainable behaviours. Millennials (born 1981–1996) and Generation Z (born 1997–2012), often labelled as 'digital natives,' constitute a significant and growing portion of event attendees. These groups are characterized by their adept use of social media, preference for mobile-first content and strong values around environmental and social issues. Platforms like Instagram, TikTok and YouTube are central to their media consumption habits and they favour visual storytelling, authenticity and interaction over static advertisements. These generations also exhibit what Nielsen (2015) termed 'values-driven consumption'. Their support for a brand or event is frequently influenced by the alignment of its practices with causes they care about, especially sustainability, diversity and ethical labour practices. Therefore, sustainability is not merely a bonus but a baseline expectation. It is a fundamental requirement. Event marketers seeking to attract and keep their interest must employ digital strategies that demonstrate and uphold these values. Examples include advertising carbon offsetting programmes, collaborations with local eco-friendly suppliers, or emphasizing accessible and inclusive practices within their event content.

In contrast, older generations, such as Generation X (born between 1965 and 1980) and Baby Boomers (born between 1946 and 1964), typically prefer platforms like Facebook, LinkedIn or email newsletters. They tend to favour informational content, such as comprehensive event schedules, logistical details and endorsements. While they might not be as responsive to visually-driven marketing or influencer endorsements, they appreciate directness, trustworthiness and practicality – qualities that can be effectively used to showcase an event's sustainability efforts. Recognizing these generational differences enables digital marketing campaigns to be not only more impactful but also more sustainable. Rather than broad campaigns that lead to unproductive engagement and unnecessary consumption of digital resources, strategies informed by demographic understanding ensure more targeted and efficient communication.

Audience expectations for sustainable events

Audience expectations for sustainable practices in events are growing in tandem with broader global awareness of climate change, resource scarcity and social inequality. Attendees now assess events not just on entertainment or educational value but also on the ecological and ethical footprint they leave behind. In fact, research by Freeman et al (2021) underscores that event attendees increasingly regard environmental responsibility as a key aspect of event quality. When these sustainable practices are not only implemented but also communicated effectively through digital marketing, they enhance the event's brand image and foster audience loyalty. The marketing strategy itself is under scrutiny. A growing number of consumers notice and reward events that utilize eco-conscious marketing methods, such as avoiding printed flyers in favour of digital campaigns, using minimalist video formats to reduce energy consumption and promoting sustainable behaviours pre- and post-event through educational social media content.

In this context, digital marketing becomes more than a vehicle for promotion – it becomes a platform for behaviour change and sustainability advocacy. Marketing can influence not just attendance but the mindset and actions of attendees before, during and after the event. For example, targeted email campaigns can provide sustainability tips ahead of the event, interactive apps can guide participants through green practices on-site, and post-event surveys can gather feedback on sustainability perceptions and suggestions for improvement. Additionally, sustainability features such as digital ticketing, locally sourced food, vegetarian/vegan options, reusable utensils, carbon offsetting programmes and recycling stations are often expected. A strong example from France that illustrates the integration of sustainability features such as vegetarian/vegan food options, reusable utensils and the inclusion of farmers' contributions in product narratives, is the *Salon du Chocolat*, an internationally renowned chocolate and cocoa trade show that has increasingly embraced sustainability in its programming and operations. The *Salon du Chocolat*, held annually in Paris, showcases not only chocolate artistry and innovation but also growing awareness around ethical sourcing and sustainability. In recent years, the event has adopted several green practices to meet rising audience expectations:

- Vegetarian/vegan options: recognizing shifting consumer preferences, the *Salon* now includes plant-based and vegan chocolate brands, catering to environmentally conscious visitors. These exhibitors highlight cocoa products made without dairy and often use alternative sweeteners or sustainable ingredients, appealing to both ethical and health-conscious demographics.

- Reusable utensils and packaging: the event encourages exhibitors to minimize single-use plastics and instead use biodegradable or reusable sampling materials. Some even provide edible packaging or compostable wrappers as part of their environmental commitment.

- Farmer inclusion in chocolate storytelling: a notable trend at the *Salon* is the spotlight on bean-to-bar producers and cooperative-based chocolatiers who centre the voices and contributions of cocoa farmers, especially from West Africa and Latin America. French artisan chocolatiers such as Bonnat and Erithaj Chocolat use storytelling and QR-code-enabled digital content on their product packaging to highlight their direct trade partnerships, sustainable farming practices and the socio-economic impact on cocoa-growing communities. These narratives are often integrated into digital marketing campaigns leading up to and during the event, aligning with audience expectations for transparency and ethical sourcing.

Understanding the target market and demographics

Understanding audience demographics, psychographics, geography and behaviour is key to crafting effective digital marketing strategies that resonate across diverse populations. Sustainability-focused events attract a wide range of attendees, from eco-conscious millennials and Gen Z to environmentally responsible families and professionals. This complexity is even greater in multicultural settings, where access to digital tools and perceptions of sustainability can differ widely.

Demographic segmentation

In India, younger, urban millennials from cities like Bangalore and Mumbai engage with green influencers and expect eco-friendly practices at events, such as digital tickets, waste management systems and water refill stations. For example, the NH7 Weekender festival promotes sustainability through digital-only ticketing and reusable merchandise, aligning with the eco-conscious values of its tech-savvy audience. In Mauritius, event organizers must cater to both tourists and locals, communicating in both French and English. For European tourists, who seek eco-friendly experiences, events like Porlwi by Light highlight sustainable transportation options and support for local artisans.

Geographic and cultural considerations

Geographic factors shape digital marketing strategies. In Australia, eco-events like Splendour in the Grass target attendees from both urban and rural areas, employing location-based services and mobile-first advertising. Popular features include a carbon offset programme and green campsite challenges, which align with the festival's emphasis on communal responsibility. In contrast, smaller regions like the Seychelles use mobile engagement strategies and influencer partnerships to promote eco-events. The Eco-Friendly Marathon, for instance, uses geotargeted ads and WhatsApp links to attract eco-conscious runners and international tourists.

Psychographic and behavioural targeting

Psychographic segmentation focuses on values and lifestyle. The Rainforest World Music Festival in Malaysia, which attracts eco-tourists and culturally curious travellers, emphasizes sustainability through biodegradable products and carbon-neutral travel options. These initiatives are promoted through niche online communities and eco-tourism blogs.

Behavioural data, such as event attendance patterns and online interaction with sustainability-related content, further refines digital marketing efforts. Platforms like Facebook Audience Insights and Google Trends can identify growing movements, such as zero-waste initiatives, helping event marketers tailor their campaigns.

Inclusivity and accessibility

Making sustainable event marketing inclusive requires understanding diverse digital engagement practices. In rural India, WhatsApp and YouTube are popular platforms for accessing content on low-cost smartphones. Audio messages, regional language videos and voice notes tend to engage rural audiences more effectively than text-heavy content. In Australia, accessibility for neurodivergent and differently-abled individuals is prioritized through digital features like screen reader-friendly websites and sensory-friendly online ticketing systems, ensuring that these features are central to the event's values rather than added extras.

Multi-channel integration across demographics

To reach a wide demographic spectrum, sustainable event marketing employs multi-channel strategies. For instance, the Goa Sunsplash Festival in India uses a mix of Instagram Live sessions for younger, digital-native audiences and email newsletters to connect with older attendees, blending social media engagement with traditional communication methods.

Feedback and co-creation with attendees

Gathering real-time feedback is crucial for ongoing improvement. Events like St Jerome's Laneway Festival in Australia use Twitter polls and mobile app surveys to collect attendee input during the event. Similarly, the Seychelles Ocean Festival engages participants by allowing them to vote on eco-initiatives they would like to see in future editions, creating a sense of ownership and aligning the event with audience expectations.

REAL-WORLD EXAMPLE Serendipity Arts Festival, Goa

The Serendipity Arts Festival in Goa, India, provides a compelling example of integrating sustainability into event marketing while maintaining cultural relevance and digital engagement. This week-long interdisciplinary arts festival attracts a diverse range of attendees from both India and abroad, showcasing music, theatre, dance, culinary arts, crafts and visual arts.

Sustainability initiatives

- Waste management: the festival collaborates with local waste management companies to ensure that 90 per cent of event waste is recycled or composted.
- Local sourcing: food vendors are sourced locally to reduce the carbon footprint of logistics and support regional economies.
- Digital ticketing and guides: QR-code-based tickets and mobile apps for event schedules reduce reliance on printed materials.
- Carbon footprint education: the festival website features a carbon calculator and encourages ride-sharing through local transport apps to minimize emissions.

Marketing strategy

- Owned media: a blog and event microsite provide behind-the-scenes content, artist profiles and sustainability initiatives, appealing to conscious cultural consumers.
- Earned media: coverage from Indian and international publications, such as *The Hindu* and *ArtReview Asia*, highlights the festival's commitment to sustainable practices.
- Shared media: Instagram Reels, featuring artist takeovers and eco-conscious influencers, spread the event's green messaging, particularly among younger audiences.
- Paid media: targeted Facebook ads in multiple Indian languages promote eco-friendly travel options to Goa, encouraging regional attendees and reducing the carbon footprint of long-haul travel.

After implementing these strategies, the festival saw a 25 per cent increase in attendance, with 40 per cent of ticket buyers citing sustainability as a key factor in their decision to attend. Partnerships with NGOs further boosted the festival's social media reach and strengthened its community relationships.

Digital tools for demographic targeting and sustainability

In recent times, sustainability has become a top priority for the global events industry. As worries about the climate intensify and various stakeholders – from governments to individual consumers – demand greater environmental responsibility, event planners are increasingly obligated to integrate sustainability into all aspects of their work, from initial planning to final execution. However, simply incorporating sustainable practices or adopting environmentally friendly logistics is not enough; it also requires reshaping how these efforts are communicated to and experienced by event attendees.

This is where digital marketing plays a crucial role, acting as a vital link between the intention to be sustainable and actual audience involvement.

The function of digital marketing in managing sustainable events has grown beyond mere promotion. Today, it serves as a key strategic tool for customizing messages, educating participants and encouraging changes in behaviour. The strength of digital marketing lies not just in its wide reach but also in its ability to segment audiences, personalize content and adapt in real time – features that are essential for effectively engaging diverse groups of attendees. Whether the aim is to promote environmentally friendly travel options, reduce the use of disposable plastics, or increase participation in recycling programmes at events, the success of these initiatives often depends on how well the message connects with specific segments of the audience.

Segmenting the audience based on demographics is crucial in this process. Factors such as age, location, online habits, values and cultural background all influence how people understand and react to messages about sustainability. For example, a Generation Z audience might respond better to TikTok campaigns featuring influencers who promote sustainability, while professionals attending a conference might prefer data-rich infographics or thought-provoking content shared on LinkedIn. Understanding these subtle differences allows marketers to create campaigns that are not only informative but also emotionally engaging and motivate people to act.

Furthermore, the increasing availability of digital tools and platforms allows event organizers to gather and analyse large amounts of data about their audience. This data-driven approach makes it possible to identify trends, divide audiences into precise segments and test different sustainability messages across various communication channels. More importantly, digital marketing provides the flexibility to adjust campaigns as needed based on user feedback and engagement, ensuring that the communication about sustainability remains relevant and impactful.

The convergence of sustainability and digital marketing also reflects a broader change in what audiences expect. Today's event attendees are not just passive receivers of information; they actively participate in creating meaning and experiences. They expect openness, personalized communication and authenticity, especially when it comes to claims about sustainability. Events that fail to meaningfully involve their audiences in these issues risk being seen as engaging in 'greenwashing' or being insincere. In contrast, those that invest in campaigns that are informed by demographic understanding and enabled by digital tools are more likely to build trust, foster a sense of community and inspire lasting changes in behaviour. In this context, the digital age provides a rich arsenal of tools for analysing audience demographics and delivering segmented sustainability-focused campaigns. These include the following:

- Computer reservations systems (CRM): these allow for the storage and segmentation of attendee data based on behaviour, preferences and demographic variables. A CRM can track interactions across platforms and personalize email content or event app experiences accordingly.

- Social listening tools: platforms such as Brandwatch or Sprout Social can provide insights into what different audience segments are saying about sustainability and events. This allows marketers to adapt messaging in real time and pre-empt concerns or criticisms.
- Data analytics platforms: Google Analytics, for example, can provide detailed breakdowns of audience demographics, traffic sources and engagement metrics, which can help fine-tune campaign strategies.
- AI and machine learning: these technologies enable hyper-personalization – delivering sustainability content based on past user interactions, preferences or even inferred values. Chatbots powered by AI can also provide sustainable event guidance and frequently asked questions (FAQs) in an energy-efficient and scalable way.
- Augmented reality and virtual experiences: these tools allow for immersive digital experiences that educate attendees on sustainability practices without requiring physical materials or large travel footprints.

Numerous examples from the event industry illustrate how demographic-driven digital marketing can support sustainability. For instance, the Glastonbury Festival (UK) is widely attended by younger, eco-conscious audiences. The festival promotes its green credentials through Instagram campaigns, zero-waste challenges and digital toolkits for sustainable travel. Its emphasis on digital storytelling and influencer partnerships reflects a nuanced understanding of its demographic base. Likewise, COP26 Climate Conference (Scotland) employed digital marketing strategies tailored to multiple global demographics, including social media campaigns for young people, livestreams for professionals and accessible formats for diverse audiences. These strategies were aligned with the event's core sustainability message. These examples demonstrate how aligning marketing practices with audience demographics can reinforce sustainable goals, enhance credibility and foster active participation in sustainability initiatives.

PESO model in sustainable event marketing

The PESO model (paid, earned, shared and owned media) by Gini Dietrich, is a media channel framework for digital public relations in an age of increasing integration across marketing communications channels and disciplines (El-Sherbini, 2023). The PESO model provides a comprehensive framework for planning and executing marketing strategies that balance reach, cost and impact. Each component of PESO has unique advantages when applied to sustainable event marketing, particularly when the goal is to create both environmental and economic efficiencies. Each marketing communication fits into one or more of the following four areas:

- **Paid media**: this encompasses various forms of paid promotion to broaden the reach of your content beyond your own channels. Examples include advertisements on social media, sponsored posts, strategies for generating leads, collaborations with influencers, pay-per-click advertising and specific event marketing campaigns.
- Earned media: this refers to publicity and attention gained through prior actions and is often linked to public relations efforts. It involves cultivating relationships with journalists, bloggers and influential figures within your specific area of interest.
- Shared media: this category includes social networking platforms such as Facebook, Instagram, TikTok, YouTube, LinkedIn and X (formerly Twitter). These platforms are valuable for nurturing connections with your audience, fostering brand loyalty and encouraging the creation of content by users themselves (User-Generated Content or UGC).
- Owned media: this refers to the content and the platforms that you directly control, such as your own articles, blogs, podcasts, email communications and videos.

The revised PESO model (2024)

According to research by Anastasiia (2024), the updated PESO model still recognizes the four fundamental media types but acknowledges considerable shifts in their influence and how they interact with each other. For instance, new platforms and evolving content expectations have arisen, including a greater emphasis on authenticity and the integration of artificial intelligence (AI). AI is now streamlining work with paid advertising channels and social networks while also shaping what kind of content users prefer. Audiences are becoming more critical and selective, which underscores the growing importance of owned media where you have direct control over the content and its presentation. Furthermore, new media platforms are gaining significance. TikTok, for example, has changed how content is approached, making video a primary format for content creators. In response to changes on X (formerly Twitter), Meta launched its own alternative platform, Threads.

According to Anastasiia (2024), content creation begins with owned media resources – personal channels or business platforms. The PESO model emphasizes independence in working with owned media, as building brand or business on publicly available platforms carries the risk of losing your work unexpectedly. Owned media includes websites, blogs, email marketing, podcasts and videos. If you do not have your own platform, you can 'rent' content on established platforms like Apple Podcast, Spotify or YouTube, as described in the real-world example below.

REAL-WORLD EXAMPLE Gart Solutions

Gart Solutions, an IT consulting firm based in Stockholm, overhauled its single-page website into a comprehensive, multi-page platform. Steps taken by the company to go global included the following:

1 Transformed their single-page website into a robust site, each page focusing on a specific service or expertise area.
2 Developed in-depth, search engine optimized (SEO) content for each page. For instance, Gart Solutions created detailed service pages like 'Infrastructure Management' and 'DevOps Services,' along with their sub-categories.
3 Established a blog section, creating a content calendar with topics relevant to their expertise. This included articles on cloud migration, DevOps best practices and IT infrastructure trends.
4 Using Weblium, they designed user-friendly, responsive prototypes for each page, ensuring a seamless user experience across devices.
5 Implemented a strategic internal linking structure to guide visitors through their service offerings and improve SEO.

Results included:

- increased organic traffic from 0 to 1000 visitors per month
- improved search engine rankings, with 1000 keywords in the top 100 positions
- enhanced user engagement, with visitors spending more time exploring Gart Solution's services.

PESO media components in event sustainability

Using PESO in an integrated strategy enables organizers to maximize impact while minimizing costs and environmental footprints. For instance, owned media can host a sustainability charter, while shared media amplifies testimonials from previous attendees, earned media builds credibility and paid media targets specific segments.

- Paid media includes advertisements such as Google Ads, social media ads and sponsored content. In sustainable events, paid campaigns are used judiciously, targeting eco-conscious demographics. For instance, the We Love Green Festival in Paris utilizes localized and time-specific Facebook Ads that only run during off-peak internet usage hours to reduce energy consumption, while maintaining engagement with urban, green-minded attendees.
- Earned media involves publicity gained through PR efforts, such as media coverage, guest blogging or influencer mentions. The Cape Town International

Jazz Festival earns significant media attention due to its green initiatives, including solar-powered stages and eco-vendor certifications, which are regularly featured in South African lifestyle and news outlets.

- Shared media refers to content shared on social media platforms, including user-generated content and engagement. Encouraging attendees to share photos and stories via a branded hashtag, such as #EcoFestEurope2024, builds trust and community. The Boom Festival in Portugal, for instance, has cultivated a loyal following by encouraging followers to document their travel choices, eco-camping setups and zero-waste practices.
- Owned media includes channels fully controlled by the event organizer, such as websites, blogs and newsletters. A good example is the Sauti za Busara Festival in Zanzibar, which uses its website not only for promotional content but also to educate attendees about carbon offsetting and local community support initiatives.

Table 10.1 highlights how each media type contributes not only to outreach but also to transparency and sustainability goals.

Table 10.1 PESO integration strategy for sustainable events (adapted from Anastasiia, 2024)

PESO component	Tool/channel	Example	Sustainable benefit
Paid	Facebook/Google Ads	We Love Green Festival (France)	Targeted low-carbon digital reach
Earned	Local and international press	Cape Town Jazz Festival (South Africa)	Green PR for audience trust
Shared	Instagram, Twitter, TikTok	Boom Festival (Portugal)	Community engagement + UGC
Owned	Festival website/blog	Sauti za Busara (Zanzibar)	Long-term impact communication

ACTIVITY 10.1

Task

Drawing from own experience, design a sustainable event marketing strategy.

Learning outcomes

- Apply theory to practice through real-world models.
- Practice team collaboration and strategic thinking.

- Learn to balance digital reach with sustainable values.
- Build cultural and contextual sensitivity.

Objective

To apply the PESO model, audience segmentation and sustainability principles in creating a comprehensive digital marketing plan for a fictional or real event.

Instructions

1 Working in groups of 4–5, each group chooses a region (e.g. Sub-Saharan Africa, Southeast Asia, Oceania, South Asia).
2 Each group must choose or create a sustainable event concept (e.g. eco-music festival, zero-waste food fair, green fashion show).
3 Develop a marketing strategy using the PESO framework:
- Paid: What platforms and budget?
- Earned: What stories or achievements could attract media?
- Shared: How to engage audiences on social media?
- Owned: What web or app-based tools will be created?
4 Identify the target market: demographic profile, psychographics and digital access constraints.
5 Include three sustainability features and describe how they will be communicated.
6 Create a visual representation (a digital poster or infographic) of their strategy

Deliverables

- Group presentation (10 mins)
- Poster/infographic submission
- One-page summary of strategy and audience analysis.

The future of digital marketing for sustainable events

As the events sector continues to struggle with the increasingly pressing need for sustainability, digital marketing has evolved beyond just a way to promote events. It has become a vital catalyst for a shift towards environmentally and socially responsible practices. The future involves seeing digital marketing as a fundamental element of designing sustainable events – integrating environmental responsibility, inclusivity for all attendees and personalized approaches based on data right into the core of event planning and execution.

Digital marketing provides unique opportunities to lessen environmental impacts, encourage eco-friendly actions and connect with audiences more meaningfully by substituting resource-intensive methods like printed materials and physical signs with environmentally-sound digital alternatives. For instance, in India, major events such as the Indian International Science Festival (IISF) and regional cultural festivals in Kerala have used targeted social media advertising, content in multiple languages and platforms optimized for mobile devices to replace traditional outreach and promote sustainable behaviours like car-pooling and proper waste disposal. Mauritius, a small island nation particularly vulnerable to the effects of climate change, has seen environmentally conscious events like the Dodo Festival and the Sustainable Island Living Expo adopt a 'digital-first' strategy. This involves reaching local communities and those living abroad through influencers, Facebook campaigns targeted by location and platforms that use less bandwidth to cater to varying levels of internet access. These efforts not only raise awareness but also weave sustainability into the marketing experience itself, demonstrating the behaviours they aim to encourage.

A key advantage of digital marketing is its ability to precisely segment and target different audiences. This allows sustainability messages to be customized based on factors like age, interests, values and where people live. This kind of demographic and psychographic segmentation makes sustainability more relevant and easier to relate to, as demonstrated by Europe's Tomorrowland Festival, which uses data insights to personalize its green messages based on ticket types, where attendees come from and how they have interacted with the festival before. Similarly, Indian platforms like BookMyShow provide organizers with tools to analyse audience demographics and send localized communications that encourage environmentally friendly choices. This personalization strengthens emotional connections and increases the likelihood of people changing their behavior, supporting the findings of Kara (2025) and Kotler and Lee (2008) about the persuasive power of communication that is relevant to the context. Furthermore, influencer marketing, which is particularly effective with digitally native generations like Millennials and Gen Z, has been crucial in shaping conversations around sustainability. By partnering with trustworthy eco-influencers and respected local figures, events in Mauritius and Europe have successfully bridged the gap between simply knowing about sustainability and acting. For example, the German GreenTec Awards and Mauritius' Eco-Fest campaigns have engaged social media creators to model sustainable behaviours, reinforcing these messages through short videos, live streams and real-time interactions that build community and a sense of shared responsibility.

Digital marketing also plays a vital role in promoting inclusivity and accessibility, two important aspects of sustainability that are often overlooked in traditional event planning. Hybrid and virtual event formats, marketed and facilitated through digital channels, allow for wider participation from marginalized, rural or international audiences, thereby making cultural, educational and business events more accessible to everyone. India's Jaipur Literature Festival, which shifted to a hybrid format in 2021, used WhatsApp, Instagram and SEO to attract remote participants from over 80 countries. Similarly, virtual events in Mauritius during the pandemic, promoted through Facebook groups for the diaspora and multilingual content, enabled engagement across borders with minimal environmental impact. In Europe, innovations like AI-powered content recommendations and real-time accessibility features have increased participation among individuals with disabilities and those who do not speak the local language, highlighting how digital marketing can support not only environmental sustainability but also social equity. After events, digital marketing tools provide valuable feedback mechanisms. From real-time analytics from event apps to AI-powered analysis of people's opinions, these systems allow organizers to gather insights from their audience, assess how well sustainability measures were received and make improvements for future events. The We Love Green festival in France, for example, provides live updates on resource use and asks for user feedback on its green initiatives, while India's Green Haat Mela uses surveys accessed via QR codes to gather attendee responses about ethical vendor practices and eco-friendly infrastructure. These tools support decision-making based on evidence and help measure the outcomes of sustainability efforts, adding accountability and transparency to events management.

However, as events become increasingly digital, we must also consider the ethical and environmental implications of the digital tools themselves. The carbon footprint of data centres, the energy used for screen time and the environmental impact of manufacturing digital devices are significant. Furthermore, digital divides resulting from socioeconomic inequalities, lack of infrastructure and limited digital literacy continue to exclude certain populations. To address this, the future must embrace the principles of 'green digital marketing,' where content is designed to use minimal energy, platforms are chosen based on their sustainability performance and digital campaigns are created with accessibility and inclusivity in mind. Europe is taking a leading role with policy-driven initiatives like France's Green IT movement, while developing economies such as India and Mauritius are investing in solar-powered technology solutions and community-based digital literacy programmes. This dual commitment to minimizing ecological impact and ethical design is essential if digital marketing is to be a truly sustainable tool. Moreover, the next generation of events professionals needs interdisciplinary skills that combine expertise in digital marketing with a strong understanding of sustainability. Universities and training institutions are beginning to respond to this need: hospitality and communication programmes in India now include modules on green marketing and Mauritius has launched workshops through its tourism board to educate local planners on digital sustainability strategies. European institutions have developed publicly available toolkits for sustainable digital events management, promoting best practices that can be adapted and used globally.

In summary, digital marketing presents both challenges and opportunities for sustainable events management. Its technological capabilities, influence on behaviour and precision in data make it a cornerstone of sustainability strategies when used ethically, inclusively and with intention. As demonstrated by initiatives across Mauritius, India and Europe, digital marketing can facilitate operations with a lower environmental impact, raise environmental awareness, enhance inclusivity for attendees and encourage changes in behaviour on a large scale. However, the real transformation lies in integrating digital marketing not as a separate communication tool, but as a strategic and values-driven instrument embedded in the entire lifecycle of event planning, from the initial design to the post-event evaluation. Reinforcing the arguments of Legrand, Chen and Laeis (2022), Buhalis and Amaranggana (2013) and Sigala (2018), the future of sustainable events will belong to those who use digital technologies not only to inform, but to inspire action, shift perspectives and build resilient communities. The path forward requires collaboration across different sectors, ongoing education and ethical innovation, ensuring that digital marketing helps create not just better events, but a better, more sustainable world.

ACTIVITY 10.2

Title:

Designing a sustainable event experience based on audience expectations

Objective

To understand how different audience demographics (Millennials, Gen Z, Gen X, Baby Boomers) perceive sustainability in events and how digital marketing strategies can be tailored to meet those expectations.

Instructions

Divide into four groups with each group representing one generational audience segment:

- Group 1: Gen Z
- Group 2: Millennials
- Group 3: Gen X
- Group 4: Baby Boomers

Scenario

You are an events marketing team preparing for an upcoming international sustainable music and culture festival. Design a digital marketing strategy that aligns with your assigned generation's media habits, values and expectations of sustainability.

Group task (30–40 minutes)

1 Identify at least three sustainability features your target audience expects (e.g. zero plastic, plant-based food, carbon-neutral travel, community inclusion).

2 Choose the digital marketing tools and platforms most relevant for your demographic (e.g. TikTok, Instagram, podcasts, LinkedIn, email newsletters).

3 Draft two sample digital messages (e.g. social post, short video idea, or newsletter headline) that communicate both the event experience and its sustainability ethos.

Summary

In an era defined by critical global sustainability needs and rapid digital advancements, the role of marketing in events management has fundamentally changed. This chapter has shown that digital marketing is more than just a tool for promotion and increasing reach, it is a crucial mechanism for weaving sustainability into the very fabric of events. As the event industry faces growing demands for environmental responsibility, social inclusivity and economic viability, digital marketing emerges as a key element in addressing these interconnected priorities through both the message conveyed and the means of communication.

The evidence presented – from local campaigns in Mauritius to large-scale festivals in South Africa and France – highlights the power of digital platforms to encourage sustainable behaviours, engage diverse audiences and reflect evolving cultural values. Innovative applications like TrashOut illustrate how involving young people, using technology and focusing on community-based sustainability goals can come together effectively. Meanwhile, examples such as Rocking the Daisies and the *Salon du Chocolat* demonstrate how ethical storytelling, inclusive branding and content that responds to audience needs can elevate sustainability from a behind-the-scenes operation to a central theme of the event experience.

Crucially, what audiences expect is no longer fixed or a minor consideration. These expectations are dynamic forces that shape strategy, influenced by generational identities, geographic realities, psychographic preferences and digital habits. Millennials and Gen Z seek authentic and value-driven experiences, while older generations prioritize clarity and trust, yet both groups demand evidence of genuine commitments to sustainability. Tailoring marketing strategies to these preferences not only improves engagement but also ensures that sustainability initiatives are inclusive, relevant to the context and impactful.

This chapter has also emphasized that sustainable digital marketing goes beyond 'what' is communicated to include 'how' and 'to whom.' Whether through paperless communication, segmenting audiences based on data, or using accessible formats for rural and differently-abled individuals, responsible marketing practices can significantly reduce the environmental and social footprint of events. At the same time, integrated frameworks like the PESO model provide strategic clarity in balancing reach with responsibility, guiding event planners in creating coherent, efficient and ethically sound campaigns.

In conclusion, sustainable digital marketing in events management is no longer optional – it is an essential part of both operations and ethics. By using digital tools not only to promote but also to educate, mobilize and transform, event marketers have the potential to shape more conscious audiences, foster long-term community engagement and turn events into platforms for systemic change. The future of event marketing lies not just in the ability to attract attention but in its power to build trust, shift behaviours and contribute to a more sustainable world – one click, one story and one event at a time.

Further reading

Font, X and McCabe, S (2017). Sustainability and marketing in tourism: Its contexts, paradoxes, approaches, challenges and potential, *Journal of Sustainable Tourism*, 25 (7), 869–83

Getz, D and Page, S J (2016) Progress and prospects for event tourism research, *Tourism Management*, 52, 593–631.

Jones, M (2014) *Sustainable Event Management: A Practical Guide*, Routledge, Abingdon

References

Anastasiia, S (2024) The PESO Model: Creating an Effective Communication Strategy, 14 August, LinkedIn

Buhalis, D and Amaranggana, A (2013) Smart tourism destinations: Information and communication, *Technologies in Tourism*, Springer, Berlin, 553–64

Canosa, A, Graham, A and Wilson, E (2020) Growing up in a tourist destination: Developing an environmental sensitivity, *Environmental Education Research*, 26 (7), 1027–42, doi.org/10.1080/13504622.2020.1768224

El-Sherbini, N N (2023) Strategic digital content marketing: The PESO model in practice, *Journal of Public Relations Research*, Middle East, 11 (47) 59–86

Font, X and McCabe, S (2017) Sustainability and marketing in tourism: its contexts, paradoxes, approaches, challenges and potential, *Journal of Sustainable Tourism*, 25 (7), 869–83

Freeman, R, Dickinson, J and Cox, T (2021) Sustainability and consumer behavior at events: Measuring perceptions and participation, *Event Management*, 25 (2), 189–204, doi.org/10.3727/152599521X16106577948084

Getz, D and Page, S J (2016) Progress and prospects for event tourism research, *Tourism Management*, 52, 593–631

Gössling, S and Hall, C M (2019) *Sustainable Tourism: A global perspective*, Routledge, Abingdon

Gowreesunkar, V and Dixit, S (2017) Consumer Information Seeking Behaviour, In: S Dixit (ed) *Handbook of Consumer Behavior for Hospitality and Tourism*, Routledge, Abingdon

Gowreesunkar, V and Séraphin, H (2020) *Marketing and Managing Tourism Destinations: International perspectives*, Palgrave Macmillan, London

Gowreesunkar, V and Séraphin, H (2022) Children as Ambassadors in Sustainability Initiatives of ANPRAS, Mauritius, In H Séraphin and V Gowreesunkar (eds) *Children in Sustainable and Responsible Tourism*, Emerald Publishing Limited, Leeds

Jones, M (2014) Sustainable Events management: A practical guide, Routledge, Abingdon

Kara, S (2025) Project-based learning to boost EFL learners' ability in writing persuasive essays, *KOYA University Journal of Humanities and Social Sciences*, 8 (1), 468–77

Kotler, P and Lee, N (2008) *Social Marketing: Influencing behaviour for good*, SAGE, London

Legrand, W, Chen J S and Laeis, G C (2022) *Sustainability in the Hospitality Industry: Principles of sustainable operations*, Routledge, Abingdon

Maingi, S and Gowreesunkar, V (2022) Child Rights and Inclusive Sustainable Tourism Development in East Africa: Case of Kenya, in H Séraphin and V. Gowreesunkar (eds) *Children in Sustainable and Responsible Tourism*, Emerald Publishing Limited, Leeds

Moyo, T and Mhlanga, O (2020) The impact of mobile marketing strategies on green tourism: Evidence from Africa, *African Journal of Hospitality, Tourism and Leisure*, 9 (3), 1–18

Nielsen, C (2015) *The Sustainability Imperative: New insights on consumer expectations*, Nielsen Company, New York

Norwood, M F, Lakhani, A, Fullagar, S, Maujean, A, Downes, M, Byrne, J, Stewart, A, Barber, B and Kendall, E (2019) A narrative and systematic review of the behavioural, cognitive and emotional benefits of passive nature exposure on young people: Evidence for prescribing change, *Landscape and Urban Planning*, 189, 71–79 doi.org/10.1016/j.landurbplan.2019.04.007

Ophoff, M G, Griese, K and Werner, K (2020) Event organisations at the interface between sustainability and digitalisation, In: *Events – Future, Trends, Perspectives*, UTB Publishers, Stuttgart

Séraphin, H and Gowreesunkar, V (Eds) (2020) *Children in Hospitality and Tourism: Marketing and managing experiences* (4), Walter de Gruyter GmbH & Co KG, Berlin

Sigala, M (2018) Implementing social customer relationship management: A process framework and implications in tourism and hospitality, *International Journal of Contemporary Hospitality Management*, 30 (7), 2698–726

UNWTO (2021) A Practical Guide to Tourism Event Sustainability. Madrid: World Tourism Organization, www.unwto.org

11 Conclusion: The future of sustainable events

Introduction

This final chapter takes a futuristic approach to the event industry (planning, designing and delivering). What will come after the Sustainable Development Goals (SDGs) run out in 2030? What about the impact of virtual and hybrid events? Is the metaverse more sustainable than live? How can the event industry be integrated within a circular economy process? Could the events industry lead the way in making sustainable practice the norm? Where might new innovations come from?

Future propositions for the events industry

Researchers have attempted to predict the future of the events industry through future propositions (FP). The most prominent research in this field includes Getz (2012) and Séraphin et al (2021). Getz's (2012) propositions regarding the future of the event industry are as follow:

- FP1: Planned, live events, both personal and societal in scale and meaning, will always be a prominent feature of civilization, in all societies and cultures.
- FP 2: Virtual events will gain in frequency and importance in response to advances in global technology and because of globalization forces and the costs or risks of travel; however, they will be in addition to and not a substitute for, live event experiences.
- FP 3: Corporate influences on the field of planned events will continue to increase, especially in terms of events produced as manifestations of marketing and branding.

- FP 4: The strategic justifications for public-sector involvement with events, especially mega-events bearing heavy costs, will be increasingly scrutinized and more difficult to defend, while social, cultural and environmental justifications will become more acceptable.
- FP 5: Generic 'events management' professionals will become the norm, forcing the various professional associations to adapt their recruitment appeal and to demonstrate their added value.
- FP 6: The events professional of the future will be competent in events management theory and applications, knowledgeable about the importance of events in society, an effective advocate for event-related policy and a constant learner within the field of event studies.
- FP 7: Even if travel and tourism collapse, possibly because of the cascading effects of global warming, another energy crisis, war, terrorism or global pandemic, events will remain important globally because they meet fundamental human needs.

Overall, Séraphin (2021) agrees with Getz (2012), although he has a slightly different view on FP1, FP2 and FP7. The counter-propositions from Séraphin (2021) are referred to as New Future Propositions (NFPs):

- NFP1: Planned, live events, both personal and societal in scale and meaning, will always be a prominent feature of civilization, in all societies and cultures. However, in time of pandemics or other crises, live events will be perturbed, before a staggered returned to normal under certain conditions and strict controls.
- NFP2: Virtual events will gain in frequency and importance in response to advances in global technology and because of globalization forces and the costs or risks of travel, but they will be in addition to and not a substitute for, live event experiences.
- NFP7: As travel and tourism collapse, possibly because of the cascading effects of global warming, another energy crisis, war, terrorism or global pandemics, events will also collapse temporarily but will remain important globally because they meet fundamental human needs.

Technology will play a major role in the future of the events industry. Both Getz (2012) and Séraphin (2021) present technology as extrinsic cues of the events industry, while also agreeing that technology is a tool that can overcome issues that are internal (prominence of events for individuals and society, cost of running events, skills and expertise of event managers, etc.) and external (crisis, war, terrorism, pandemics, etc.) to the event industry. Trends in technology that could potentially impact the event industry are shown in Table 11.1.

Table 11.1 Top 20 new technology trends (adapted from AI Uncovered, YouTube, 2025)

Technology trends	What the technology trends are about
Artificial intelligence (AI) and machine learning (ML)	Making decisions with minimal human intervention
5G technology	Connecting devices simultaneously while enabling them to communicate
Internet of Things	Connecting devices
Edge computing	Automation
Block chain technology	Securing transactions
Augmented reality (AR) and virtual reality (VR)	Immersive digital environment / Immersion in a virtual space
Quantum computing	Solving complex problems
Robotic process Automation (RPA)	Repetitive tasks, allowing employees to focus on higher value tasks
Enhancing cyber security	Protection of data
Sustainable technology	Reducing the environmental impacts of industries
Human augmentation	Enhancing human abilities
AI augmented development	Automated code generation
Industry cloud platforms	Boost operation efficiency
Smart apps	Improving customer engagement and organization efficiency
Democratized generative AI	Creating new content (texts, music, etc)
Continuous threat exposure countermeasure	Monitoring and addressing vulnerability in real time
AI trust, risk and security management	Building ethical and transparent AI systems and addressing risks
Platform engineering	Scaling operations efficiently
Machine customers	Machine making autonomous purchasing decisions as it predicts needs without human intervention
Augmented connected workforce	Enhancing productivity in hybrid model of working for teams collaborating from different locations

The following table provides a few examples of how these trends could impact on the event industry (Table 11.2).

Table 11.2 Top 20 new technology trends and their impacts on the event industry

Technology trends	Example of potential impacts on the event industry
Artificial intelligence (AI) and machine learning (ML) Edge computing Quantum computing AI augmented development Machine customers	Risk assessment design Strategies to address issues arising during an event could be automated
5G Technology Internet of Things Smart apps Democratized generative AI	Offer attendees more options in terms of sharing their experience with a wider audience. Offer event organizers additional marketing options
Block chain technology Enhancing cyber security AI augmented development Continuous threat exposure countermeasure AI trust, risk and security management Machine customers	Useful for event organizers who will have fewer complaints to deal with, while attendees will feel more confident when processing payment and/or sharing personal data These tools (particularly machine customers) could also help with customer relation management (CRM)
Augmented reality (AR) and virtual reality (VR) Democratized generative AI	Enhanced experience for attendees For event organizers, it pauses the questions of investments and skills to manage these tools Such tools could be considered as competitive advantages for more competent event managers
Robotic process automation (RPA) Industry cloud Platforms Platform engineering Augmented connected workforce	Help event companies to reduce the number of staff as the technology can process bookings, payments, etc., leaving staff to focus on other activities
Sustainable technology AI augmented development	Could play a major role in the image and reputation of event organizers, and his Economic performance and sustainability is considered a good selling point
Human augmentation	Potential to offer a wider and more extravagant range of entertainment, which could impact positively on the experience of attendees

The following activity provides an opportunity to discuss technology and the future of the event industry.

ACTIVITY 11.1

Using the information in Tables 11.1 and 11.2, develop your own propositions regarding the future of the event industry.

1. Select three trends in technology
2. Discuss how these trends will impact (both positively and negatively) the future of the events industry. Justify your point of view with evidence.
3. Do you agree with Getz (2012):
   - FP1: Planned, live events, both personal and societal in scale and meaning, will always be a prominent feature of civilization, in all societies and cultures.
   - FP 2: Virtual events will gain in frequency and importance in response to advances in global technology and because of globalization forces and the costs or risks of travel; however, they will be in addition to and not a substitute for, live event experiences.
   - Give reasons for your answers.

Activity 11.2 will help you to take a reflective and critical approach to your future career.

ACTIVITY 11.2

Visit uk.indeed.com and enter 'events management' in the job title search bar. What are the most common jobs in events management?

1. What skills, qualities, experience and qualifications are most required?
2. Identify a job you are interested in and state what it is that interests you.
3. In a decade, what jobs do you think will be available in the industry? Are they going to be different types of jobs? Justify your answer.
4. What skills, qualities, experience and qualifications will be required for future employees in the events industry? Justify your answer.
5. Identify a job that does not exist yet in the event industry that you think will appear in the future. Then, design a job description and person specification for this job.

6 Do you agree with Getz (2012)?

   o FP 5: Generic 'events management' professionals will become the norm, forcing the various professional associations to adapt their recruitment appeal and to demonstrate their added value.

   o FP 6: The events professional of the future will be competent in events management theory and applications, knowledgeable about the importance of events in society, an effective advocate for event-related policy and a constant learner within the field of event studies.

   o Give reasons for your answers.

Events and their purpose: a futuristic approach

As discussed in this textbook, EDI, SDGs and TBL are concepts that play a major role in discussions around sustainability in the events industry. From these discussions it is clear that what particularly matters is that events must have a social purpose and address societal issues. The economic dimension of events remains important but is now taking a 'back seat', as indicated by Alberts and Niendorf (2021) who place 'profit' as the last dimension to be achieved by society (Figure 11.1).

For Craig (2013) the 'profit' dimension is out of the equation (Figure 11.2).

Future events will be planned around three axes and/or questions:

1 What societal issues will be addressed?
2 What processes will be put in place to reduce/remove the negative impacts on the environment?
3 How will we finance and generate income from the event (*not* profit) to make it viable in the long term?

Figure 11.1   The triple bottom line: people, planet, profit (adapted from Alberts and Niendorf, 2021)

People > Planet > Profit

Figure 11.2   Planet and people (adapted from Craig, 2013)

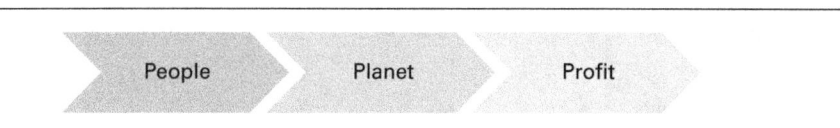

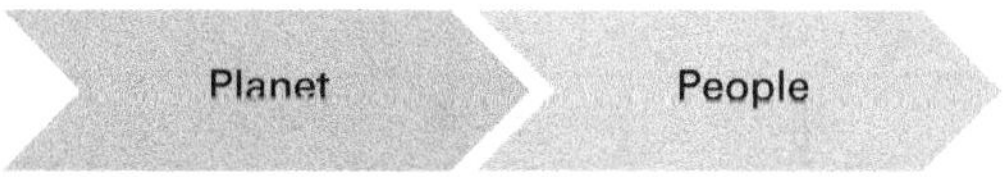

Figure 11.3 Innovation for sustainable events (I4SE)

These three research questions could be the starting point of the Think Tank for Innovation for Sustainable Events (I4SE) and are the parameters to take into consideration when developing event concepts. The outcome of all these parameters put together is the framework presented in Figure 11.3. Despite the urgency of sustainability in events, it is important to keep the fun and edutainment dimensions (Poris, 2006; Séraphin and Chaney, 2024; Yallop et al, 2025).

The model for sustainability suggested in this chapter alongside the entire philosophy of this textbook is articulated around a new approach of events management. Innovation is important in the process of challenging how we approach and how we do things. Indeed, Chaney et al (2025) argue that convictions of being good at something and/or mastering it make individuals 'dumber' as subjective knowledge correlates with closed-mindedness.

Despite the fact the framework in Figure 11.3 suggests a futuristic approach to planning, designing and delivering events, it should be noted that many events have already adopted this approach, as demonstrated in the real-world examples below. This suggests that this framework approach should be more widely spread.

REAL-WORLD EXAMPLE   Haiti Je Connais Live Challenge

Context

A diaspora consists of people coming from the same country but living away from their home country (Bordes-Benayoun, 2002). A diaspora is heterogeneous because people leave their home country for a variety of reasons: victims/refugees, trade, imperial expansion, labour and cultural/hybrid/postmodern diaspora (Seraphin et al, 2021). Within the diaspora can be found first-generation diaspora members, born in the home country who migrated to a host country. The second-generation diaspora was born in the host country, but whose parents were born in the home country. Meylon-Reinette (2009, 2010) argues that first-generation diaspora remains very close to the home country, while the second-generation onwards are less and less attached to the home country. This is referred to as de-diasporization and is a major issue for some destinations as the diaspora who send remittances back to their home country are major economic stakeholders (Séraphin et al, 2021).

Haiti is a destination known to be the first independent black republic in the world and one that struggles for stability and democracy. As a result, the country has diaspora scattered around the world and so de-diasporization is starting to be an issue within this community (Meylon-Reinette, 2009, 2010; Séraphin et al, 2016).

The event

To overcome the negative image of the destination and to educate the second-generation onwards, some members of the diaspora based in France decided to tackle de-diasporization by developing an app called *Haiti Je Connais*. The aim was to educate in a fun way (edutainment) the younger members of the diaspora. They also organize an annual live event in Paris, France called *Haiti Je Connais Live Challenge*, where both younger members and adults of the diaspora can take part in a general knowledge quiz that covers different aspects of the culture of the destination.

Haiti Je Connais Live Challenge is a small/local cultural event (friend fun, empowering fun, competitive fun, family fun) organized by a Parisian charity called *Evolution d' Haiti* (EVOH) which began in 2015 by members of the Haitian diaspora. The focus of the charity is 'people' (TBL), while addressing SDG 4 (Quality education).

Further reading:

App Haiti Je Connais: https://haitijeconnais.com/home

Haiti Je Connais Live Challenge 2023: www.facebook.com/HaitiJeConnais/videos/1292386338342923/

EVOH: www.evoh.fr/

Summary

A lot has already been done by the events industry when it comes to sustainability, but there is still more to do. Education of future managers/event organizers in sustainability is perhaps one of the most effective tools that could be used by the industry. The following New Future Propositions (NFPs) could be formulated (adapted from Getz, 2012):

- NFP5: The event professional of the future will be competent in planning, designing and delivering sustainable events. Indeed, they will be knowledgeable about the societal importance of events and how to minimize their negative impacts.
- NFP6: As effective advocates of sustainable event-related policy and constant learners within the field of event studies, the event professionals of the future, because of their skills, expertise and values, will force the various professional associations and business owners to adapt a 'responsible' recruitment strategy.

The new generation of event organizers/planners should play a major role in unlocking positive changes in the industry through transformational leadership and enterprise reform and transparency. The new generation of consumers will also play a major role in the sustainability of the industry. Indeed, Yeoman (2013) suggests that as time passes, consumers and event organizers are more educated towards sustainability, which makes them highly sensitive to ethical consumption.

The use of technology and social media is likely to play a major role in making the event industry sustainable. Indeed, 'youth are an easily identifiable market, relatively homogenous, highly aural and visual, globally connected and increasingly technologically dependent' (Miffling and Taylor, 2007: 1323). As for social media, it is used by the new generation as a tool for the accumulation of social capital (Yeoman, 2013).

As the future is unpredictable, only time will tell if the propositions formulated in this textbook are accurate. Like Samuel Johnston in *Rasselas Prince of Abyssinia*, this textbook provides a conclusion in which nothing is concluded. This is an approach often used so that readers can make up their own mind (Smith, 1996).

Further reading

For training and courses in events management, visit UCAS: www.ucas.com/

References

Alberts, H C and Niendorf, B D (2021) Interdisciplinary learning about people, planet and profit in Germany, *The Geography Teacher*, 18 (3-4), 158–63

Bordes-Benayoun, C (2002) Les diasporas, dispersion spatiale, expérience sociale, *Autrepart*, 22 (2), 23–36, doi.org/10.3917/autr.022.0023

Chaney, D, Trelohan, M and Moroz, D (2025) When thinking you're good makes you dumber: An investigation of consumers' earned dogmatism, *Journal of Business Research*, 194, 115351

Craig, D H (2013) Healthy planet, healthy people, *Health Education*, 14 (5), 9–13

Getz, D (2012) *Event Studies: Theory, research and policy for planned events*, Routledge, Abingdon

Melyon-Reinette, S (2009) *Haïtiens à New York City: Entre Amérique noire et Amérique multiculturelle*, L'Harmattan, Paris

Melyon-Reinette, S (2010) De la dédiasporisation des jeunes Haïtiens à New York, Études Caribéennes, 16 August, doi.org/10.4000/etudescaribeennes.4628

Miffling, K and Taylor, R (2007) Investigating the importance of youth culture in successful youth events, *The Journal of Contemporary Issues in Business and Government*, 13 (2), 65–80

Poris, M (2006) Understanding what fun means to today's kids, *Young Consumers*, 7 (1), 14–22

Séraphin, H and Chaney, D (2024) Identifying and understanding the intersectional cues that matter for customers in speed dating events, *Event Management*, 28 (6), 933–48

Séraphin, H, Butcher, J and Korstanje, M (2016) Challenging the negative images of Haiti at a pre-visit stage using visual online learning materials, *Journal of Policy Research in Tourism, Leisure and Events*, 9 (2), 169–81

Séraphin, H, Gowreesunkar, V and Canosa, A (2021) Destination marketing organisations: the need for a child-centred approach to diaspora tourism, *Tourism Planning & Development*, 20 (3), 468–80

Smith, D H (1996) Patterns in Samuel Johnson's *Rasselas*, *Studies in English Literature, 1500–1900*, 36 (3), 623–39

Yallop, A C, Séraphin, H and Hamdan, O A (2025) Rethinking the relationship between dating services and the hospitality industry through speed dating events: a partner ecosystem strategy, *Event Management*, 29 (4), 565–83

Yeoman, I (2013) A futurist's thoughts on consumer trends shaping future festivals and events, *International Journal of Event and Festival Management*, 4 (3), 249–60

YouTube (2025) Top 20 new technology trends www.youtube.com/watch?v=KvN3JXICzdM

INDEX

Note: Page numbers in *italics* refer to figures or tables.

A Greener Festival (AGF) 43, 80, 158, 176
Abba Voyage 196
AC. *See* alternating current (AC)
academia 27, 28, 197
accessibility 30–31, 41, 71, 94, 188, 240, 248–49
accountability 74, 80, 163, 175, 196, 233, 249
acoustics 219–20
adaptability 233
advocacy groups 80–81, 83
AEV. *See* Association of Event Venues (AEV)
African Union Agenda 2063 235
AGF. *See* A Greener Festival (AGF)
AI. *See* artificial intelligence (AI)
AIF. *See* Association of Independent Festivals (AIF)
All England Lawn Tennis Club (Wimbledon) 103
Allegiant Stadium 157, 174–75
alternating current (AC) 220
ANPRAS (African Network for Policy, Research and Advocacy for Sustainability) 235
anxiety disorders 197
Apple Podcast 244
artificial intelligence (AI) 8, 244
Arts by the Sea 112–13
Ascot Racecourse and Arsenal Football Club (Emirates Stadium) 103
Association of Event Venues (AEV) 103
Association of Independent Festivals (AIF) 193
Australian Tennis Open 73
autism 30
AV (audio visual) 91, 194, 227
awareness campaigns 79

B2C (business to consumer) 216
Baby Boomers (born 1946–1964) 237
Baby Jumping Festival 167, 169
Baku 42
Ballie Gifford 121
BASIS. *See* British Association for Sustainable Sport (BASIS)
Batec Mobility 30–31
Battle of the Orange 168, 169
BCOPS (Behaviour, Communication, Operations, Policy and Strategy) 173–76
Behaviourism 138–39
Berlin International Film Festival 76
Biophilia 141–43
Birmingham Commonwealth Games (2020) 41
Birmingham Commonwealth Games (2022) 162
Boardmasters Festival 198–99, 204

BookMyShow 248
Boom Festival (Portugal) 246
Boomtown Festival 123–24
BOPA (Body of Persons Approval) 190
Boston Marathon 77
Brandwatch 243
Brexit 202, 206
British Association for Sustainable Sport (BASIS) 103
British Standard 8901 101
British Standards Institution 101–02
Brockwell Park 159
B-Side Festival (UK) 30
Bun Festival (Hong Kong) 167, 169
Bun Scrambling Competition 167

calendar events 18, 122
Campaign for the Arts 200
cancellation 66, 192, 195–96, 198–99, 203–04
Cape Town International Jazz Festival 245–46
carbon emissions 70, 75, 117, 119, 124, 145, 157, 175, 212
carbon footprint 65, 79, 98–99, 226, 233, 249
   emissions 98, 157
   measurement 117
   reduction strategies 68, 78, 146
Carbon Market Watch 117
carbon offset programmes 70, 76–77, 78
carbon offsets 233
catering 7, 78, 148, 211, 221–23, 238
   hotels 90
   suppliers and services 124
   venues 100, 219
   water resources 70, 97
catering costs 2, 33
Cavendish London hotel 43
ceremonial functions 225
certification schemes 88
child-centric events 3–5, *4*, *5*
Children and Young Persons Act (2008) 190
Children of Winchester Festival (UK) 122
circular economy 76–78, 97, 113, 124, 163, 171, 215
circular living 124
Cirkulär Festival 160–61
climate change 1, 42, 101, 134, 202, 233, 237, 248
'Climate Pledge Arena' 101
Coachella (USA) 30
Coca-Cola Music Experience (Spain) 30

Index

co-creation 7, 132, 147–48, *148*, 150, 240
Code First Girls 150
co-designers 147
commercial objectives 234
community bonding 71
community engagement 64, 70–73, 80, 165, 174, 236
   liaisons 164
   staff and 101
   stakeholders 123
   strategies 180
community groups 128, 164, 176, 200
community messaging 171
community partnerships 176
community relations 123, 124
community-led events 124
composting programme 97
conferences 42, 91, 155, 178, 194, 225, 233
Conferences of the Parties 42, 126–27, 202
content marketing 235
contingency planning 8, 191
contingency plans 185
contingent valuation methods (CVM) 158–59, 181
Convention Centre Dublin 92
Co-Op Live Arena 204
COP. *See* Conferences of the Parties
COP26 Climate Conference (Scotland) 243
COP26 Climate Summit (Glasgow) 78
co-produced events 122
co-producers 147
coral reefs 168
core groups 185–89, *186*, *187*
   risk management at events for children, young people 190–91
   safety events for children and young people 189–90
corporate events 18, 24, 150, 176, 194, 225
Covid-19 1, 13, 20, 110, 192–94
Creole culture 233
crime rates 71
CRM (Computer reservations systems) 242
crowd management 8, 184, 191, 196–99
crowd psychology 197
cultural
   appreciation 82
   authenticity 63, 72
   events 18–19, 71, 112, 167
   expression 70, 72
   festivals 68, 71, 80, 194, 225, 248
   heritage 71, 106, 198
   identities 70–72
customer engagement 28, 171
customer satisfaction 49, 102, 121, 196
CVM. *See* contingent valuation methods (CVM)

Daisies app 236
dating industry 6, 21, 27, 46, 48
Day of the Dead 169
Deepwater Horizon oil spill (2010) 118
deforestation 146
demographics 6, 158, 236, 239–43, 245, 248
destination marketing organization (DMO) 103
digital marketing
   audience expectations 236–38
   digital tools for demographic targeting and sustainability 241–43
   future in sustainable events 247–50
   introduction 233–34
   sustainable events and 234–36
   understanding target market and demographics 239–41
digital storytelling 243
digital ticketing 76, 238
digital tickets 239
digital toolkits 243
digitalization 233
'Dinner Date' 47, 48, 53–54, 58
disability 29, 40, 121, 149, 188
Disability Discrimination Act (1995) 40
disposable plastics 242
diversity 71, 72, 149–50, 187, 237
DMO. *See* destination marketing organization (DMO)
Dodo Festival 248
'doughnut economics' 66, 72

Earth Action Day Area 25
Earth Day Organisation (EDO) 25
earthquakes 42
Eco-Fest campaigns 248
#EcoFestEurope2024 246
eco-friendly activities 79, 80
Eco-Friendly Marathon 239
eco-friendly venues 56
ecological awareness 82
ecological integrity 63
ecological stewardship 234
economic
   benefits 68, 70–71, 73, 74, 75, 192
   growth 22, 67, 73, 114, 198
   inefficiency 223
   priorities 77
   viability 64, 68, 75, 91, 170, 234, 251
EDI. *See* equality/equity, diversity and inclusion (EDI)
Edinburgh Festival Fringe 72, 80, 121
Edinburgh International Book Festival 121
EDO. *See* Earth Day Organisation (EDO)
El Playon volcanic eruption (1658) 167, 169
El Salto del Colacho (Devil's Jump) 167
email campaigns 235, 238
email newsletters 237, 240
EMP. *See* event management plan (EMP)
Employment Equality (Age) Regulations (2006) 40
Employment Equality (Religion or Belief) Regulations (2003) 40

Employment Equality (Sexual Orientation) Regulations (2003) 40
endorsements 237
energy efficiency 66, 70, 74, 76, 95, 171
entertainment costs 2, 33
entertainment value 70–71
environmental
 audits 80
 degradation 67, 223
 goals 77, 201–02
 impacts 49–50, 63, 65, 75, 114, 146, 248
 issues 42, 236
 responsibility 64, 102, 103, 174, 234, 236, 241, 248
 stewardship 1, 22, 170
Equal Pay Act (1970) 40
Equality Act (2006), Part 2 40
Equality Act (2010) 40, 185, 187–88
Equality Act (Sexual Orientation) Regulations (2007) 40
equality/equity, diversity and inclusion (EDI) 2, 7, 40–41, 132, 185–87, 259
equipment costs 2, 33
Equity and Inclusion Enforcement Act (2021) 40
ethical concerns 223
ethical sourcing 171, 238–39
ethnicity 6, 40, 67, 187
Event Cycle (2025) 215–16, *217*
event industry 2, 9, *14*, 21, 26, 28, 33, 63, 74, 79, 121, 194
 ambidextrous management approach 47–48
 Covid-19 impacts on 13, 192
 digital marketing 234–36
 events professionals as agents of change 24–26
 framework 161–62, *161*
 future propositions for 254–59, *256, 257*
 key phases 155–56
 key strategies 57–58
 partner ecosystem strategy 26–28
 pre-event staffing 162–65
 role of disempowered groups 29–31
 team building 165–66
 technology and social media *256, 257*, 263
 triple bottom line 22–24, *23, 24*
 see also planned events
Event Industry Forum 25
event management plan (EMP) 111, 202
event managers 56, 89–91, 92–95, 100, 174, 102, 214, 222, 233
event organizers 2, 8, 43, 48, 49, 56, 64–65, 77, 111, 113, 120, 122, 125–26, 133, 159–60, 176, 188–89, 197–99, 201–04, 236–37, 239, 242
event planners 74, 88–89, 98–100, 103–04, 116, 134, 137, 140, 149, 151–52, 218–19, 223, 241, 252
event planning
 change in society 196

crowd management 196–99
financial considerations 192–96
impacts of political landscape 200–02
long-term planning 203–04
see also core groups
event psychology 132, 138–40
Excel London 97, *98*
exhibitions 18, 91, 118, 194, 235
Expo 2000 World Fair 101
external stakeholder 113–14, 116, 117, 118, 120
Extinction Rebellion 42

Facebook 233, 235, 237, 248
Facebook Ads 245
Facebook Audience Insights 240
face-to-face events 94
family events 30
FAQs. *See* frequently asked questions (FAQs)
Farnborough International Exhibition Centre 124
Festival Inclusivo por la Diversidad Asturias (Spain) 30
Festival International Kreol 233
FFB. *See* Fossil Free Books (FFB)
FIFA Women's World Cup (2023) 77
FIFA World Cup Qatar (2022) 116–17
financial incentives 76, 77
Florida Keys Underwater Music Festival (UMF) 168
food redistribution programmes 75
food waste 70, 78, 145, 167, 223, 230
Formula 1 Dutch Grand Prix 77
Formula E 14, 43
Fossil Free Books (FFB) 121
fossil fuels 42, 202
FPs. *See* Future Propositions (FPs)
free entry festivals 169–70
freelancers 112, 194–95
Fridays for Future 42
fund-raising events 19
furniture 94, 105, 144, 211, 219, 223–24, 230
future planning 111, 162, 175, 181, 203
Future Propositions (FPs) 13, 254–59

'Game for Everyone' 41
Gamescom Exhibition (2023) 216
gamification techniques 79
Generation X (born 1965–1980) 237
Generation Z (born 1997–2012) 237, 239, 242, 248, 251–52
German GreenTec Awards 248
Glastonbury (UK) 30
Glastonbury Festival 68, 75, 79, 80, 174, 197, 243
global events 78, 169–70, 241
global warming 42, 98, 255
Goa Sunsplash Festival 240
Green Deal 76
Green Globe 103, 104
'Green Guardians' programme 171–72

Green Haat Mela 249
Green IT movement (France) 249
Green Plan 2030 77
Green Sense Events 145–46
Green Team Coordinators 163
Greenbelt Festival 192
greenhouse gas emissions 42, 212
greenhouse gases 98
'greening events' 13–14
Greenpeace 80
#GreenStars 235
greenwashing 7, 13–14, 77, 118, 120, 242
guest experience 107, 224
Győr Kids Festival 29, 122

Haiti Je Connais Live Challenge 261–62
hallmark events 20
Hampshire 123–24, 192
Hampshire Business Show 18
Hannover Principles 101
Hay Festival 121
HE. *See* higher education (HE)
Health and Safety at Work Act (1974) 185
Heineken Greener Bar initiative 77
Helix model 27–28
Hellfest (France) 30
hospitality 6, 13, 24, 73, 100, 221, 249–50
   food waste 223
   industry 21, 27, 46, 48, 57
   sporting venues 91
host community 7, 64, 70–71, 73, 122, 124, 134
host organisations 7
human resources 165, 195
Human Rights Act (1998) 40

Ice Storage Thermal Unit (ISTU) 92
IISF (Indian International Science Festival) 248
inclusivity 30–32, 71, 72, 161, 233–34, 240, 248–49
indoor events 143, 185, 221, 224
industry reform 29–30
influencer partnerships 235, 239, 243
Innovation for Sustainable Events (I4SE) 260, 261
Instagram 236, 237, 240, 249
Instagram campaigns 243
institutional theory 176
intangible resources 27, 210
integrated values 30
interactive apps 238
internal stakeholders 111–13, 114
International Children's Games 122
International Confex 125
international festivals 233
International Organization for Standardization (ISO) 43, 102
intersectional events 21
intersectionality 132, 149–51, 153
ISO 14000 102

ISO 20121 8, 102, 161–62
ISO 20121:2024 122
ISO 9001 102
ISTU. *See* Ice Storage Thermal Unit (ISTU)

Jaipur Literature Festival 249
Julie's Bicycle 124, 125, 158, 176

key performance indicators (KPIs) 137, 158, 160–62
keynote speakers 225
Kids TEDx 29–30
'knowledge cities' 28
Kolb's Reflective Cycle 53
KPIs. *See* key performance indicators (KPIs)

La Tomatina 20
Lake of Stars Festival 235
large-scale annual events 114
large-scale events 70, 71, 72, 74, 76, 174
large-scale festivals 165, 251
Las Bolas de Fuego (El Salvador) 167
Las Vegas Sphere 196
Latin America 238
leadership positions 187
lean manufacturing 215
LGA. *See* Local Government Association (LGA)
life-cycle events 19, 21
LinkedIn 237, 242, 244
local authorities 41, 105, 113, 125–26, 176, 198
local communities 19, 64–65, 67–68, 75, 79–80, 119, 132, 248
Local Government Association (LGA) 112
local suppliers 56, 73, 93, 99, 101, 218, 222
logistical constraints 148
logistical details 237
Lollapalooza (USA) 30
Lollapalooza India 2025 25
London Olympics (2012) 67, 70, 118, 160, 176
London After Dark festivals 27
loneliness 41, 48–49
longer-term relationships 116
Lopburi Monkey Banquet 168
Lopburi Province 168
'Love the Farm, Leave No Trace' campaign 174
low-risk events 185

major events 20, 74, 75, 77, 248
Makkah 19
Mallorca Live Festival (Spain) 30
Manchester City Council 125
marginalized groups 71, 80, 149
MCDA. *See* multi-criteria decision analysis (MCDA)
media interactions 171
meetings, incentive travel, conferences and exhibitions 118
mega-events 18, 57, 67, 73, 74
Melbourne Food 78

Index

Meta 244
MICE. *See* meetings, incentive travel, conferences and exhibitions
migrants 30
Millennials (born 1981–1996) 237, 239, 248, 251–52
minority cultures 71
Monkey Buffet Festival. *See* Lopburi Monkey Banquet
multi-criteria decision analysis (MCDA) 4
music festivals 30, 72, 79, 168, 194, 199
Music of the Spheres tour 25
Music Venue Trust 193, 201
music venues 90, 201, 204
MVP (Music Venue Properties) 201

National Health Service (NHS) 200–01
National Society for the Prevention of Cruelty to Children (NSPCC) 190
natural elements 142
natural materials 142, 143
natural resources 42, 56, 106, 168, 169, 212
Net Zero Strategy 77
Newspeak 13–14, 57
NFPs (New Future Propositions) 255, 262
NHS. *See* National Health Service (NHS)
noise pollution 71, 159
non-governmental organizations (NGOs) 75, 80–81
non-recyclable materials 70, 134
non-renewable resources 106
non-use value 158–59, 181
Notting Hill Carnival 68, 71, 198, 203
NSPCC. *See* National Society for the Prevention of Cruelty to Children (NSPCC)
nZero 157, 174–75

Olympics 67, 91, 102, 203
operational costs 135
operational planning 162–63
Out of the Box Festival of Early Childhood (Australia) 122
outdoor events 194, 221
overnight events 94
'Own Our Venues' project 201

Paris Agreement (2015) 127
Paris Olympics (2024) 57, 76, 171–72
Parkes Elvis Festival 65–66
Partnerships for Forest Forum 146
Penta Helix model 27
PESO (paid, earned, shared, owned) model 9, 243–46, *246*, 252
'phygitalisation' 46
physical assets 210
'Plan-Do-Check-Act' approach 176
planned events 132, 254
    definition 14–17, *15*, *15–17*
    existing typologies 17–21, *18*, *19*

TBL and 24
    updated typology 21–22, *21*
podcasts 233, 244
policy reforms 80
portable staging 221
positive branding 134
positive relationships 165
post-modern society 12
power imbalances 148
Primavera Sound (Spain) 30
PRM (people with reduced mobility) 30–31
PRME (Principles for Responsible Management Education) 24, 25, 43
procurement 73, 74, 78–79, 99, 124
    event registration and ticketing 217–18
    sustainable 210–17, *212*, *213–14*, *217*
professional standards 99
profit margins 110–11, 192
props 144–45, 211, 221, 223–24, 230
Protect Brockwell Park (PBP) 159
psychic income 22, 43, 59
psychographics 239
public events 165, 206
public relations 171, 204, 243, 244
Pullman Jakarta Central Park 104
Purple Guide 41
purpose-built venues 91
push-notifications 146–47
Pyramid Stage 75

Qatar World Cup 57
QR codes 249
Quad Helix model 27

Race Relations Act (1976) 40
Rainforest World Music Festival (Malaysia) 239
Rasselas Prince of Abyssinia (Johnston) 263
Reading Festival (UK) 30
real-time updates 146–47
recycling 79, 95–97, 135, 174, 242
    bins 96–97, 104
    stations 171, 238
redistribution programmes 75, 78
reforestation projects 78
religious buildings 89
religious ceremonies 225
renewable energy 70, 75–76, 77, 80, 98–99, 176
Research Institute for Disabled Consumers 187–88
resource management 75
resource scarcity 237
resource utilization 233
resource-based view (RBV) theory 165
Rio Carnival 20, 80
Rio Olympics (2016) 68, 74, 75
risk control plan 185, *187*
risk management 184–85, 187, 190–91
Rocking the Daisies festival 235–36, 251
romantic loneliness 48–49

Roskilde Festival 79
Running of the Bulls 167

safety advisory group (SAG) 125
Saidai-ji Eyo Hadaka Matsuri 168–69
Salon du Chocolat (Paris) 238, 251
San Fermin festival 167
Sauti za Busara Festival (Zanzibar) 246
SDGs (UN Sustainable Development Goals) 6, 13, 25–27, 40–41, 76, 134, 162, 176
SEA. *See* Sustainable Event Alliance (SEA)
Seasons for Change 112
Secret Garden Party Festival (UK) 193, 203
self-efficacy 174
self-employment 194
seminars 225
sensitisation campaigns 235
sensory-friendly spaces 149
Serendipity Arts Festival 240–41
Sex Discrimination Act (1975) 40
Seychelles Ocean Festival 240
Shambala Festival 113
shared values 71, 111, 128
showcase events 18
sign language 31, 149
Singapore Grand Prix 77
single-use plastics 68, 75, 76, 78, 79, 80, 137, 238
Slovene child benefit programme 81–82
SMART. *See* Specific, Measurable, Achievable, Relevant and Timebound
smartphones 152, 240
social cognitive theory 174
social equity 68, 170
social identities 71, 149
social identity theory 197
social responsibility 30, 45–46, 75, 134
societal expectations 176
socioeconomic groups 6, 67
Specific, Measurable, Achievable, Relevant and Timebound 137, 138, 158
speed dating events 21, 27, 41, 46
Splendour in the Grass 239
sponsors 48, 75, 77–78, 105, 113–14, 125, 134, 236
sponsorship 2, 77–78, 113–14, 118, 124–25, 150
sporting complexes 89
sporting events 17–18, 20, 79, 91, 118, 165, 194
sporting venues 91, 94, 103
St Jerome's Laneway Festival 240
Stadium 974 116–17
staff training 174, 227–28
staffing costs 2, 33
stakeholder engagement 30, 64, 67, 74, 110–11, 114, 124, 181
stakeholders 7, 26–28, 33, 45–49, 57–58, 67–68, 75–77, 79–81, 88, 155–56, 159, 165, 174–75, 180, 195–96, 241
  communication and expectations 115–17
  considerations and challenges 115–27
  decision making 118
  ethics and transparency 118–21, *119*, *120*
  role in event planning 122–26, *123*, *126*
  types of 111–15, *115*
  vulnerable stakeholders 121–22
Steamboat Springs 66
Street Child United (UK) 122
subject-matter experts 225
Super Bowl LVIII 75
suppliers 28, 41, 48, 75–76, 113, 155, 165, 176, 181, 236
  behaviour 174
  cancellation impacts on 195–96
  catering 221–23
  requirements 226–27, *226*
  role of venue 99–100, 104–05
  services and 116, 124
  vendors and 78–79
  venue and 218–19
  see also procurement
Sustainability Action Plan 112
sustainability measures 64, 75, 114, 249
sustainability metrics 171
sustainability pledges 79
Sustainable Event Alliance (SEA) 80
sustainable events 45–46, 55–58, 126
  ambience and décor 144–46, *145*
  attendee engagement and satisfaction 151–52, *152*
  attendees and participants 79
  benefits of designing 134–35
  biophilic design 141–42
  brainstorming 135–36
  characteristics of 66–67
  co-creation in event design process 147–48, *148*
  digital signage 146–47, *146*
  economic targets 73–75
  environmental targets 70
  event organizers 75–76
  government bodies and regulatory agencies 76–77
  idea development 132–34, *133*
  intersectionality, equality, diversity and inclusion 149–51
  introduction and definition 63–64
  local communities 79–80
  NGOs and advocacy groups 80–81
  role of children 81–82, *82*
  role of psychology 138–41, *139*, *140*, *141*
  social targets 70–72
  sponsors and corporate partners 77–78
  suppliers and vendors 78–79
  sustainability goals setting 136–38, *136*, *137*, *138*
  sustainability targets 68–75, *69*
  theme selection 141

variability 67–68
see also event industry
Sustainable Island Living Expo 248
sustainable practices 7, 75, 78–80, 88–89, 95, 110, 113, 118, 123, 132, 135, 152, 156, 230, 166–67, 169–71, 237, 241–42
   ambidextrous management approach 47–48
   applications in event management 40–45, *44–45*
   evaluation of experiences 50
   evaluation of objectives 49–50, *50*
   future staging of sustainable events: recommendations 55–58, *55*, *56*, *58*
   key elements for individuals attending events 53
   loneliness as societal issue 48–49
   questions for consideration 50–52, *51*, *52*
   self-evaluation 53–54, *54*
   sustainable events: planning and designing 45–47, *46*
symbolic interactionism 174, 180
Sziget Festival (Budapest) 30

TALC. *See* Tourism Area Life Cycle (TALC)
tax breaks 77
technical skills 165
technical specification
   equipment and staging 220–21
   sound and lighting 219–20
third-party contractors 100
Threads 244
TikTok 237, 242, 244
Tokyo Marathon 79
Tokyo Olympics (2020) 76–77, 78
Tomorrowland Festival 75–76, 248
tourism 6, 13, 64–65, 73–75, 201–02, 233
   child-centred rights approach 81
   event hosting 67–68
   event organizers and 75–76
   role of governments and regulatory bodies 76–77
   sponsors and corporate partners 77–78
   suppliers and vendors 78–79
Tourism Area Life Cycle (TALC) 203
trade shows 194
transformational leadership 29–30, 46, 262
transparency 74, 118–21, 128, 211, 235, 246, 249
transport manager 112
TrashOut campaign 235, 251
tree planting 118–20, *120*
triple bottom line (TBL) 2, 5–6, 22–24, 156–57, 170, *259*
Triple Crown Baseball Tournament 65–66
two-way radios (walkie talkies) 220

UK Festival Awards 123–24

UK LIVE Event Freelancers Forum 194–95
UN Environment Programme 234
Underwater Music Festival 169
UNEP report 74
unusual events 166–70
   low cost or no cost events 169–70
   support and interests of participants 168–69
unusual venues 90–91, 107

Venice Carnival 20
venue costs 2, 33
venue grading 88, 101–03
venue management
   expectations of clients and event attendees 103–04
   future of sustainable venues 106–07
   role of the venue in event planning 104–05
   selection 75, 92–94
   staff and community engagement 101
   sustainable venue 95–100, *95*, *96*, *98*, *99*
   types of event venues 89–92, *89*
   venue grading and sustainability certification 101–03
   venue selection 92–94, *93*
venue managers 89, 218
virtual events 2, 14, 20–21, 33, 249, 254, 255
virtual networking 147
visitor attractions 89, 90, 94

waste management 22, 70, 76, 96–97, 159, 167–68, 176
   food 223
   policy 13, 67, 92, 236
   programmes 80
waste production 96, 233
waste reduction 75, 76, 79, 80, 171, 174
waste segregation 79, 166, 171
We Love Green Festival (Paris) 245, 249
WeAreTechWomen 150, 151
WeeFestival 122
wellbeing 7, 56, 59, 122, 142
WhatsApp 233, 239, 240, 249
Wine Festival 78
work–life balance 195
World Body Painting Festival 169
World Travel Market 18
WRAP (2021) 223

X. *See* Twitter

YouTube 237, 240, 244

Zentive 145
'Zero Plastic' initiative 233
zero-waste challenges 243
zero-waste initiatives 70, 75, 233

Looking for another book?

Explore our award-winning books from global business experts in Marketing and Sales

Scan the code to browse

www.koganpage.com/marketing

From 4 December 2025 the EU Responsible Person (GPSR) is:
eucomply oÜ, Pärnu mnt. 139b – 14, 11317 Tallinn, Estonia
www.eucompliancepartner.com

www.ingramcontent.com/pod-product-compliance
Lightning Source LLC
Chambersburg PA
CBHW071137300426
44113CB00009B/1003